DATE DUE

The **Smart** Step-Family

RON L. DEAL

The **Smart** Step-Family

BETHANYHOUSE
Minneapolis, Minnesota

Published by Bethany House Publishers
11400 Hampshire Avenue South
Bloomington, Minnesota 55438

Bethany House Publishers is a division of
Baker Publishing Group, Grand Rapids, Michigan.

Printed in the United States of America

Library of Congress Cataloging-in-Publication Data

Deal, Ron L.
   The smart stepfamily : seven steps to a healthy family / by Ron L. Deal
      p. cm.
Includes bibliographical references.
ISBN 0-7642-2657-6 (perm. paper)
   1. Stepfamilies. 2. Remarried people—Family relationships. 3. Stepparents.
4. Parenting. 5. Stepfamilies—Psychological aspects. I. Title.
   HQ759.92 .D4   2002
   306.874—dc21   2002009985

To my wife and best friend, Nan,
Three diamonds.
All my love, for all my life.

Acknowledgments

Like any healthy stepfamily, this book has taken a long time to develop. And like any healthy stepfamily, this book is the result of a careful integration of people, ideas, backgrounds, and relationships. I am grateful to so many who have offered their encouragement and talent along the way—this book could not have been created without your help.

Special appreciation goes to Ashleigh Short Givens and David and Robbie Hutchins for their early reviews of the manuscript and technical writing input. You helped this project get noticed and ultimately published—thank you. Also, a special thank-you goes to Rebecca Warnick for her administrative support and to the Southwest Church of Christ elders for their encouragement. Your vision for a family ministry that extends beyond the Jonesboro community has resulted in a ministry whose borders, by God's grace, are expanding daily. I couldn't have done this without your blessing.

Others whose friendship and professionalism have made this journey possible include H. Norman Wright, Steve Laube and the Bethany House team, Dr. Margorie Engel and the Stepfamily Association of America's board of directors and institute faculty, and the researchers and clinicians whose work is referenced throughout this book. I must especially acknowledge the work and influence of Dr. Emily Visher, whose life has come to an end, but whose inspiration and research will live on. This book stands on the shoulders of her scholarly research, shared writing with her husband, John, and personal stepfamily experience. Yet equally impacting was her encouragement of me as a young writer and teacher. I am exceedingly grateful for her influence and wisdom. Also, to the original Southwest Step-by-Step education group, I say thanks. You boldly supported each other and shared your stories with me so that I might help others. You have blessed my life; I hope you have been blessed in return.

To my dearest friends and spiritual partners, Randy and Judy Lewis, Gregg and Elisa Barden, Shawn and Arlene Mayes, and Jeff and Misty Floyd (Faith Camp rocks!)—your encouragement and faith have challenged me to be used by God through this book and seminar ministry. Let's give him the glory! And finally, a very special word of appreciation goes to James and Dana Caldwell, whose willingness to share their life has taught others and me so much about the stepfamily journey, and whose friendship has enriched my life deeply.

RON L. DEAL is family life minister for Southwest Church of Christ and a licensed marriage and family therapist, licensed professional counselor with the Better Life Counseling Center. He presents his *Building a Successful Stepfamily* seminar nationwide and is on the institute faculty and advisory council for the Stepfamily Association of America. Ron, his wife, and their sons live in Jonesboro, Arkansas.

Contents

A MESSAGE TO THE CHURCH

Introduction

Have you ever tried to put together a 3-D jigsaw puzzle without instructions and without a picture on the box to show you what the final product should look like? Try adding a blindfold. Sounds impossible, doesn't it? In fact, it doesn't even sound fun to try. Attempt to combine members of two (or more) different households and you'll encounter similar frustrations.

Putting together or *integrating* a stepfamily is one of the most difficult tasks for any family in America today. Integration involves combining two unique family styles, various personalities and preferences, differing traditions, pasts, and loyalties. Yet most people make the decision to bring two families together without consulting the instructions (i.e., God's Word) or developing a shared image of the final product (the picture on the jigsaw puzzle box). Blinded with a well-intentioned ignorance, couples march down the aisle a second or third time, only to discover that the building process is much more difficult than they anticipated—and the rewards are few and far between, especially in the beginning. But the odds of your success increase dramatically when you take off your blindfold and see a picture of how a healthy stepfamily looks and acts.

WORKING SMARTER, NOT HARDER

The purpose of this book is to give you just that—a healthy picture of a successful Christian stepfamily based on God's instruction manual. And believe it or not, it can be done if you work smarter, not harder. Working smarter means understanding the dynamics of stepfamily life and development, and making intentional decisions about how you will grow together emotionally, psychologically, and spiritually.

If you are currently married and perhaps finding that your three-dimensional puzzle is depending on a fragile foundation, read this book with an eye for what you can change. Once you've developed concrete ideas for putting the pieces of your family together, begin working the plan cautiously but with much determination. You'll be amazed at God's power to heal your heartaches and turn your unstable or crumbling puzzle into an edifice that is safe, beautiful, and built on a firm foundation.

If you are currently single, divorced, or widowed and are considering marriage, and if one or both of you have children, you've turned to the right source. There are many hidden challenges in stepfamily life, and you need to be as prepared as you possibly can. Taking off your blindfold and seeing clearly the journey ahead is the best choice you can make. Indeed, your decision to form a stepfamily by marriage needs to be an informed choice; otherwise you may regret the decision once the challenges hit you head-on. I once heard Elizabeth Einstein, a stepfamily author, lecturer, and stepfamily member, tell a group of ministers that they should make it very difficult for persons to form stepfamilies simply because the challenges are so great.[1] She, more than most, knows that successful stepfamilies can bring great joy and fulfillment to the lives of children and adults. But she also understands that a great deal of work and determination is required to develop a healthy stepfamily and that most stepfamily marriages simply won't survive. You cannot afford to go into marriage armed only with "better than last time" intentions. The process demands that you know and understand more than that. This book will tell you what you need to know.

Please know that this book has grown out of the belief that the home is the primary context in which we learn and experience the character of love. Ultimately, the experience of love points us toward a loving God. It is my firm belief that stepfamilies can build those experiences and demonstrate the character of love just as can biological families. One of the ways we come to know our heavenly Father is through the love we experience in our earthly relationships. Reciprocally, our knowledge of and commitment to him in turn strengthen our family bonds. Truly, faith and family are intrinsically and dynamically linked. Thus, building a smart stepfamily is spiritual food for each member of your home (even the generation yet to come). It is my prayer that this book will help you build a spiritual two-way bridge with one lane moving you toward God while the return lane brings you back home with greater commitment and clarity of heart. Let the journey begin.

The Israelites groaned in their slavery and cried out, and their cry for help because of their slavery went up to God. God heard their groaning and he remembered his covenant with Abraham, with Isaac and with Jacob. So God looked on the Israelites and was concerned about them.

—EXODUS 2:23b–25

PART ONE

Headed for the Promised Land!

Can you imagine what freedom must have been like to the Israelites? For some four hundred years they had been oppressed by the Egyptians, held in bondage against their will, and forced to live as slaves. For years the Lord had heard their cries, and now the time had finally come for freedom. It's hard to imagine the joy, relief, and utter exuberance the Israelites must have felt. They were going home! But where, exactly, was home?

Moses, a rather unsung hero at the time, through God's power had become their leader. A pillar of cloud by day and a pillar of fire by night made it obvious that God was leading his people to the Promised Land. Yet the joy and celebration of being set free was soon quenched when the Israelites found themselves hemmed in by the Red Sea on one side and an angry Pharaoh, who had changed his mind about letting them go, on the other. In their terror the Israelites cried out, "Was it because there were no graves in Egypt that you brought us to the desert to die? What have you done to us by bringing us out of Egypt? . . . It would have been better for us to serve the Egyptians than to die in the desert!" (Exodus 14:11–12).

Freedom from slavery was what the Israelites pleaded for, and yet oppression and bondage actually became attractive to them as soon as the journey became difficult. Indeed, this wasn't the only occasion about which the Israelites complained and pleaded to return to Egypt. The security of slavery was often more inviting than the insecurity of traveling an unmarked road to an unknown destination. They just hadn't learned how to trust God to give purpose and provision in unfamiliar territory.

Many stepfamilies walk this same journey.

CHAPTER ONE

Through Wilderness Wanderings

"Was it because there were no graves in Egypt that you brought us to the desert to die? What have you done to us by bringing us out of Egypt? . . . It would have been better for us to serve the Egyptians than to die in the desert!" Moses answered the people, "Do not be afraid. Stand firm and you will see the deliverance the Lord will bring you today" (Exodus 14:11–13).

It is nearly a universal experience for the adults in stepfamilies, and it occurs soon after remarriage. I'm referring to disillusionment. Believing that remarriage will release them from the bondage of divorce, loss, loneliness, and painful emotions, couples pick up their children and possessions and launch into the wilderness toward the Promised Land. The wedding seems to mark a release from oppression. *At last,* they think, *I am loved and important again. And my children will have the benefit of a two-parent family. This is going to be great!* But eventually the realities of stepfamily life trip over unrealistic fantasies, and disillusionment sets in.

Remarriage for most adults seems to be their second (or third) chance on life. Life hasn't worked out the way they planned, and the trip has been painful. But things are looking up—they've fallen in love again and the dream of a normal family life has returned. A new journey of hope has begun. The journey, however, almost always takes some unexpected turns. For example, your spouse's dedication to his or her children was noble before the wedding, but now seems to be a challenge to the marriage; a teenager living in one of the other homes decides to live with you; parenting styles differ more than you expected, and conflict erupts frequently. The trip is filled with uncertainty, and parents realize they feel lost much of the time. The daily grind continues, but progress is slow in coming. Life seems to go in circles. It's easy to get lost in the wilderness.

DON'T LOOK NOW; WE'RE BEING PURSUED!

Just as the Israelites quickly found themselves caught between the Red Sea and Pharaoh's army, so stepfamilies shortly after remarriage find themselves caught between the future and the past. Behind them, debilitating pain and loss from the days of bondage are quickly pursuing. Anger, resentment, rejection, and guilt siphons the energy from people's emotional tanks, while losses too numerous to count (especially for children) make for cautious emotional investments in new stepfamilies. Indeed, the pain of the past makes for a tremendous fear of the future. Consider these statements from the Thomas family:

> BIOLOGICAL MOTHER, JUDY: *"I'm afraid it's not going to work, and we'll get divorced. And then three times I've failed. I'm afraid Frank's [her new husband] going to get aggravated with his stepchildren—my kids—and he's going to walk, 'cause there's only so much he can take. I'm afraid my kids are going to turn against me because they didn't want Frank as their stepfather. It would just be another failure."*

> OLDER SON, JOHN (AGE SEVENTEEN): *"I'm afraid of getting close to anyone. I'm not very trusting. With all I've had to live through, I keep waiting for it to happen all over again: the constant blaming and getting stuck in the middle. And I won't let it ever happen again."*

> MIDDLE DAUGHTER, SUSAN (AGE FIFTEEN): *"I ain't afraid of nothing. I'm not scared of anything. I mean, if you broke up, it wouldn't be the first time. I might be a little worried where we'd go or something like that.*

But as far as you breaking up, I mean, two times gets you ready for it to happen at any moment."

YOUNGER SON, RANDY (AGE FOURTEEN): *"I try to get closer sometimes but then the fear happens and I hide out from doing things with Frank and keep farther apart from him than I should be. . . . I want to get close, but not too close, for fear of something that might happen in the future."*

STEPFATHER, FRANK: *[regarding his marriage]* "I'm afraid to be in another relationship where I'm nobody and have no say about what's going on in the house. [Regarding the stepchildren] I'm afraid that if we don't change things right away, they're going to grow up and we'll never have a relationship. They'll just be stepkids who come and visit at holidays. I don't want it to be that way."

The pain of their collective past is driving their fears of the future, which, in turn, is leading them to be guarded and untrusting in the present. If these heartaches and losses are not successfully resolved for this family and yours, the result will be a tired, disillusioned couple unable to draw close to each other, let alone meet the emotional needs of their children. Painful emotions from the past must be resolved in order for you and your children to move on.

FACING A SEA OF OPPOSITION

Looking to the future is difficult when the fear of further loss looms before you. Yet that is just the beginning. A sea of opposition and challenges lie ahead for most stepfamilies. Common uncharted waters include:

- achieving marital intimacy after being hurt;
- parenting and stepparenting roles and rules;
- questions of spiritual integrity and church involvement;
- how to integrate the members of a stepfamily over time;
- dealing with ex-spouses and co-parenting issues;
- helping children emotionally and spiritually;
- handling sexual pressures between unrelated persons;
- issues of money management and financial autonomy.

Stepfamily life can be overwhelming and intimidating. It's not uncommon for persons to start wondering, much like the Israelites did, if maybe they should return to the bondage of divorce or single-parent living. Sure, it was miserable and unfulfilling, but at least they knew what they had. Disillusionment quickly gives birth to grumbling, complaining, and conflict. Emotions run high and problems escalate. The stepparent, who from an outsider's position can more clearly see and feel the disharmony in the home, often voices this disillusionment first. The biological parent who is still blinded by the fog of new love frequently discounts requests for change. Slowly but surely, this builds distance in the couple's relationship at a time when they can't afford to be out of touch.

The temptation to return to bondage continues: "What have I done? Maybe I shouldn't have left being single. Besides, it appears that the God I prayed to for so long has abandoned me (I'm sure I deserve it) and condemned me to flounder on my own." Wrong! While I doubt that the God of the universe will reveal a path to you with a cloud of fire, he most certainly will provide strength and direction for your journey, even when the path seems dismal.

If there is one message that stepfamilies need to hear, it's this: *There is a stepfamily Promised Land of marital intimacy, interpersonal connectedness, and spiritual redemption! God has not abandoned you, even though you may have lived a life of sin and shame, or even though you doubt his presence in your life. If you will listen, trust, and continue walking by faith, you will hear him confirming your journey, offering guidance, healing, and providing a path on dry ground. But you must trust him.* Don't be like most remarried couples who end their journey in divorce within the first three years; they quit before ever crossing the Red Sea. God beckons you to remain persistent and see your family through to the Promised Land. There is a reward to be gained. But you must hold God's hand and walk through your sea of oppositions.

IS THE JOURNEY DIFFICULT FOR ALL STEPFAMILIES?

Stepfamilies vary greatly. Some have children from just one spouse and involve only one household if, for example, the death of a parent ended the first biological family. (This is not to imply that the death of a parent makes stepfamily living easy.) Other stepfamilies are much more complex with "yours, mine, and ours" children, two or more ex-spouses, and plenty of stepparents and stepgrandparents. These factors plus the different levels of involvement children have with parents and stepparents make it hard to predict how much a family will struggle. I've worked with stepfamily adults who had horrible first family experiences and find stepfamily life easy. Others assume they will have an easy transition because they have an amicable relationship with their ex-spouse, and the children appear (before remarriage) to like their future stepparent. However, they later discover many complications that challenge their marital strength and faith in God.

Not all stepfamilies have a difficult journey, but most will experience unexpected challenges. Some will face a great many barriers. It is important to remember that the number of barriers you face comments neither on you nor on whether or not you should have married. Once you say, "I do," your original wisdom, or lack thereof, in creating this family is irrelevant. When encountering opposition, too many people convince themselves that it wasn't a good idea to marry in the first place. They then begin looking for a way out.

When stepfamily life gets tough, remaining dedicated to your commitment is a day-to-day decision. A man once drove six hours to talk with me about his stepchildren and marriage. He hoped that once I heard him describe the sea of oppositions he was facing, I would give him "permission" to leave the marriage. I did not (and he was terribly annoyed). What I did do was agree with him that the marriage, in its present condition, was not something anyone should keep, nor was God honored by an angry, resentful relationship. I suggested that with guided help he could choose to work on his marriage and remain open to how the God of the impossible might intervene on their behalf. Furthermore, avoiding divorce by tolerating a miserable marriage, I suggested, does not honor God. Commitment requires that you strive for a better life together, even when you don't feel like putting forth your best effort or have convinced yourself the marriage should have never happened in the first place.

SO YOU'RE CONSIDERING REMARRIAGE . . .

To those of you who are perhaps engaged or considering remarriage, I am so glad you are reading this book now. I can't tell you how many couples attending my *Building a Successful Stepfamily* seminar have said, "Why didn't anyone ever tell us these things before we married? We could have saved ourselves a lot of grief if we would have only known." So by all means, keep reading with these intentions:

- Use this book to enlighten yourself to the possible struggles you may face in your stepfamily journey.
- Equip yourself and your relationship with practical strategies to meet the challenges.
- Use the stories and information here to help you make an informed decision about remarriage.

Remarriage and stepfamily life can be filled with many blessings, but the journey probably won't start out that way. You'll have to work diligently to reach the Promised Land. To that end, have you truly considered the costs? Do you know what the costs are? This book will help you identify them. In addition, I recommend that you find a group of stepfamilies or an individual stepfamily in your congregation and ask them some questions:

- What do they wish they had known before they remarried?
- What are their three greatest challenges?
- How could they have better prepared themselves for stepfamily living?
- What painful emotions from the past did they not resolve well enough prior to remarriage?
- Where are they in the journey, and what still lies ahead?
- What blessings have they experienced and at what price?

The lure of marriage is tremendous. *Finally,* you think, *someone to take care of me. I just feel so good when I'm with him.* But stepfamily life is so much more than just your marriage. God's plan that two single people leave their families of origin and cleave solely to each other doesn't occur in stepfamilies. The marriage begins with children who dramatically impact the marriage. Biological families, when they experience upheaval, can survive riding on the back of the marital relationship because it precedes the children and hopefully has remained strong through the transition to parenthood. In stepfamilies, the parent-child bonds predate the couple's relationship, often making the marriage the weakest relationship in the home. And it's tough to strengthen your marriage when parenting issues constantly push marital closeness to the back burner. Being in love with someone who "makes me feel good again" is just the beginning of what it takes to survive. So, please, do yourself and your children a favor— find out everything you can and count the cost before deciding to remarry. Date the person for at least two years, giving yourself plenty of time to develop an understanding of your intended *and* his or her children. Too many couples date while the children are with the baby-sitter; the dating partner can easily be shielded from a real life, day-to-day experience with the future stepchildren. You need to know what you're getting into on every level. If after much prayer and courting you do remarry, give it everything you've got, and trust God to lead you through.

THE GOD WHO HEALS

Shortly after delivering Moses and the Israelites from Pharaoh's army, the Israelites journeyed through the Desert of Shur. For three days they traveled, and the only water they found was bitter and not fit for consumption. Again the people complained, and again God provided for his people. God had Moses throw a piece of wood into the unpalatable water, turning it sweet. In reference to the miracle, God then refers to himself as Jehovah-Rophe, the "Lord who heals you" (Exodus 15:26). In so doing, God declares a promise. If his people will listen to his voice and do what is right in his eyes, he will heal—he will make the bitter waters of their life sweet again. That same promise is available to stepfamilies. I believe that our God is just waiting for a chance to heal your past hurts and to alleviate all that pursues you. But that's not all he offers. To those who are faithful, he will provide strength to keep their stepfamily commitments, and he will provide wisdom to overcome the obstacles that lie ahead. He wants you to be successful. But you can't rely on yourself. Depend on him and he will clear a path.

FOOD FOR THE JOURNEY

Water was not all that God provided for the Israelites. He also caused manna and quail to rain down upon the people. Similarly, I suggest two types of food to help nourish your journey: practical information and support from fellow travelers. This book will provide the practical stepfamily information. After laying down some key stopping-stones for the stepfamily journey, I will discuss common challenges to the Christian stepfamily and provide practical guidance.

But don't stop there. I highly recommend you find another couple or a group of couples and meet together on a regular basis. I have been involved in support and therapy groups for a number of years, and stepfamily groups are among the most dynamic I've seen. The common stories that are shared and the pressures and crises that are experienced together create an incredible bond among group members. That's why you'll find a study guide intended for group use at the end of each chapter. A recommended group format is to read each chapter and come together to discuss the questions. This helps you process the information, internalize it, and apply it to your home. When you've finished this book, read another and continue the process. Then, once your family has reached smoother waters, start inviting other couples to join you. You or another couple may "lead" the group, but the format can remain a self-responsible discussion group. If you have a minister or stepfamily educator who will help support the group, ask them to join you. Lives will be touched, including your own.

IS IT ALL WORTH IT?

Tim was remarried, but after three years he was just beginning to understand how difficult the journey was going to be. His life experience had shown him that the stepfamily journey can be tough, and now he was hearing me confirm that in a live seminar. During one of the breaks, this thirty-eight-year-old upright man asked an honest question: "I'm just not sure it's worth all the work. I mean, I'm beginning to think the payoff can't be worth all this hard work. It feels like I'm married to my wife, and she's still married to her kids. That makes it very hard for me to work at liking and accepting them. If you don't know what you'll have in a few years, is it worth the effort?"

He spoke for many people who silently wonder if they're heading down a dead-end street. My answer to such doubt is, it's not a dead-end street. It *is* worth the effort. The Israelites discovered the Promised Land to be everything they dreamed. Not all stepfamilies have all their expectations realized, but with hard work and commitment, it is possible to achieve many or all of the following.

PROMISED LAND PAYOFFS

"Focusing on the strengths in a stepfamily is essential, especially in the early stages, for creating a positive outcome," says Elizabeth Einstein, author and marriage and family therapist in Ithaca, New York. "It's too easy to identify problems early on and get stuck." In 1997, I attended one of Elizabeth's "Strengthening Stepfamilies" workshops where this leading stepfamily educator identified the following stepfamily strengths.[1] With her permission, I liken them to Promised Land Payoffs. Not all stepfamilies will experience all of these Payoffs, but with hard work and commitment it is possible to achieve many of the following:

- Marital Satisfaction
- Healthy Marriage Models for Children
- Role Models for Children
- Restored Well-Being in Children
- Adaptability and Flexibility
- Mistakes, Lessons Learned, and Healing
- Personal Growth and Spiritual Commitment

Marital Satisfaction

Couples can create mutually satisfying, intimate, God-honoring marriages within stepfamilies. Undoubtedly there are a number of barriers to overcome (see chapter 5), but remarriages can be healthy relationships. Furthermore, I've observed that couples that endure the adversity of the journey, frequently have a bond that is powerful enough to withstand anything. There is strength and a sense of victory after surviving what for some is a difficult journey.

And how long does it take for couples to find an increase of satisfaction? E. Mavis Hetherington reports, in her highly scientific book *For Better or For Worse: Divorce Reconsidered*,[2] that it takes most couples five to seven years to get through the tensions of stepfamily life, such that their stress level declines to match that of a husband and wife in a first marriage. Furthermore, surviving their tumultuous early years seems to give couples a staying power that keeps them going . . . and growing.

Marital satisfaction is a process. Keep pursuing it.

Healthy Marriage Models for Children

A strong remarriage is critical for the relational development of the children. Stepfamily children, especially those who have lived through a parental divorce, need to witness and learn from a healthy marital relationship. This counteracts the negative and destructive patterns of interaction they witnessed in their parent's previous marriage (and since the divorce). Instead of arguments filled with yelling and personal agendas, they watch two people who maintain a win-win attitude negotiate the best solution for their family. Instead of a distant relationship between two people living parallel lives, they witness two people giving time and attention to their relationship. Instead of an unbalanced relationship, where one spouse is constantly chasing an ever-distancing, never available spouse, children see a husband and wife who continually seek to sacrifice for the other out of love. Children desperately need positive marital role models. If not, they are likely to repeat destructive relationship patterns. Indeed, children of divorce have a much higher risk of divorce in their own adult relationships. However, positive relationship models can counteract destructive ones.

It's worth mentioning that many children do not welcome their parent's remarriage, especially in the beginning. They may even fight the stepparent's efforts to join the family, and be antagonistic. This is normal, as children hold on to the dream that their biological parents will remarry. Despite the children's resistance, a strong stepfamily couple will have positive benefits for them over time. The key is to remember that during the early integration years, children may resent the stepparent's presence in the home. Maintain a long-term perspective and live as if a healthy marriage is just what the kids desire. Someday they may come to appreciate your marital commitment.

Some time ago a woman sent me an anniversary card she received from her stepdaughter. Debbie had kept the card because it meant so much to her. It made her realize just how much her stepdaughter was watching and learning from her marriage. Nearly a decade into her remarriage, Debbie received the card, which read, "Glad to see you two still haven't lost the magic. Happy anniversary, Mom and Dad!" The handwritten note inside the card was even more encouraging: "Happy Anniversary! I just wanted to thank you for the wonderful Christian example of how a marriage should work. The way you solve conflict with humor is fun to watch. When the time comes for the Lord to bless me with a mate, I hope I am as lucky as the two of you are! I love you both, Kara."

Now, that's what I call a Promised Land Payoff!

In addition to a healthy marriage model, a healthy stepfamily marriage provides the structure children need to grow and develop as individuals as well as the structure the family needs to develop as a unit. The old saying "As goes the marriage, so goes the family" is true in stepfamilies as well. However, there is an equally valid statement in stepfamilies: As goes the stepparent-stepchild relationship, so goes the family. That will be the center of discussion in chapter 7. For now, let it be said that a stable marital relationship is the backbone to a stable stepfamily journey.

Role Models

The parenting team is comprised of all the adults who are interacting with the children in some form of parental role. Many stepfamily children have at least four role models, while others have more (if grandparents, uncles, stepparents, etc. are part of the parental team). When the adults of the parental team are living responsible, God-fearing lives, stepchildren actually have more positive family role models than children of nuclear (biological) families. (This is not to suggest that children in intact families are somehow at a disadvantage.) Children can be blessed significantly when lots of loving adults are involved in their lives.

For example, contrary to the popular "wicked stepparent" myth, stepchildren don't always hold stepparents in contempt. Listen to the words of one boy who nominated his stepfather for a Fathering Hall of Fame award:

> My daddy's name is Jimmy. He is my stepdad, but he has always been there for me since I was very tiny. He has a job and works every day. He takes me fishing and swimming. He even gives me my bath every night. I think he is very special, and I love him a whole bunch. He does more for me than anybody—he is a

super daddy. He heals my cuts with medicine and bandages. He even cooks for me sometimes. And puts me in my bed at night and covers me up. I love my daddy 'cause he is a super dad.

Another example comes from Debbie, a good friend of mine, who showed me her son's high school graduation photo. Her son was being hugged on one side by his father and stepmother and on the other by his mother and stepfather. The picture not only symbolized this young man's achievement but it also told the story of two ex-spouses and two new spouses who worked hard for six years to create a cooperative relationship on behalf of their son. The result was a well-adjusted eighteen-year-old who could openly love both his parents and his stepparents without fearing hurt feelings from any of them. They in turn could openly love him, share their talents and abilities with him, and feed his self-esteem and sense of personal worth. What a blessed child!

Restored Well-Being in Children

In 1998 James Bray published research culminating the first ten-year longitudinal study of stepfamilies in America. His research revealed that a loving, well-functioning stepfamily over time can negate many of the detrimental psychological impacts of divorce on children. While not all of the negative effects can be reversed, it is certainly a message of hope for parents and children. It seems that with time, healthy stepfamilies can have benefits that counteract the negative costs of divorce.

In addition, Bray says a "strong, stable stepfamily is as capable of nurturing healthy development as a nuclear family. It can imbue values, affirm limits and boundaries, and provide a structure in which rules for living a moral and productive life are made, transmitted, tested, rebelled against, and ultimately affirmed."[3] The key here is a "strong, stable stepfamily." This isn't created overnight, but affirms that dedication to healthy stepfamily integration has significant rewards for children. If that's not a reason to endure the journey to the Promised Land, I don't know what is.

Adaptability and Flexibility

Learning to be flexible is a must for stepfamilies. So many adjustments needed to survive the journey require flexibility from each person. This ability to adapt can become a valuable characteristic that individuals carry with them throughout life. Our world is changing at remarkable speeds given today's technological advances. The ability to change and go with the flow is a skill that can be used in many areas of one's life.

Mistakes, Lessons Learned, and Healing

Without question, stepfamily life offers people a second chance. Learning from our mistakes and then applying ourselves to new relationships are qualities of successful people. In stepfamilies, children get to see their parents grow as persons, spouses are challenged to greater personal responsibility in their marriages, and individuals are invited to wrestle with difficult emotions. Lessons are learned and healing takes place. For example, one key emotion in stepfamilies is grief. Most persons enter remarriage before they or their children have sufficiently grieved the losses of the past. Stepfamilies who grant permission for grief expression help bring healing to the hurting. Indeed, you might think of stepfamilies as grief support groups, with each person carrying some measure of grief. Finding support, openness, and acceptance within the stepfamily home despite feelings of hurt, anger, or sadness is a healing phenomenon reflective of the biblical admonition to bear one another's burdens (Galatians 6:2). This is why I encourage stepfamilies to view this Promised Land Payoff as part of their spiritual ministry to one another.

Personal Growth and Spiritual Commitment

Sometimes the stepfamily journey is filled with great discouragement. What results is an opportunity to deepen our faith and rely on God's Spirit. One stepmother put it this way: "I don't know how I would have made it without God's unending power and this fellowship of people to encourage me." The biblical author James noted the benefits of struggles as well: "Consider it pure joy, my brothers, whenever you face trials of many kinds, because you know that the testing of your faith develops perseverance. Perseverance must finish its work so that you may be mature and complete, not lacking anything" (James 1:2–4). The stepfamily journey can be a spiritual trial of great magnitude. Holding tightly to God's hand throughout the journey results in a closer relationship with the Father and a greater trust in his power to lead.

The Israelites experienced many periods of doubt; perhaps you do too. But undoubtedly, when they stopped to look back, they could see the hand of God and how many times he had acted on their behalf. Perhaps you haven't looked back recently. Perhaps the barriers that stand in front of you now are fueling your doubt and pessimism. Stop for a few moments. What has God done to help you navigate your journey? In what ways has his Word provided insight for decisions and encouragement for patience? How has trusting in his truths about marital fidelity, kindness toward your enemies (perhaps your ex-spouse or stepchildren), and having a servant's heart helped you and your family to overcome obstacles along the way?

Is there a Promised Land for stepfamilies who don't quit, who faithfully follow their Lord, and who learn all they can about navigating the journey? Absolutely. And it's well worth the effort!

Questions for Discussion

Work through the following questions on your own before sharing them with your spouse. Some of the questions are appropriate for children as well. Before talking with your children or stepchildren, take into consideration their ages and your overall relationship with them. In addition to discussing these questions with your spouse (or dating partner) and children, share your answers with your discussion group.

FOR ALL COUPLES

1. What aspects of your past did you hope remarriage would "cure"?
2. Which of the following emotions have you felt in the past? Which still haunt you from time to time? Anger. Bitterness. Depression. Sadness. Longing. Hurt. Resentment. Guilt. Fear. Pain. Rejection.
3. In what ways did you experience disillusionment, and at what point did you realize things weren't working out like you expected? How have you adjusted your expectations?
4. In what ways was your remarriage another loss for your children? How can you be sensitive to that loss without being guilt-ridden (or easily manipulated because you feel guilty)?
5. Look again at the list of uncharted waters on page 19. Which of these represent areas of growth for you or your stepfamily? What areas do

you consider to be the priority growth areas right now?

6. In what ways have you or your stepfamily members experienced God's leading or his healing hand? Be sure to share with your stepfamily how you see him at work in your lives.

7. What Scriptures have been helpful or inspiring to you recently? If you haven't been reading the Bible much lately, how can you begin to do so again?

8. Share a time with your spouse when you weren't sure the work was worth the effort. If that time is now, what do you need to help you stay determined? If you trusted God to bring you through, what would you be doing differently than you are now to work in that direction?

9. Which, if any, of the Promised Land Payoffs have you experienced to some degree already?

CASE STUDY IN STEPFAMILY FEARS

Read again the fears from the Thomas family on pages 18 and 19, and then answer the following questions. Remember that when fears are left to govern your behavior, you will find yourself limited in your range of responses. An integrating stepfamily cannot afford to be controlled by fear.

1. Which fears of the biological and/or stepparent can you relate to and why?

2. What are you doing to prevent these fears from becoming a reality?

3. Think through your previous losses and painful family experiences (either family of origin or first marriage). How do your current fears connect with those experiences? How have they sensitized you to avoiding more pain in current relationships?

4. If you weren't hamstrung by the past, how would you be different in the present?

5. Consider the fears mentioned by the children. Which might your children also feel?

6. What have you done to try to prevent your children's fears from becoming a reality? In what ways could these protective efforts be sabotaging new relationships?

FOR PRE-REMARITAL COUPLES

1. In what ways do you feel intimidated and frightened after reading this chapter?
2. What might this new relationship be rescuing you from?
3. What challenges are you beginning to see that you had not thought about before?
4. Think of a stepfamily couple that you can interview. Ask them the following questions. If possible, start attending a stepfamily support group to help you make a more informed decision about remarriage.

   - What do you wish you had known before you remarried?
   - What are your three greatest challenges?
   - How could you have better prepared yourselves for stepfamily living?
   - What painful emotions from the past did you not resolve prior to remarriage?
   - How long have you been traveling this journey?
   - What blessings have you experienced and at what price?

CHAPTER TWO

Key Stepping-Stones

"It's been a real struggle trying to be a stepmother to my husband's son. We butt heads quite often, and my husband doesn't know how to help. Usually he and I start arguing about his son, but before long we're arguing with each other. It's been three years, and I just thought things would be so much better by now. But they seem to be getting worse."

Without question, this stepmother is struggling. I receive numerous e-mails such as this, and most of them come from good-hearted Christians who are discouraged with their journey. The Promised Land can seem so far away when daily problems continually drain your energy. The real question is, can you persevere while trying to understand what obstacles stand in the way and what solutions will help you overcome them? Remember, continue to walk in faithfulness and trust that God will provide strength and wisdom when you ask him (James 1:5–8).

God calls us to Christlikeness. We should continually seek to live as Christ lived and take on his attitude of sacrifice. The qualities of Jesus form stepping-stones upon which we walk both spiritually and relationally. A few key stepping-stones will enable stepfamilies to overcome obstacles and take advantage of the opportunities that come their way. Essentially, stepping-stones are important attitudes and perspectives that will enable you to endure the wilderness and cross your sea of oppositions. As you read these key qualities, assess which ones you have already put to work and in what areas your family needs to improve.

Spiritual Integrity and Christlikeness

This stepping-stone goes straight to the heart of any successful family. All individuals within your stepfamily must voluntarily put themselves under the lordship of Jesus Christ. This is not just a "good idea" or an external statement of religiosity. This is an internal, personal commitment to follow Christ and to accept his gracious forgiveness of the sin that separates us from God. Living in faithful response to this grace will ripple into every other relational aspect of your stepfamily. For example, only when we truly understand how much we have been forgiven can we extend forgiveness to those that have hurt us deeply. Furthermore, just as Christ was not swayed from acting fairly toward those who falsely accused him, stepparents who seek to imitate Christ, for example, can find ways of rising above their stepchildren's manipulative ploys. Christ's spiritual integrity, that is, his doing what was right despite the negative attitudes of those around him, becomes a much needed model for how we are to treat one another. When his integrity becomes yours, a transformation will begin in your home that defies the odds.

Spiritual integrity also communicates who is in charge of the stepfamily. When God's rules for holy living become the guiding light for family decision-making, husbands and wives no longer have to battle each other for power and control. They are unified in their strivings to honor Christ. But, oh, how our pride keeps us from following his directions! I'm told that the following is a radio conversation that took place off the coast of Newfoundland.

Canadians: Please divert your course 15 degrees to the south to avoid a collision.

Americans: Recommend you divert your course 15 degrees to the north to avoid a collision.

Canadians: Negative. You will have to divert your course 15 degrees to the south to avoid a collision.

Americans: This the captain of a U.S. Navy ship. I say again, divert your course.

Canadians: No. I say again, you divert your course.

Americans: THIS IS THE AIRCRAFT CARRIER USS *LINCOLN*, THE SECOND LARGEST SHIP IN THE UNITED STATES ATLANTIC FLEET. We are accompanied by three destroyers, three cruisers, and numerous support vessels. I demand that you change your course 15 degrees north; I say again, that's one-five degrees north, or countermeasures will be undertaken to ensure the safety of this ship.
Canadians: This is the lighthouse. Your call.

Don't we sometimes try to tell Jesus—our Lighthouse—which way is right? We argue with him about which way is best when we are the ones who need to follow his directions, for he will not steer us wrong. But ultimately it *is* our call—whether we will submit to his lordship or undertake our own self-serving countermeasures.

Christlikeness demands a commitment to personal holy living. When the individuals of a stepfamily make this declaration and live accordingly, they set themselves up for success. People are not filled with drugs or alcohol, but with the Spirit of the living God. Parents work to keep their minds from being consumed with material possessions and instead fill their thoughts with things from above (Colossians 3:1–14). Sexual boundaries are maintained so as to protect against infidelity, pornography, and stepfamily incest. Men challenge themselves to be the servant-leaders of their home (Ephesians 5:25) and, in so doing, set a standard of sacrifice for everyone else. And persons continue to study the Scriptures in order to keep in step with the Spirit (Galatians 5:25). There are, of course, thousands of Scripture texts that address relationships and cast a spotlight on godly living. Let's sample just a few. Read the following and apply them specifically to the relationships within your stepfamily. Ask yourself how you might live with and/or relate to your spouse, ex-spouse, children, and stepchildren.

> Put to death, therefore, whatever belongs to your earthly nature: sexual immorality, impurity, lust, evil desires and greed, which is idolatry. Because of these, the wrath of God is coming. You used to walk in these ways, in the life you once lived. But now you must rid yourselves of all such things as these: anger, rage, malice, slander, and filthy language from your lips. Do not lie to each other, since you have taken off your old self with its

practices and have put on the new self, which is being renewed in knowledge in the image of its Creator. (Colossians 3:5–10)

Therefore, as God's chosen people, holy and dearly loved, clothe yourselves with compassion, kindness, humility, gentleness and patience. Bear with each other and forgive whatever grievances you may have against one another. Forgive as the Lord forgave you. And over all these virtues put on love, which binds them together in perfect unity. (Colossians 3:12–14)

Love is patient, love is kind. It does not envy, it does not boast, it is not proud. It is not rude, it is not self-seeking, it is not easily angered, it keeps no record of wrongs. Love does not delight in evil but rejoices with the truth. It always protects, always trusts, always hopes, always perseveres. Love never fails. (1 Corinthians 13:4–8a)

Finally, brothers, whatever is true, whatever is noble, whatever is right, whatever is pure, whatever is lovely, whatever is admirable—if anything is excellent or praiseworthy—think about such things. Whatever you have learned or received or heard from me, or seen in me—put it into practice. And the God of peace will be with you. (Philippians 4:8–9)

But the fruit of the Spirit is love, joy, peace, patience, kindness, goodness, faithfulness, gentleness and self-control. (Galatians 5:22–23a)

Do not let any unwholesome talk come out of your mouths, but only what is helpful for building others up according to their needs, that it may benefit those who listen. (Ephesians 4:29)

The application of these texts can be profound for your family. For instance, you might find it much more difficult to argue with your ex-spouse if you "don't keep a record of wrongs." Compassion can help you to be sensitive to your spouse who feels caught between love for you and love for his or her children. Gentleness with a stepchild who has made it perfectly clear he doesn't want you around, is a high calling, but will eventually help open the door to your stepchild's heart. Finding and focusing on what is "praiseworthy"—instead of rehashing what is upsetting—helps create energy for problem solving and gives you hope for the future. And finally, not letting your children hear "unwholesome talk" about the other household is a gift, just as "building up" your children's stepparents (especially the stepparent in the other home) is a gift.

Negative comments about your children's other stepparent (the ex-spouse's new spouse) are usually an attempt to keep your children's loyalties. Parents don't realize they already have their children's loyalties; a stepparent can never replace a biological parent in a child's heart. Negative comments are simply unnecessary. If you are successful in getting your children to become uncooperative and disrespectful toward the stepparent, stress is created in the other home, which is then carried back into your home by the children. In other words, unwholesome talk about the other home is an effective form of self-sabotage! We should all be reminded that God's way really does work best. We can argue with his directions or comply with the Lighthouse. Which are you doing?

Listening

The second stepping-stone involves one of the hardest skills in relationships—listening. If stepfamily members are not willing to hear one another, they can't know how to love and honor one another. Listening is a process by which persons set aside their own agendas long enough to tune in to someone else. This allows you to see another perspective and gain insight into that family member's feelings, desires, and goals. In contrast, an unwillingness to listen and value the perspective of another results in feelings of invalidation and unimportance.

Outsiders in stepfamilies are those who are not biologically related to other stepfamily members. They frequently feel discounted and pushed out of discussions and decision-making because, as they are told, "you just don't understand" the history behind a given problem or circumstance. Such invalidation brings about resentment and a sense of unacceptance. Even though opinions will differ, everyone in a stepfamily has the need to be heard.

When conflict erupts, the biblical admonition to "be quick to listen and slow to become angry" is of tremendous value (James 1:19). During conflict, most persons want so badly to be heard that they talk over others, or are devising their next comment when they're supposed to be listening. Proverbs 18:13 reminds us that, "he who answers before listening—that is his folly and his shame." It takes great discipline, but people who can apply the principle of *listening first to understand the other before trying to be understood,* will find their conflicts de-escalating and more productive.

Understanding

Listening is the skill that makes understanding possible. It can be difficult to fully understand someone else's perspective, but standing in another's shoes in order to see the world from that person's point of view is a good first step. Individuals within stepfamilies have each traveled a different journey. Biological children and stepchildren, for example, experience their stepfamily quite differently. Biological parents experience the stepfamily differently than do stepparents. The adult experience is different than the children's. To put yourself in the shoes of the other persons in your family is a tremendous act of courage. You may find, for example, that a stepdaughter's resentment of you is not farfetched given how she has been hurt by others in the past. Or you may discover that your husband's style of discipline makes sense once you understand what he experienced in his first marriage and family of origin.

The key is to put yourself in the shoes of another and wonder what it must be like to be that person. Ask yourself:

- What losses has he or she experienced? (Make a list of the losses your children have experienced, and you'll be humbled by what they have been forced to give up.)
- How do the other members of our stepfamily treat this person? How do I treat him or her?
- What is it like for children to live in the other home?
- What challenges does he or she face in trying to belong?
- What responsibilities, roles, relationships, etc. does he or she have that I don't have to deal with?
- What is his or her favorite part of this family?
- What part does he or she care for the least?

Ask this family member to share the answers to some of these questions with you. Listen intently and strive to understand how these aspects impact his or her daily life with you. Such understanding will help you develop empathy for each member of your family, which in turn helps you relate more effectively.

Perseverance

Life is filled with trials, tribulations, and challenges. It is the norm for all types of families (biological, single parent, and stepfamily). This is especially true at the beginning of the stepfamily journey; in fact, uncertainty, disillusionment, and discouragement commonly characterize the first few years. But the stepping-stone of perseverance can carry you through these difficult times.

What I'm talking about is being determined and sticking with your marriage and family when the going gets tough. Henry Blackaby in *Experiencing God*[1] talks about the "crisis of belief" that Christians experience when God's will becomes evident. When God speaks his desire for us, whether through Scripture or circumstance, we face a crisis of belief. Will my belief lead to action and take me wherever God has directed—even if I personally don't want to go there—or will my belief remain simply words? I wish I could share with you how many Christians have sat in my therapy office and said they were unwilling to persevere, even though they knew God didn't want them to give up on their marriage. Determination is not a convenience. It is a crisis of belief. In effect, determination says, "Trusting God to be faithful as the Lord of Possibilities, I will be faithful and persevere in my marital responsibilities even if this marriage and family is not what I want it to be."[2] Determination, then, can be quite costly, but it also paves the way for a growing relationship.

Commitment

Determination, when combined with the decision to persevere, results in a strong commitment to building your stepfamily. The bedrock of this commitment is dedication to your spouse. Nothing can be more important in any family; after all, the stepfamily begins as two people vow to love, honor, and cherish one another for a lifetime. But sometimes we need to be reminded that our marital vows were not multiple-choice. The preacher probably didn't let you choose: "I'll take richer, for better, and in health— but I won't commit to poorer, for worse, or in sickness."

A few years ago I heard about a young man who approached the minister during the wedding rehearsal and made him an offer. "Look, I'll give you $100 if you'll change the wedding vows. When you get to me and the part where I'm to promise to 'love, honor, and obey' and 'forsaking all others, be faithful to her forever,' I'd appreciate it if you'd just leave that part out." He then gave the minister the money and walked away. At the wedding, when it came time for the groom to state his vows, the minister looked him straight in the eye and said, "Will you promise to prostrate yourself before her, obey her every command and wish, serve her breakfast in bed every morning of your life, and swear eternally before God and your lovely wife that you will not ever even look at another woman, as long as you both shall live?" The groom gulped, looked around, and of course said, "Yes." He then leaned toward the minister and hissed, "I thought we had a deal." As the minister slipped the $100 bill back into the groom's hand, he whispered, "She made me a much better offer!"

Commitment means remaining dedicated to the vows we expressed on our wedding day. Couples then make a decision every day of their life whether or not they will live up to those words. If they choose not to, their stepfamily will not survive the journey.

Patience

Stepfamily integration hardly ever happens as quickly as adults want it to. It just doesn't happen on their timetable. Stepfamily researcher James Bray discovered that stepfamilies don't begin to think or act like a family until the end of the second or third year.[3] Furthermore, Patricia Papernow, author of the book *Becoming a Stepfamily*, discovered that it takes the average stepfamily seven years to integrate sufficiently to experience intimacy and authenticity in step relationships.[4] Fast families can accomplish this in four years, if the children are young and the adults are intentional about bringing their family together. However, slow families, according to Papernow, can take nine or more years. In my experience, very few adults come into their stepfamily believing it will take this long. They want a quick, painless blending process. In fact, if they had known the journey would take so long, they might not have signed on in the first place.

You see, the stepfamily is filled with complex dynamics that take most adults by surprise. Family therapists have long recognized that divorce doesn't really end family life; it just reorganizes it. In effect, it spreads your family out over multiple households. Emotional and relational dynamics that preceded the divorce continue even though the family living arrangements have been restructured. Even new relationships become part of the larger family. Have you noticed, for example, that when your ex-wife's new mother-in-law has a crisis, it impacts your home? Your children are emotionally impacted, and it may force your ex-wife to change her visitation schedule, which, of course, dramatically affects your life and plans.

Stepfamilies need to realize that all the people sharing a home with your children and stepchildren are part of your "expanded" family. Start counting, and the total number of people can be exasperating! From a mathematical perspective, the number of possible interactions in a stepfamily containing children who move back and forth between two homes, and who have stepparents who have biological children of their own, can be thousands of times greater than a biological family's possible interactions. That's why family therapists and stepfamily educators Emily and John Visher point out that stepfamilies don't have a family tree, they have a family forest! This complex forest simply takes time to integrate.

A seminar participant once asked me what he could have done differently to build a relationship with his stepdaughter. He described how he took his new twelve-year-old stepdaughter out shopping and to get ice cream whenever possible. He asked her what activities she liked doing and then made sure they did them together. In his words, "I tried and tried, but she never warmed up to me, so I gave up." Bewildered by the scenario, I asked for more information. He had become this girl's second stepfather after her mother divorced a second husband. The girl's biological father was uninvolved in her life, leaving a deep wound in her heart. Her first stepfather was aloof, distant, and critical. I suggested to the gentleman that, because of them, he had two strikes against him when he remarried her mother. But the real clincher came when I asked how long he attempted to win his stepdaughter's heart. *Three months.* He gave up after only three months. You see, he simply didn't take into consideration all that this girl had been through and how long it takes for step relationships to develop. His intentions were good. His actions were on target. He just wasn't patient enough.

Flexibility

Have you ever tried to force a square peg into a round hole? Because the stepfamily is different from a biological family, you need to learn flexibility. The rituals, expectations, and assumptions our society trains us to have about family life become our square pegs that, when forced into the round stepfamily hole, just don't fit. Again, it's not that the biological family mold is necessarily better; it is just different.

What would happen if while riding a bicycle you made a 90-degree right-hand turn by turning the handlebars the same way you would a car steering wheel? You'd flip right over the handlebars and face-plant on the ground! The bicycle is a different vehicle than a car and requires different movements to steer it correctly. If you try to steer your stepfamily the exact same way you would a biological family, you're bound to flip over a time or two. Almost immediately some rituals, styles of parenting, and expectations will work just as they do in biological families, and others will eventually work well once the family has bonded together. Other ways of relating, however, will always be different, requiring flexible handling.

Humor

In the midst of a chaotic moment, humor is definitely the best medicine for stepfamilies. Humor brings a perspective that helps you to step back from the crisis or circumstance and see it in a whole new light. In fact, you might even enjoy a good laugh.

I often reference two cartoons that make this point clear. The first pictures a man reading a piece of mail to his wife. "It's bad news, Anne," he says. "The traffic judge assigned to our case is my first wife." The ability to chuckle at the predicaments of life will save your soul from worry and anxiety. The second cartoon pictures two young children standing in the front yard. The little girl is pointing at the boy, reminding him, "Your dad cannot beat up my dad because your dad is now *my* dad, remember?"

Incidentally, that cartoon took on new meaning when I applied it to Jesus—the most famous stepchild who ever lived. Think about it: He wasn't raised by his natural father. Joseph was his stepdad. Yes, it is a unique circumstance, but you still can't avoid the fact that the Creator of the universe entrusted his Son to be raised by a stepfather. Picture Jesus as an eight-year-old talking to his stepsiblings. "Oh, no. Believe me, your dad cannot beat up my Dad!"

Learning to laugh at yourself and your circumstances is not about denying problems or responsibilities. It is about not taking yourself too seriously so you can gain perspective on your circumstances.

SHARE YOUR TRAVELOGUE: A TOOL FOR DEVELOPING COMPASSION AND UNDERSTANDING

How many of the key stepping-stones does your family possess now? Just where is your stepfamily in this journey to the Promised Land? Are you just beginning, toward the end, or somewhere in the middle? I'm sure you have definite ideas, but your children may view it differently. As I mentioned earlier, there are similarities in how persons experience their family life, but the differences in stepfamilies can be profound because each person in the stepfamily has traveled a different path to where they are now. Listening shows respect for the other's experience and helps you to maintain a humble attitude about your own. Understanding comes when you see your stepfamily through the eyes of others. Both help you to respond to their needs.

Patricia Papernow has developed the travelogue as an effective tool that helps stepfamilies listen and understand one another.[5] The technique is based on the notion that if people in your family went to a foreign country for a month, upon their return you would probably ask them for a travelogue, that is, the story of their journey. You'd ask where they ate, what food they liked, what famous sites they saw, what was most exciting or disappointing, etc. You'd want to know what the journey was like for them. Showing similar interest in each family member's biological, single-parent, and stepfamily journey affirms the person's experience and can teach you what it is like to be him or her. CAUTION: While this tool can facilitate bridge-building between family members, it can also reveal great pain in others and might reveal parts of yourself that need changing. Only the courageous and determined should read on.

At a family meeting (see chapter 8), ask each person to share his or her *travelogue*, that is, a personal account of their stepfamily journey. Remember, the task is to maintain enough curiosity ("tell me more") and empathy ("that must be tough") in the face of differences and disappointments so that each person is able to share joys, pains, heartaches, and experiences without fear of retaliation or rejection. As people share, everyone must maintain a non-defensive attitude. Focus on listening, not defending yourself.

To begin, say something like: "You know, everyone in our family has traveled a long way to get to where we are. And even though we're in the same family, we've probably traveled different paths to get here. Maybe we could share what it's been like so far. Starting with your first family and single-parent years, let's all take turns and talk about what this journey has been like until now. The rest of us will listen just as if we're listening to someone who's been to a foreign land. We'll ask questions and try to imagine what it must have been like for whoever is talking."[6]

Once you've opened the door to honesty and understanding by sharing your travelogue first, keep the conversation going by giving the children a chance. Here are some questions that might help.

- What was the good and bad of your parents' divorce (our divorce) for you?
- How did your life change after that?
- What have you lost that hasn't been regained?
- What do you think has changed for others?
- During the single-parent years, what was good or okay for you? What was a pain? How was life different for you?
- What was your first impression of your future stepparent/stepchildren?
- How did life with your mom/dad/children change once the remarriage occurred?
- What hopes or dreams did you have for this stepfamily that haven't come about yet?
- What painful emotions have you been feeling lately?
- What fears do you have about this stepfamily or yourself?
- Describe insider and outsider roles with older children. First, ask everyone to share whether they are an insider or outsider and why. Then discuss what it would be like to be in the other's (insider/outsider) shoes.

- Discuss the common myth of instant love (see chapter four) and share how you envision love developing between stepfamily members.
- End your travelogue meeting in prayer.

The travelogue exercise can be repeated in your home over time. Family meetings are the perfect time to ask questions and be updated on everyone's travels. Biological parents might also find one-on-one time with each child to discuss their current travelogue.

KEEP STEPPING

The journey to the Promised Land is not always an easy one, but then again, what in life is easy? In this chapter I've suggested that maintaining key attitudes and qualities—*stepping-stones*—will advance your journey in the Lord.

- *Spiritual integrity* demands that we allow Jesus to be Lord over our heart and home.
- *Listening* and *understanding* help family members develop compassion and empathy for one another.
- *Perseverance* will help you stay the course when the going gets tough.
- *Commitment* expresses itself in dedication to fulfilling your marital vows.
- *Patience* means enjoying your stepfamily as it is, instead of pushing everyone to arrive at the Promised Land on your schedule.
- *Flexibility* includes changing your assumptions of how things should be and opening yourself to creative solutions to common problems.
- *Humor*—the gift that focuses on the bright side of dark moments.

I have sought in this chapter to give you hope on your journey. In the next section we will examine seven smart steps that nearly all stepfamilies must take to reach the Promised Land. The dynamics of stepfamily life can be challenging, but they are not impossible. Keep stepping.

Questions for Discussion

FOR ALL COUPLES

1. Have you had any informal travelogue talks? What did you learn?

2. Discuss the pros and cons of having everyone present for the travelogue discussion vs. only biological parents and children.

3. What is one of your chief frustrations or complaints about your stepfamily right now?

4. On a scale of 1 to 10 (with 10 being the highest), rate your personal level of spiritual integrity. What spiritual challenges stand in front of you and how are you addressing them?

5. Describe a time when you tried to force your will on God. What was the outcome?

6. Choose one of the Scripture passages on pages 35 and 36 and share how applying that verse will help your stepfamily's growth.

7. If you asked your children and your spouse whether they felt you were a good listener, what would they say? In what ways does defensiveness keep you from listening well?

8. Identify the person you have the most conflict with or the child to whom you are the least bonded. Share what you think it would be like to be that member of your stepfamily. Consider his or her losses, sense of belonging, fears, responsibilities, and hurts.

9. Read James 1:2–4. If the testing of our faith produces perseverance (which in turn helps us mature), how has the testing of your stepfamily helped you grow as an individual?

10. List three things you could do this week to express your dedication (commitment) to your spouse.

11. In what ways have you been impatient with the status of your stepfamily bonds? How have you tried to force or pressure people to love one another?

12. In what ways is your stepfamily different than a biological family? Share some of the flexible solutions you've already discovered that help.

13. Share a humorous occasion or story from your stepfamily's life. If you can't think of one immediately, try to step back from your circumstances in order to see the humorous side.

FOR PRE-REMARITAL COUPLES

1. Feel free to begin having travelogue discussions as a couple and with your children. Keep in mind that before the wedding most children cannot adequately anticipate all they will feel. Be sure to ask them again later. How might you go about having travelogue discussions now?

2. Which of the stepping-stones characterize your relationships now?

PART TWO

Seven Steps in the Journey

An old Chinese proverb states that a journey of a thousand miles begins with just one step. While the stepfamily journey involves many challenges, there are a few major steps that must be handled well. This section of the book provides the nuts and bolts to integrating a stepfamily.

Each chapter discusses a key step in the integration process. It's likely that you won't take each of these steps just once. You'll probably find yourself navigating them again and again as children grow, and relationships in your and the other household change. These seven steps create a dance that must be danced repeatedly before harmony is achieved on the dance floor of life.

CHAPTER THREE

Smart Step One: STEP Up!

Discover a redemptive God who loves,
forgives, and provides strength
and direction for the journey

*"When we were utterly helpless, Christ came at just the right time and died
for us sinners. Now, no one is likely to die for a good person, though someone might be willing to die for a person who is especially good. But God
showed his great love for us by sending Christ to die for us while we were
still sinners. And since we have been made right in God's sight by the blood
of Christ, he will certainly save us from God's judgment. For since we were
restored to friendship with God by the death of his Son while we were still
his enemies, we will certainly be delivered from eternal punishment by his
life. So now we can rejoice in our wonderful new relationship with God—
all because of what our Lord Jesus Christ has done for us in making us
friends of God"* (Romans 5:6–11 NLT).

When I started doing therapy and speaking with stepfamilies, I had no
idea how important Step One would be to their overall development. I was
conscious of everyone's need for a personal relationship with God (that
was a given). But what I didn't understand was how frequently stepfamily
individuals (adults in particular) seem to be paralyzed by the belief that
they are unworthy of God's love and forgiveness. Commonly there is a fear,
confusion, and sense of alienation from God.

THE RALLY CRY RESPONSE

I believe God has called me to educate and equip stepfamilies for healthy living. Furthermore, I consider it part of this calling to shout a rally cry to church leaders, inviting them to better minister to stepfamilies in their communities (see chapter 12). However, the rally cry response has been met with some opposition by those who are concerned that stepfamily ministry somehow condones (or encourages) divorce or adultery. In addition, there is hesitation from a few who wonder if ministering to the remarried is the equivalent of abandoning God's design for marriage. Let it be understood that I want to uphold and teach God's ideal that one man and one woman be married for life (and any remarried person with a Christlike perspective on life will agree that God's ideal is best). In no way should we compromise God's plan for the foundation of our homes. My desire to educate and equip stepfamilies, then, is not about condoning a past. It is, rather, an effort to help stepfamilies walk hand in hand with their Lord in the present.

You see, the problems and pressures of stepfamily life are a distraction from that which really matters—making Jesus the Lord of your life and sharing your faith with the children under your care. Satan knows that one of the greatest influences on your life is your family, and if he can mess it up, then he will likely get you as well (and the next four generations to come!). But if you dedicate your family to God, then you're well on your way to finding the strength and answers you need to make your family successful. Satan would much rather you be distracted, discouraged, and defeated!

And that's exactly where many stepfamilies end up—feeling that they don't belong in church and believing they aren't good enough for God's grace. What contributes to that? First, let's examine a stepfamily's relationship to the church.

Spiritually Marginalized From God's Hospital Church

- "Thanks for recognizing that we're not the church's dirty little problem."
- "I never thought I could go back to church again."
- "Once the divorce happened, the majority of the church members

had nothing to do with any of us, including my children. I was working at a bank, and one of the deacons refused to stand in my line because I was a divorced person. . . . When you go through a divorce, you need your family and [church] friends' support. I received no support from the church; instead, I was treated like a second-class citizen."

Second-class citizens. That well sums up how many stepfamilies are made to feel. They don't reflect God's ideal family constellation, so they just aren't quite good enough. One couple I have grown to love and appreciate very much was studying with a preacher who was trying to help them come back to the Lord after a number of prodigal years. When the preacher discovered they were divorced and remarried, he closed his Bible, looked at them, and said, "I'm sorry. Your background and past might infect everyone else, so we can't have you in our church." He then turned and left their home.

Can you imagine? A man claiming to proclaim the grace of God told them they were so sick they needed to be quarantined from the hospital! I thought hospitals were for the sick, for those who need healing. I guess I missed the part of the Bible that says only perfect people belong in church. I should add that God wasn't finished with this couple. After hearing this preacher's condemnation, they visited the church where I serve as family life minister. After much prayer and repentance, this couple resurrected their relationship with Christ, and we eventually put them to work leading our stepfamily support group. Together they have blessed numerous lives and continue to serve their King.

But the message divorced and remarried persons sometimes receive from the church is only half the problem. Stepfamily adults often become spiritually marginalized due to their own sense of guilt and unworthiness.

Spiritual Shame

- "I am not sure if I am accepted by God because of my remarriage. I am almost afraid to read the Bible, because I'm not sure what I may find."
- "I have tried to get my life back on track, but as a divorcee, that stigma and my own guilt combined to make me feel like an outsider.

That outsider feeling made me not want to give up my sinful life. Satan would step in and say, 'Why should you commit to this church? They look at you weird; they know you are divorced. If they do not care about you, why should you care about them or be committed to their God?' So before I could develop any ties to a local church, I would lose interest in getting my life straight. I would quickly return to my life of sin—lost, frustrated, and now even more embarrassed."

Feeling unworthy of God's love is often self-imposed. Yes, sometimes it's an excuse to avoid responsibility, and sometimes it flows from a legalistic theology that believes we have to earn our salvation. But no matter its origin, the impact is the same: People keep their distance from God and his church.

"Okay, Ron," people have interjected before, "just how does God feel about me and my stepfamily situation? I mean, if we could ask him, what would he say?" Well, perhaps he feels about you the same way he felt about the imperfect families of the Bible. Let me illustrate.

THE FAMILY OF PROMISE

Nan, my wife, and I waited a number of years before having children. Once we began making plans to conceive a child, I began praying for God's insight and wisdom into how I should be as a father. Furthermore, I began searching the Scriptures to find a healthy, faithful family that could serve as a model for me. My training in marriage and family therapy had primarily focused on the dynamics of change with dysfunctional families, so I needed to see more of what a functional family looked like. Besides, I wanted to see how faith and family dynamics would integrate to make a "perfect combination." So I began to survey the families of the Old Testament.

Murder is not new to us in America. Besides the violence in the streets, it has become common within our schools, suburban neighborhoods, and even within homes. Yet the first incident of family homicide came from Adam and Eve's family. Cain was so jealous of his brother's favor in God's eyes that with premeditation he lured him to a lonely place and killed him (Genesis 4:1–8). Not a good start for this world of ours, huh?

And then there's Noah and his sons, Shem, Ham, and Japheth (Genesis 9:20–27). We're all aware of their incredible faithful journey on the ark, but are you aware of what happened later? Noah got drunk one night, leaving himself naked and exposed to his son Ham. The older brothers respectfully covered their father's nakedness, but the damage had already been done. Noah cursed Ham for the shame he experienced (wasn't Noah partly responsible?) and blessed the older two brothers. In effect, Noah set the brothers against each other, and a pattern of jealousy and competition continued yet another generation.

My search then led me to the "family of promise." Abraham is well known for his faithful walk with God and for God's promise to make him into a great nation. Eventually, in fact, the seed of Abraham would bring the Messiah, the Savior, Jesus Christ himself. As I surveyed biblical families I remember thinking, *Adam and Noah's families were disappointments, but surely I'll find a good model family here.*

In Genesis 12:13–20 Abram coerced his wife, Sarai, to lie to the Egyptians in order to save his life. "Say you are my sister," he told her. Because Sarai was a beautiful woman, Abram feared that Pharaoh would have him killed in order to have Sarai for himself. Wives, if your husband refused to own you in public and was willing to put you in jeopardy in order to save his own skin, how would you feel? Furthermore, what if he gave you to another man, knowing he would take you to be his wife and have intercourse with you—now how would you feel? What if he did it *twice*?!

Believe it or not, Abraham (God had changed his name) again said—this time to Abimelech—that Sarah was his sister. He feared Abimelech, the king of Gerar, would have him killed, so he handed her over to become another man's wife. In case you're wondering, this is not what Promise Keepers has in mind for husbands! Abraham was a man of great faith. But he was far from the perfect husband. (See Genesis 20.)

But the pattern of selfish husbandry doesn't stop there. Isaac, Abraham's son, who probably wasn't even born when his father disowned his mother, told the same lie about his wife, Rebekah. He too feared for his life, so he told the king of the Philistines that Rebekah was his sister (Genesis 26:1–11). Abraham and Isaac's lies were eventually found out, but not before a great many people were hurt by the deception. Has lying and deception ever cost you peace in your home?

In chapter 5 we'll examine further the expanded family dynamics of Abraham's home. But for now remember that while Sarah was barren, she suggested Abraham take her maidservant, Hagar, to be a second wife so they could conceive a child through her (Genesis 16). But once Hagar conceives, jealousy and competition become the name of the game between Sarah and Hagar. Anger, bitterness, and favoritism are the result.

I called this home an "expanded family" because there were multiple wives and competition for how the children would be treated by the biological father, Abraham. Some are calling the stepfamily of modern America an "expanded" family. Indeed, the dynamics of Abraham, Sarah, and Hagar mirror the dynamics of today's stepfamily with ex-spouses and children moving between homes. We'll examine those dynamics more in the chapter on marriage. Suffice it for now to say that Abraham's expanded home was full of anger, jealousy, competition, bitterness, and loyalty conflicts. And these negative qualities are handed down to yet another generation.

In Genesis 27 we read of how Abraham's daughter-in-law, Rebekah, conspired with her favored son, Jacob, to deceive her husband, Isaac. If it worked, Jacob would receive a critically important blessing meant for Esau. Jacob had already cheated his brother out of his birthright, but he wanted more. He wanted a special position, because the other brother and his descendants would serve the one who received the blessing. Rebekah and Jacob's plan worked, and a divided house became even more divided as Esau set out to avenge his loss and kill Jacob. Talk about sibling rivalry! But we're not finished studying the "family of promise."

Jacob then passes on the family pattern of favoritism to his son Joseph, who was his father's favorite. Jacob even gave him a special robe to signify his love. Joseph's brothers, however, didn't appreciate Joseph's favored status, so they devised a plan to kill him. Only at the last minute did they stop short of murder and decide instead to sell him into slavery. Can you imagine? And you thought your stepchildren were being inconsiderate of your biological children.

No, my attempt to find the model biblical family was not successful. Indeed, within a few generations of Abraham there were family power struggles, failures to become properly individuated from parents, family secrets, exploitive and coercive relationships, marital game-playing that led to triangulation, parent-child alliances, vindictiveness, anger, and sibling rivalries. But that's not all.

The family pathology within the family of promise continues to mushroom through the family of David. Even though the Bible does refer to him as a "man after God's own heart," David's behavior included premeditated murder to cover an affair, an out-of-wedlock pregnancy, and a son who replicates his father's disgrace by raping his half-sister. Later another of David's sons would avenge his sister's humiliation by hunting down and murdering the brother who raped her.

Are you feeling any better about your stepfamily situation?

So much for the family of promise being a model family for us to emulate. And the other families of the Bible, in both Old and New Testaments, are not much better. In truth, God's ideal for the family is evident in Scripture, but an ideal model family to imitate is not. So why would God insist that generations of family dysfunction be detailed in the Bible and serve as an everlasting testimony to the history of his people? *Because God is more concerned about providing redemption in the lives of his people than in promoting self-reliance and personal accomplishment.* The failures of the family of promise resulted in their dependence on God. It is God who forgives and restores us; not even Abraham, Isaac, Joseph, or David were deserving of his mercy.

GOD'S REDEMPTION

Entering into this fullness is not something you figure out or achieve. It's not a matter of being circumcised or keeping a long list of laws. No, you're already *in*—insiders—not through some secretive initiation rite but rather through what Christ has already gone through for you: he destroyed the power of sin. If it's an initiation ritual you're after, you've already been through it by submitting to baptism. Going under the water was a burial of your old life; coming up out of it was a resurrection, God raising you from the dead as he did Christ. When you were stuck in your old sin-dead life, you were incapable of responding to God. God brought you alive—right along with Christ! Think of it! All sins forgiven, the slate wiped clean, that old arrest warrant canceled and nailed to Christ's cross. (Colossians 2:9–14 THE MESSAGE)

Did you hear that? The apostle Paul is screaming the good news—we can't earn our worthiness. Our worth, the possibility of forgiveness, and a right relationship with God have come about because of Christ's saving work on the cross. While we were stuck in our sin, Christ died for us, giving us the hope of redemption. Not all stepfamilies are born out of sinful behavior, but some are. And the good news is that no matter what decisions or sins you may have committed in the past that led to your current stepfamily situation, God wants you back. And he's provided a way through Christ to make it happen.

The portrait of families in the Bible is a series of broken relationships in need of redemption. Not a single family in the entire Old or New Testament was so exemplary that God held it up as a model or pattern for us to follow. Indeed, the great faithful men of the Bible had to rely on God's grace too. And despite their imperfections, God used them for his purposes.

The answer to the question "How does God feel about me and my less-than-perfect family situation?" is this: God loves and forgives the imperfect people in stepfamilies the same way he loves and forgives the imperfect people in biological families. Furthermore, people in stepfamilies are not "second-rate Christians," simply because there is no such thing as a "first-rate Christian." We're all sinners and all less than perfect. All our families are less than ideal. And we all need a Savior.

You may be plagued by guilt, shame, and remorse over your past and present. You may have had an affair or abandoned your spouse, which resulted in divorce; you may have been neglecting your children since the divorce, and their faith is suffering because of you. You may be harboring anger at your ex-spouse for the hurt he or she caused you and the children. Or perhaps a mean-spirited church leader pushed you away from believing you could be forgiven, and previous friends have isolated themselves from you. You may have lost touch with God and find it hard to pray and spend time with your church family. If so, don't look now, but you're being pursued. Pursued by a God who desperately wants you to STEP UP to meet him.

His desire for you is the same as it was for Abraham, Isaac, Jacob, and David—God wants you to daily surrender your will and follow him. His desire for your family is the same as it was for any imperfect biblical family—that you make him the cornerstone upon which the house is built (Psalm 127:1).

If there is distance between you and God, decide today to humbly accept Christ's offer of forgiveness, dedicate your life and marriage to the Lord, and make Him the architect of your new home. It's a decision you'll never regret. If you don't, you may be destined to repeat the past. If your walk with the Lord is solid, keep right on stepping.

I hope this chapter has either opened your eyes to God's incredible redemption or encouraged you to continue basking in his grace. Ultimately, *The Smart Stepfamily* is aimed at helping all members of your family strengthen their relationship with the Creator of life. Truly, what good would it do to develop a healthy stepfamily but have no relationship with God? "And how do you benefit," Jesus wondered, "if you gain the whole world but lose your own soul in the process?" (Matthew 16:26 NLT).

The stepfamily's journey to the Promised Land begins and ends with stepping up to a redemptive God. No other step is nearly as important. And while no other step costs as much as emptying self to carry a cross, no other step is as easy. For our effort to step up is successful only because of our Savior's willingness to step down to the point of our greatest need.

Questions for Discussion

FOR ALL COUPLES

1. How does the survey of Old Testament families make you feel about your stepfamily?
2. On a scale of 1 to 10 (with 10 being the strongest), how strong is your relationship with Christ? How strong is your spouse's relationship with Christ?
3. To what degree have you been alienated from him in the past? What was happening at that time?
4. What messages have you received from the church that discouraged your walk?
5. In what ways do you feel unworthy of God's grace and forgiveness?
6. What parts of your life (such as self-reliance, pride, or selfish desires) do you hold on to? What is difficult to surrender?

7. What hurts have you had difficulty letting go of? Share about your journey toward forgiveness.

8. Realizing that the ground is level at the foot of the cross—that is, we're all in need of a redeemer—what do you need to do individually and as a couple to begin living in a right relationship with Christ?

9. Whether your relationship to Christ is just beginning or going strong, list three habits that would deepen your knowledge of God's Word and his will for your life.

CHAPTER FOUR

Smart Step Two: STEP Down

Adjust your expectations and learn how to cook a stepfamily

"Therefore I tell you, do not worry about your life, what you will eat or drink; or about your body, what you will wear. . . . Look at the birds of the air; they do not sow or reap or store away in barns, and yet your heavenly Father feeds them. Are you not much more valuable than they? . . . So do not worry saying, "What shall we eat?" or "What shall we drink?" or "What shall we wear?" . . . But seek first his kingdom and his righteousness, and all these things will be given to you as well. Therefore do not worry about tomorrow, for tomorrow will worry about itself. Each day has enough trouble of its own" (Matthew 6:25–26, 31, 33–34).

If the Israelites had known that they would face the Red Sea, be pursued by Pharaoh and his army, and face great tests of their faith, do you think they would have ever embarked on the journey to the Promised Land? More than once they considered going back because the costs of the trip were much more than they had expected. They always are. Perhaps that's why God didn't tell them what was in store. Instead, he simply called upon them to trust him with what stood directly in front of them. All the Israelites had to do was trust God's faithfulness with each step they took. I think we would all find the journeys of life much less worrisome if we could just be faithful to God with what stands in front of us and not fret over what tomorrow may hold.

We cannot help but have expectations of what lies ahead. And because love and romance are natural blinders, expectations are often filled with unrealistic visions for how stepfamily life will proceed. Knowing the remarriage divorce rate is at least 60 percent, would you form a stepfamily if you believed you would soon join those making up that statistic? Of course not. No one assumes he or she is destined for marital failure or even distress. We assume, whether it is a first marriage or a remarriage, that love will conquer all.

During pre-remarital counseling I consider it my job to break through the fog of "being in love" and give couples a realistic picture of the challenges, as well as the rewards, of stepfamily life. But I'm amazed at how easily the challenges are discounted and minimized. "I can see how that might impact someone else," they say, "but we're different. The kids are getting along just fine, and God has obviously brought us together; this must be right." Reader beware: If you allow unrealistic expectations to drive the way you attempt to bring your family together, you are in for a great deal of disappointment.

When our expectations of what should happen in a stepfamily are not met, disappointment and disillusionment are sure to result. If solutions can't be found and the disillusionment solidifies, people commonly begin to wonder if the marriage was a mistake. "Perhaps this wasn't such a good idea, after all. I had no idea his children would be so defiant or that he would be so controlling over my parenting. I wonder if I should have dated longer before agreeing to marry him?" Did you hear that? Embedded in her doubt was the first look back toward Egypt. "Maybe I *should* just go back to my previous life." It's subtle, but the erosion of commitment has begun.

Whether you are not yet married, or a few years down the road, use this chapter to examine your expectations and listen to what is realistic. Learning to accept "what is" versus "what you think should be" is critical to your emotional well-being and dedication. It also sets you up to relax in the Lord's timing, rather than be overtaken by the myths common to stepfamilies.

MYTHS AND UNREALISTIC EXPECTATIONS

The following are common myths and unrealistic expectations that stepfamilies face.[1] Closely examine your assumptions about each.

Love Will Happen Instantly Between All Family Members

This represents the ultimate fantasy of stepfamily life. Somehow, by some miracle of God, each adult and child in the stepfamily home will come together in love despite their different backgrounds, losses, and bonds with other extended family. While this belief is understandable, it simply is not true. Even worse, when parents force persons together in order to make the dream come true, the exact opposite frequently occurs. Putting unrelated persons in the same house does not mean they will love and care for one another. In fact, what is realistic is that love and care may or *may not* develop at some point in time. And if it does, it assuredly won't happen instantly. Learn to relax and make acceptance and respect for one another your goal. Love in the sense of "love your neighbor" is attainable; love in the sense of deep family bonds may or may not be achieved.

We'll Do It Better This Time Around

A frequent mistake made by couples is comparing the new relationship to the former one(s). It's as if this marriage is competing against the legacy of the previous one(s). Nothing could be further from the truth. In fact, living in the present with a constant eye on how it compares to the past forces you to live in the past (and that didn't work out so well the first time). Of course, both partners should examine how they contributed to the demise of a previous marriage and learn from their mistakes, but the new marriage is simply a different marriage. Some things will be similar, but many things will be different. You cannot make up for past losses, mistakes, or sins, so don't use this marriage to redeem your good name. Live in the present and accept your stepfamily for what it is.

Everything Will Fall Quickly Into Place

Want to bet? In chapter 2 I mentioned that the stepping-stone of patience is critical to stepfamily development. Becoming disillusioned with how your family is progressing is an almost universal experience, because progress never happens on your timetable. Remember, the average stepfamily takes seven years to integrate, according to Patricia Papernow, a leading stepfamily researcher.[2]

Before remarriage, the last thing any parent wants to assume is that the emotional work required before their children bond with their stepfamily will take seven or more years. Most parents have seen their children suffer enough, and they don't want them to suffer further because of a decision to remarry. Parents want to believe that their children will be okay and the new spouse will find his or her place. Thus, the power of hope blinds pre-remarriage couples to the realities of stepfamily integration.

Despite the length of time generally required for integration, stepfamilies needn't be overwhelmed by what lies ahead. Don't forget, all God calls us to do is to be faithful with what stands directly in front of us. The journey may have many bends or mountains to climb, but facing the current challenges with determination is what matters most. This means we must trust God to provide direction and resources when challenges present themselves. Replacing an "everything will fall quickly into place" expectation with a "God will see us through the journey—however long it may be" attitude of trust will bring much needed patience and peace to your journey.

Our Children Will Feel As Happy About the Remarriage As We Do

Stepfamilies are born out of loss. That is a sobering fact. Perhaps a parent was lost to death, or a marriage ended in divorce. Perhaps this stepfamily was born out of an out-of-wedlock pregnancy with a biological parent now living elsewhere. Whatever the loss, parents watch their children suffer and nothing excites them more than thinking that the gaps in their children's lives could be filled by a new family. This desire to repair children's emotional well-being creates the assumption that children will quickly enjoy the new home. What a blow it is for parents to realize that remarriage is a gain for them, but another loss to their children. Children want their biological parents to remarry or the dead parent to come back to life. For the most part they're not interested in a replacement adult; assuming they will treat this new person as they did the old is a huge myth.

The truth is children will feel confused about the remarriage, both happy and angry, sometimes both at once. And parents who expect their children to feel positive about their choice to remarry may be setting themselves up for great disappointment.

Blending Is the Goal of This Stepfamily

The most common term used to refer to the stepfamily is "blended family." But serious stepfamily therapists, educators, and researchers do not use the term "blended family" simply because most stepfamilies do not blend—and if they do, someone usually gets *creamed* in the process!

The key reason it's not the term of choice: Blending is not the goal. When cooking, blending is a process by which you combine ingredients into one fluid mixture: think of a fruit smoothie or a cream soup. Rarely can it be said that a stepfamily becomes one in a relational sense. More realistic is a process by which the various parts integrate, or come into contact with one another, much like a casserole of distinct parts. For example, biological parents and children will always have a stronger bond than stepparents and stepchildren, even if all goes well. And biologically related children will always have a tighter connection with blood relatives. This is not to say that different members of a stepfamily cannot be close. Many will develop deep emotional bonds, but there will always be a qualitative difference.

John was a very conscientious stepfather. He impressed me with his commitment to the Lord and desire to be a positive influence on his stepfamily. Yet he was longing for something deeper. "Why doesn't my stepson show as much desire for a relationship with me as he does with his dad?" John asked. "His dad is a jerk—he breaks promises to spend time with *David,* he forgets his birthday, and when they are together he drops David off at his grandmother's house. I've been with David since he was four, and even now, ten years later, David prefers spending time with his father. Why does that hurt so much?"

I had spent a fair amount of time with David and knew that he greatly respected and loved his stepfather. Yet the pull to know his dad was tremendous (as is frequently the case with an unavailable noncustodial parent). A blood relationship, for David, was thicker than his mom's marriage. The reason John hurt so much was that he still carried the hope that he and his stepson would be one fluid mixture. They had not and probably would not "blend," but they had already integrated quite well. John was simply placing the bar too high. Stepping down his expectations would have resulted in less hurt and a greater awareness of his current connection with his stepson.

So if blending is not the goal, then how do you cook a stepfamily?

HOW TO COOK A STEPFAMILY: WHAT NOT TO DO

Whether you realize it or not, you likely have an assumed integration style. By that I mean a set of assumptions about how your family ought to come together. Let's use cooking as an analogy to identify some integration styles that generally don't work.

Blender. We've already noted that this mentality assumes all ingredients can be whipped together into one smooth mixture. This assumes each ingredient will relate to the others in the same uniform fashion. There is no uniqueness granted to the different ingredients and little space for diversity.

"Why can't I build a relationship with my stepdaughter? She was sixteen when I married her mother. The other kids were ten and eight, and I haven't had any trouble building a bond with them." Keeping in mind that time is essential to relationship development, building a bond with teenagers is extremely slow going because they are gradually moving away from the family. It is quite normal for a stepparent to have close bonds with one stepchild, be working on bonds with another, while experiencing a distant relationship with an older child. Relationships will be different within the same stepfamily, not one fluid mixture.

Food Processor. These stepfamilies chop up one another's history and attempt to instantly combine all ingredients with rapid speed. When love doesn't occur right away, persons are left feeling torn to pieces; no one remains whole.

A classic example of this mentality is the adult who demands that the stepchildren call their stepparent "daddy" or "mommy." It is as if the child is told, "We've chopped up your real dad and thrown him to the side. This is your new dad." Some parents actually think their children will buy that!

Another example is stepfamilies that assume they can't honor traditions that were established in the first family or single-parent family, because it would leave someone out. What they fail to realize is that chopping up the tradition also chops up the people who honored it. It results in another loss and invites resentment toward the new family.

Microwave. These families refuse to be defined as a stepfamily and seek to heat the ingredients in rapid fashion so as to become a nuke-lier family (pun intended). They avoid labels like stepfamily and the implication that they are different from any other family. People tell me they resent being called a stepfamily, because it makes them feel second-rate. There is nothing inherently wrong with being a stepfamily; it is neither better nor worse than other family types, just different.

Let me emphasize this point. No matter how desperately you may want your stepfamily to be like biological families, it is not. It is true that every stepfamily has aspects that are reflective of biological families. But every stepfamily also has unique characteristics that differ from biological families. Some parts function the same; some don't.

A major barrier to healthy stepfamily adjustment is a parenting team that denies this reality. Consciously or unconsciously people often try to make their home to be just like their family of origin or their first family— only better. After all, the Brady Bunch did it. Why can't we?

One stepmother demonstrated her microwave mentality in an e-mail, questioning an article I had published: "I was disturbed after reading your article," she began. "I am a stepmother of two wonderful girls. I became their stepmother when they were four and two. Shortly afterward, their biological mother abandoned them, and we have not seen or heard from her in almost four years. Don't get me wrong," she continued, "I consider this a blessing." [For whom, I wondered.] "My point is, I am the girls' mother. No step or halves or any other modifier. . . . Our family can and does function like any other family."

Right now this stepmother obviously feels good about her role and stepfamily. For that I am grateful. But I wonder how she will feel as "the girls' mother" if their biological mother happens to reappear hoping to resurrect her relationship with her two daughters. Or perhaps the girls will entertain fantasies about their mother and keep her present, if only in their thought life. Perhaps they will someday seek her out, trying to discover more about their genetic and cultural heritage (as do many adopted children). I'm pleased that this stepmother feels so close to her step-daughters. But whether she wants to accept it or not, she lives in a stepfamily, not a biological family.

Coming to accept your unique challenges and opportunities as a stepfamily is a tremendous first step to finding creative solutions to your dilemmas. If you refuse to admit a difference, you inadvertently shut off your ability to learn new, more effective ways of relating.

One woman refused to believe that her second husband would treat her son any differently than his children. "If he loves me, he'll love my son," she told herself. That, of course, was not the case. While most stepparents try hard to treat their stepchildren the same as their biological children, differences commonly occur. Various levels of bondedness influence our natural reactions to people. While this stepfather should strive for equity in how he treats his children and hers, his wife should understand that differences will occur.

Pressure Cooker. This family cooking style results in ingredients and spices (that is, rituals, values, and preferences) being put under pressure to meld together completely. The family is under great duress, and since expectations are so high, the lid often blows off the pot.

"I know your stepfather is a little demanding and more strict than I, but can't you just get along?" This child is under great pressure to conform because his mother needs him to. Her emotional health seems to be riding on her son's acceptance of his stepfather. Talk about setting yourself up for disappointment!

Another example of the pressure cooker mentality is stepfamilies that assume the answer to every conflict in holiday ritual is to combine the traditions. *Paul* and his children developed a meaningful Christmas tradition in which each person opened one gift on Christmas Eve and the remaining gifts the following morning. However, his new wife, *Sharon*, and her children held the tradition of opening all the gifts Christmas morning after a special breakfast. In a panic, Paul called a few weeks before their second Christmas together. "I'm dreading Christmas this year. Last year Sharon and I combined our holiday traditions and it was disastrous. To honor my family we had all the children open a gift Christmas Eve, and to honor Sharon's family we had breakfast and opened the remaining gifts. But no one liked the outcome. Everyone acted as if we were at a funeral instead of a celebration, and eventually Sharon and I ended up in a fight that lasted through New Year's Day. What are we supposed to do this year—go to our separate corners and pray no one throws a punch?" I'll discuss surviving holidays in chapter 8, but for now understand that combining rituals works sometimes, but pressuring people to be okay with the combination can sabotage the results.

Tossed. Like a salad, this style throws each ingredient into the air with no consideration as to where it might fall. The ingredients keep some of their integrity, yet are expected to fit together with the other pieces. Examples of this style can be subtle or extreme.

When one child is spending time at their other home, remaining children often believe they can play with the absent child's toys or belongings. Children should be taught that even though someone is temporarily in the other home, the absentee's stuff is not free game. If *Susie* wants to wear her stepsister's sweater, she should call her at the other home and ask her permission. If *Brooke* wants to play with her stepbrother *Cole's* video game, she needs to call and ask his permission or establish ground rules before he leaves the house. Respecting one another's possessions is important because it teaches people to honor others; it also communicates belonging to the child who is spending time at the other home. "You may be at your dad's house, but you still have a place here."

More extreme examples of the tossed integration style are noncustodial parents who make frequent moves and expect their children to emotionally handle the disruption in visitation schedules. Parents who expose their children to a revolving door of dating partners or live-in lovers and those who engage in Velcro marriage (a series of stick-and-peel marriages) are also tossing their stepfamily about. This exposes the children to a variety of unstable living environments, changes in school and social arrangements, financial insecurity, and unhealthy relationship models.

One parent kept secret from her two younger children the fact that their older brother had a different father (from a previous marriage). Her personal shame of making some poor decisions early in life and fear of her children's reaction led her to hide the truth from them. Tossing children around while covering the taste of the truth with the right "dressing" does not bring integrity to stepfamily integration. Thankfully, this mother was finally able to tell her children the truth before they heard it from someone else.

CULINARY INSIGHTS FOR COOKING A STEPFAMILY

"So if all of these integration styles are generally not helpful, what style should we use?" I recommend a Crockpot cooking style. Stepfamilies choosing this style understand that *time* and *low heat* make for an effective combination. Ingredients are thrown together in the same pot, but each is left intact, giving affirmation to its unique origin and characteristics. Slowly and with much intentionality, the low-level heat brings the ingredients into contact with one another. As the juices begin to flow together, imperfections are purified, and the beneficial, desirable qualities of each ingredient are added to the taste. The result is a dish of delectable flavor made up of different ingredients that give of themselves to produce a wondrous creation.

The key to Crockpot stepfamilies is *time* and *low heat.* I've already stressed the importance of being patient with the integration process and not trying to force love, care, or togetherness; perhaps you've noticed that the one common element of the food processor, microwave, pressure cooker, and blender integration styles is an attempt to quickly combine the various ingredients (people, rituals, and backgrounds). Such an effort almost always backfires, bringing a backlash of anger and resentment.

Stepfamilies need *time* to adjust to new living conditions, new parenting styles, rules, and responsibilities. They need *time* to experience one another and develop trust, commitment, and a shared history. They need *time* to find a sense of belonging and an identity as a family unit. None of these things can be rushed. People who are trying to prove to their parents, friends, church, minister, or *themselves* that their remarriage decision was right for everyone, need their family to "blend" quickly. But they are often greatly disappointed and feel like failures. A slow-cooking mentality, however, brings relief from the pressure to show everyone you can get along because you assume from the beginning that it will likely take years for your stepfamily to integrate. It also invites you to relax in the moment and enjoy the small steps your stepfamily is making toward integration, rather than pressuring family members to move ahead.

Cooking with *low heat* refers to your gradual, intentional efforts to bring the parts together. It is working smarter, not harder. To illustrate the Crockpot mentality at work, let me apply some Crockpot approaches to the previous examples of what not to do.

A Crockpot stepfather, as opposed to the blender stepfather, would not worry excessively about why he isn't bonding with his teenage step-daughter or assume he and the kids should all blend to the same degree. Slow-cook stepparents understand the cardinal rule of relationship development with stepchildren: Let the stepchild set the pace for the relationship. If she is receiving of the stepfather, let him return the child's affections. If she remains distant or standoffish, he shouldn't force himself upon her. Find ways of managing rules and getting through life (see chapter 8), but don't insist a child welcome your authority or physical affection.

The food processor adults had a similar struggle. They hoped the children would want to refer to their new stepparent with a term of endearment. When this didn't happen naturally, the food processor parents demanded they do so. But a Crockpot adult would understand (even while wishing it were otherwise) that a stepparent can be "daddy" to his youngest stepchild, "James" to his next oldest, and "Mr. James" to the teenager. Crockpot stepfamilies recognize the emotional and psychological attachment children have to biological parents and don't force them to change those attachments.

The microwave-turned-Crockpot mother will accept that her husband will struggle to respond fairly to her children. As a Crockpot mom, the formerly frustrated pressure cooker mom will not immediately respond with anger to her son who is uncooperative with his stepfather. She will look past his oppositional behavior to see a boy who is struggling with loss, unable to connect with his biological father, and discouraged with his family circumstances. And Paul, the pressure cooker stepfather who tried to meld two Christmas traditions, would allow his stepfamily to develop an entirely new Christmas tradition. He and his wife, for example, might have a series of family meetings with the children to discuss their preferences and wants. It may be they decide on an entirely new tradition to honor each family's history by alternating how gifts are opened, or they may decide to let each parent and their children keep their own tradition.

This last idea refers to "mini-family" activities. Early in a stepfamily's integration process it can be helpful to maintain separate family traditions and rituals by giving parents permission to spend time with their children without the step relations present. Stepparents need to give their new spouse and stepchildren time to be alone, without intrusion. The biological parent can play games with her children, while the stepparent enjoys a personal hobby or goes shopping with his children. Such mini-family activity helps children get uninterrupted time with their biological parent and siblings, honoring their need for attention from the ones they love most. It also affirms to children that they have not completely lost access to their parent. As helpful as compartmentalized mini-family activities can be, however, those without a Crockpot mentality often perceive segregated time as an indication of family division.

Troy and *Meredith* called me with a typical integration struggle—what to do with free time on Saturday afternoons. Prior to the remarriage, Troy and his children—*Josh*, eleven, and *Emily*, nine, enjoyed spending their Saturdays doing activities together. Whether miniature golfing, playing softball with friends, or riding bikes in the park, their priority was doing something together. Meredith and her sons—*Terry*, thirteen, and *Joe*, eight, had a different preference for free time. They valued independent time away from each other so each could pursue his or her particular interests. Meredith considered it her "down time" to relax and read a good book, Terry enjoyed playing with friends, while Joe mastered his latest computer game.

At the time they called, Troy and Meredith had tried everything they could to create a "blended family." They challenged one another and the kids to take turns spending their Saturdays doing activities together or apart. One week they would all go miniature golfing only to discover that Meredith's kids complained they were missing out on their fun. Joe would then pester Emily when he got bored, quickly turning the outings into arguments. First the kids would whine and complain, and then Troy would suggest to Meredith that she needed to better control her son. She would feel attacked and defensive about her parenting and resent Troy's "controlling" behavior.

The next week they would try to let everyone experience the joys of "doing your own thing." But inevitably one of Troy's children would try to join Meredith's children in some activity, resulting in arguments and slamming doors.

"We've tried everything," they insisted.

"No," I responded, "you've just tried many cooking styles, hoping to create a biological family that does everything together. What you need to do is back off, and honor one another's past by spending time with your kids doing what you like most."

"You mean he should go golfing with his kids, while the boys and I do separate things? That wouldn't be a family afternoon at all," Meredith challenged.

My response was sobering. "Yes, it would. It would be a stepfamily afternoon." I went on to explain that pressuring the various ingredients to blend was blowing the lid off the pot. Troy and Meredith needed to accept their family as different so they could discover a creative solution. Mini-family activities might not *feel* like a good solution because they were trying to steer their family as they would a biological family. Accepting their stepfamily as one *in the integration process* would help them to see that *for now*, this was the best solution. After cooking a little longer—giving the family time to come together—another solution might become more appropriate.

Unrealistic expectations often set couples up to overcook their stepfamily. Trying to force, pressure, or quickly cook the ingredients of your home will likely result in a spoiled dish. But stepping down your expectations and giving your stepfamily time to cook slowly will move you closer to the Promised Land.

Recommended Family Activity

As a couple, ask all the children to help you in the kitchen with a project. Have a recipe ready for a Crockpot dish of your choice. Let everyone add one ingredient to the pot. As they do, talk about how your family is like this dish. Note to the children that you are not stirring or blending the ingredients by hand but are relying on the Crockpot to bring everything together slowly over time. Also, talk about how long it takes to cook foods in a Crockpot and that for every hour, your stepfamily may need a year. Allow people to ask questions. At the end of the cooking time, sit down together as a family and enjoy the meal. As you eat, wonder with the children what the food would have tasted like at the beginning of its cooking time. Pray together at the end of the meal, asking God to give your family patience as you "cook together."

Questions for Discussion

FOR ALL COUPLES

1. In what ways has this chapter been a discouragement to you? How has it given you hope?
2. When did you first realize that your expectations were not becoming reality?
3. In what ways have your expectations been met successfully? Celebrate your successes and share what is going well for your home.
4. Which of the following myths have you been guilty of believing? Identify each and express what you hoped would come about as a result.

   • Love will happen instantly between all family members.
   • We'll do it better this time around.
   • Everything will fall quickly into place.
   • Our children will feel as happy about the remarriage as we do.
   • Blending is the goal of this stepfamily.

5. Which of the following integration styles have you been guilty of? What have been the results? Give an example.

   • Blender
   • Food processor
   • Microwave
   • Pressure cooker
   • Tossed

6. How does the Crockpot cooking mentality go against your natural desires and assumptions for how a stepfamily should integrate?
7. In what way is it relieving to know that time is important to the integration process?
8. What "low heat" approaches have you utilized already (even if you

didn't realize it was important until now)?

9. What fears do you have that force you into a high-heat mode of response?

10. In what ways do you need to implement a low-heat mentality? What would you have to change about yourself?

11. How appropriate are mini-family activities for your stepfamily at this time? In what way might you implement this idea over the next month? Make a plan and share with your support group the outcome. Evaluate its effectiveness and decide whether to try it again.

FOR PRE-REMARITAL COUPLES

1. How is this book opening your eyes to the challenges of stepfamily life? List your hopes for how your future stepfamily will be an exception to the rule.

2. Now list reasons why you believe your remarried family will successfully integrate.

3. How might these hopes and reasons blind you to reality?

4. As a couple, discuss the following expectations. A stepmother expressed them two years into her remarriage. How do you identify with her desires? How realistic do you believe them to be?

   - I thought my husband would appreciate how overwhelming and difficult it would be for me to care for his children.
   - I thought that raising his children would fill my need to be a mother.
   - I thought I would have more say in the children's visitation schedules (e.g., when we watch them for their mother, when they spend the night at a friend's house, etc.).
   - I expected to fit in, to be welcomed by his children, and to be treated well.
   - I expected to immediately take priority over all his other relationships, even his children.

CHAPTER FIVE

Smart Step Three: Two-STEP

Your marriage must be top priority

"Haven't you read," he replied, "that at the beginning the Creator 'made them male and female,' and said, 'For this reason a man will leave his father and mother and be united to his wife, and the two will become one flesh'? So they are no longer two, but one. Therefore what God has joined together, let man not separate" (Matthew 19:4–6).

Every family, including the stepfamily, is founded on the marital relationship. Yet the complexity of stepfamily life makes nurturing the marital relationship a tremendous challenge. It is easy for the marriage to get lost in the stepfamily forest.

For the first time in over three decades the divorce rate for first-time married couples has begun to drop. The latest predictions estimate that 42–45 percent of first-time married couples will divorce. Until recently, however, the divorce rate hovered around 50 percent for all marriages, and in the late '80s researchers at the University of Wisconsin were predicting that first-time married couples had a 67 percent chance of divorce.[1] Thank the Lord, the divorce rate is beginning to move downward.

However, the divorce rate among remarried partners seems to remain unchanged. Remarriages make up 46 percent of all weddings conducted in America today[2] and a full 60–65 percent of them will end in divorce (most within five years).[3] Another way to view the impact of this statistic is through the eyes of children. Half of all children will watch their parents divorce at some time; half of those children will watch at least one parent divorce a second time.

Without question the remarriage divorce rate is high. And the presence of children has much to do with it. The rate of divorce is 50 percent higher in remarriages with stepchildren than in remarriages without.[4]

So we must ask ourselves: Why is divorce higher in remarried couples than in first-time marriages? What unique stepfamily dynamics make marriage difficult? Before answering those questions, let's remind ourselves of the qualities of successful marriages.

GOD'S DESIGN FROM THE BEGINNING

The beautiful story of Genesis 2 is of a God who provided a partner for man and for woman. Two people who would complete each other, share intimacy, work side-by-side in child rearing, and reflect God's love to each other. The mystery of marital oneness (Ephesians 5:31–32) was created by God for humankind. And marriage was created for a purpose.

I like to think of marriage as God's spiritual buddy system. From the beginning God was at the center of the marital relationship. He was the focal point for Adam and Eve's relationship, giving purpose and instruction for life. Marriage, like all of God's activity in this world, is meant to usher people into relationship with him. He loves us with his whole heart and desires to be known by us. Marriage, then, is about knowing God and sharing his love with another, who, in turn, loves us in such a way that we are drawn toward God. It's a love-triangle unlike any in Hollywood. In fact, the closer we draw to God as individuals, the closer we come to our mates; the closer we become in marriage, the more intimate we become with God.

This spiritual intimacy is at the heart of Christian marriage and forms the basic divine purpose of marriage for all times, places, and cultures. Healthy, growing marriages seek to build on this foundation. Couples who place God at the center of their existence, whether a second, third, or fourth marriage, put him in charge of their will, their choices, their money, their vocation, and their relationship. Such a couple, while never achieving marital perfection, will undoubtedly experience some of God's richest blessings. This holy love triangle has two parts: each partner's relationship to God and their relationship to each other.

EACH PARTNER'S RELATIONSHIP TO GOD

At the core of Christian marriage are two people who fully submit themselves to the lordship of Jesus Christ. The challenge of discipleship—to deny self will, take up our cross, and follow Christ (Mark 8:34–35)—is a daily decision for the Christian. Previously we discussed the spiritual challenges brought on by shame and guilt over an unchangeable past. Stepfamilies need to be reminded of God's redemptive power to save. Second Corinthians 5:21 boldly proclaims our position before God: "God made him who had no sin to be sin for us, so that in him we might become the righteousness of God." There is no greater message for anyone, in any family. The priority in life is relationship with God, not relationship with your stepchildren or even your mate. But relationship with God does provide strength and wisdom for our journey together on earth.

Many of the ideas in this book for building stepfamily relationships are so contrary to our cultural understanding of how to do family life, you won't be able to implement them if you don't have the power of the Holy Spirit working in your life. For example, Jesus said, "Love your enemies and pray for those who persecute you" (Matthew 5:44). Well, what if your enemy is your ex-spouse . . . or your stepson? How can you rise above their actions to love them if you don't have the Spirit's strength? Your motivation to overcome evil with good (Romans 12:21) must be fueled by self-denial and an appreciation for what Christ has forgiven you.

Another significant outcome of our love relationship with the heavenly Father is the identity and worth provided for us through Christ's sacrifice on the cross. Listen to the words of Titus 3:4–7:

> But when the kindness and love of God our Savior appeared, he saved us, not because of righteous things we had done, but because of his mercy. He saved us through the washing of rebirth and renewal by the Holy Spirit, whom he poured out on us generously through Jesus Christ our Savior, so that, having been justified by his grace, we might become heirs having the hope of eternal life.

Did you hear that? Despite our sinfulness we have been reborn and made new in Jesus Christ. More than that, we have become heirs of the King. Therein lies our identity—I am an heir of God, a person of surpassing value. Through Jesus I have a worth that doesn't have to be earned, but is simply a by-product of God's saving grace.

As a therapist, I understand the importance of self-esteem and the significance it plays in people's lives. But I believe that even more important is "God-esteem." This comes about when persons realize and accept their worth in God, not because of what they've done to obtain his approval, but because of what Jesus did for them on the cross. God-esteem is humbling because it can't be earned. Yet it is liberating to those who are disciples of Christ because it frees us to offer our lives to God, not out of obligation or payment, but in loving response to his gift of grace.

Furthermore, accepting the truth of God-esteem is a gift to your marriage. Let me explain. Centuries ago Bernard of Clairvaux described four levels of love.[5] The first two levels we can hardly call love from any biblical standpoint, but unfortunately describe many of the relationships of those in our world today. The first level is "to love myself solely." Self-love or narcissism is the goal here and is not interested in the needs of the other person. The second form of love is not much better: "to love you for my sake." This form of love is rooted in selfishness as one person uses the other for personal gain. The third form of love is a huge jump in quality from the previous two: "to love you for your sake." This form of love respects the value of the other person and wants good things for him or her. It looks out for another's interests. For most, this form of love sounds like the best there is—a mutually respectful relationship, where each serves the needs of the other. But Bernard of Clairvaux thought there to be one form of love higher than this.

"To love myself for your sake" is a self-respecting love that offers its best to the other. It is rooted in the awareness of my God-esteem. When you accept your worth in Jesus Christ, you can honor your spouse, cope with struggles, and even disagree about your family life, without fear of personal rejection, because your identity is secure. You are not dependent on your family for your sense of self, but on your God.

Incidentally, this last form of love sounds much like Jesus, who said the second greatest command is to "love your neighbor as yourself;" that implies that a healthy self-respect makes loving another possible. Where does that healthy self-respect come from? The greatest command—to love the Lord with all my heart, mind, soul, and strength—indicates that it is through my love relationship with God (Matthew 22:37–39).

So how is accepting my identity in Christ a gift to my marriage? When my worth as a person comes from God, I don't have to get it from you. It's great when marriage affirms us, but having God-esteem means it isn't devastating to our worth when the marriage doesn't affirm us. I can stand firm in the face of rejection because your momentary distance doesn't crush my worth.

It is my observation that this is critical in stepfamilies because rejection is so common. If you are a stepparent, for example, you need to know your identity is in God when your spouse is confused about your needs and is more attentive to his children than to you. You need to know you have a worth that cannot be taken away when a stepchild repeatedly ignores your attempts to join the family or refuses to even acknowledge your presence in the room. And a biological parent needs a healthy dose of God-esteem when her adolescent children choose to live in the other household. Without question such a transition will bring tremendous loss and sadness. But it doesn't define your identity or your worth—God does. People in stepfamilies need to know the source of their worth. It makes enduring the journey so much easier.

PARTNERS' RELATIONSHIP TO ONE ANOTHER

Building a marriage that can thrive in the stepfamily home requires two solidly committed disciples of Christ and a healthy couple relationship. It is imperative that stepfamily couples learn all they can about healthy marital relationships and give constant attention and energy to strengthening their marriage. It is quite evident that many of the problems children and families face have their roots in a weak marriage. And stepfamily couples have more than the average share of stressors that erode their relationship. If building and solidifying the marriage is not a priority to both partners, it will undoubtedly suffer the consequence of mediocrity. I recommend that couples attend a marriage enrichment weekend at least once each year, as well as take advantage of marriage classes offered in your local congregation, read books, and listen to Christian radio programs on the family. You need every tip you can get.

Beyond the spiritual aspects already discussed, stepfamily couples must learn to set goals for their marriage, develop trust and a sense of companionship, establish commitment, cultivate a satisfying sexual relationship, and build communication and conflict resolution skills. It is beyond the scope of this book to address all the areas of a healthy marriage. However, let's briefly review a few of the qualities that are most pertinent to stepfamily marriages before turning our attention to two specific barriers stepfamily couples face.

Establishing a Commitment to Go the Distance

The following story was first told by Max Lucado. It captures the kind of dedication that stepfamily couples must have to insure a lifetime of love.

The People With the Roses

John Blanchard stood up from the bench, straightened his army uniform, and studied the crowd of people making their way through Grand Central Station. He looked for the girl whose heart he knew, but whose face he didn't, the girl with the rose.

His interest in her had begun thirteen months before in a Florida library. Taking a book off the shelf, he found himself intrigued, not with the words of the book, but with the notes penciled in the margin. The soft handwriting reflected a thoughtful soul and insightful mind. In front of the book, he discovered the previous owner's name, Miss Hollis Maynell.

With time and effort, he located her address. She lived in New York City. He wrote her a letter introducing himself and inviting her to correspond. The next day he was shipped overseas for service in World War II. During the next year and one month the two grew to know each other through the mail. Each letter was a seed falling on a fertile heart. A romance was budding.

Blanchard requested a photograph, but she refused. She felt that if he really cared, it wouldn't matter what she looked like.

When the day finally came for him to return from Europe, they scheduled their first meeting—7:00 P.M. at Grand Central in New York. "You'll recognize me," she wrote, "by the red rose I'll be wearing on my lapel."

So at seven o'clock he was in the station looking for a girl whose heart he loved but whose face he'd never seen.

I'll let Mr. Blanchard tell you what happened.[6]

A young woman was coming toward me, her figure long and slim. Her blonde hair lay back in curls from her delicate ears; her eyes were as blue as flowers. Her lips and chin had a gentle firmness, and in her pale green suit, she was like springtime come alive. I started toward her, entirely forgetting to notice that she was not wearing a rose. As I moved, a small provocative smile turned her lips. "Going my way, sailor?" she murmured.

Almost uncontrollably I made one step closer to her, and then I saw Hollis Maynell.

She was standing almost directly behind the girl. A woman well past forty, she had graying hair tucked under a worn hat. She was more than plump, her thick-ankled feet thrust into low-heeled shoes. The girl in the green suit was quickly walking away. I felt as though I was split in two. So keen was my desire to follow her, and yet so deep was my longing for the woman whose spirit had truly companioned and upheld mine.

And there she stood. Her pale, plump face was gentle and sensible; her gray eyes had a warm and kindly twinkle. I did not hesitate. My finger gripped the small worn blue leather copy of the book that was to identify me to her. This would not be love, but it would be something precious, something perhaps even better than love, a friendship for which I had been and must ever be grateful.

I squared my shoulders and saluted and held out the book to the woman, even though while I spoke I felt choked by the bitterness of my disappointment. "I'm Lieutenant John Blanchard, and you must be Miss Maynell. I am so glad you could meet me; may I take you to dinner?"

The woman's face broadened into a tolerant smile. "I don't know what this is about, son," she answered, "but the young lady in the green suit who just went by, begged me to wear this rose on my coat. And she said if you were to ask me out to dinner, I should tell you that she is waiting for you in the big restaurant across the street. She said it was some kind of test!"[7]

The key to any marital relationship is single-mindedness and dedication—even in the face of more attractive alternatives. When what you hoped for in this remarriage is not what you see coming at you, it will be dedication that helps you stay the course and make the right choices. John and Hollis went on to enjoy over forty years of marriage together. It started off with dedication and it endured with dedication. Nearly every stepfamily couple faces a time when they feel trapped between the sea of opposition and their past. At those moments, what appears to be much more attractive is returning to single life. But maintaining a single-mindedness to fulfill the commitment you have made and reach the Promised Land will empower you to make the difficult but right choices. Your stepfamily can't survive without it.

Communication Skills and Resolving Conflict

Commitment is the attitude that keeps you investing in your marriage. Good communication skills and the ability to resolve conflict takes you through the sea of opposition. You can never learn enough about how to communicate with your spouse—or your ex-spouse, children, and mate's ex-in-laws, for that matter.

Communication is the life-blood of your relationship. A number of years ago a Castrol commercial showed how draining their synthetic oil from a car engine wouldn't stop the engine. Engines drained of standard oils soon locked up. They simply couldn't function without something reducing the friction. Effective communication reduces friction in your marriage.

Stepfamilies experience higher levels of conflict during the first few years, a time when the couple is trying to bond their relationship. If couples are unable to talk, argue, and negotiate decisions constructively, they can easily experience marital "lock up." But couples that competently handle conflict will discover a deepening of their mutual trust and confidence in their marriage. Don't underestimate the importance of communication and conflict skill training for the success of your marriage.

THE MARITAL LOVE BANK

Dr. Tom Milholland, one of my graduate professors, made a statement about marriage I'll never forget: "Couples who don't invest in their marriage will always find it in decline. Marriage is like the grandfather clock in your dining room; if you don't wind it up every now and then, it stops working." Nothing could be more accurate.

Sheryl and *Tom's* story was familiar to me. They arrived at their first therapy session with resentment in their eyes and distance evident in their physical posture. "It's like he switched after we got married," she began to explain. "Before we married he took me places, sent me nice gifts, and said nice things about my children. It's like he was on the hunt, and I was his reward. And I loved it. But now all we do is talk about the kids' schedules, his ex-wife's latest boyfriend, or what's happening at work. He hasn't shown an interest in me in months."

It is very common for an emotional shift to occur after the wedding. Couples stop focusing on winning the heart of the other and turn to the concerns of their instant family. Understandably and predictably there will be a decline in energy put into the relationship. However, couples must remember to invest in their love account from time to time or they will wake up one day to discover the account is bankrupt. Consider the marital love bank.

Every person and every relationship has an emotional love bank. Marital accounts, for instance, are either in the red or in the black. Sometimes accounts are bankrupt and sometimes they're paying significant dividends on the investments made.

The account works just like a bank account. You keep your marital account in good standing by making sure the balance is always on the plus side. This requires, at a minimum, more deposits than withdrawals and the deposits must be of greater cumulative value than the withdrawals. *Deposits* are anything positive that you contribute to your relationship; *withdrawals* are any negatives that take away from the marriage or hurt the relationship.

To keep their accounts in the black, couples make two kinds of deposits: occasional large sums and regular small investments. Occasional large sums include things like a weekend getaway, a cruise, or giving an expensive gift. These significant deposits can boost a relationship for months, but are usually expensive and, therefore, can't be contributed very often. Besides, the regular small investment is more productive over the long haul. These investments come in the form of simple, small, daily behaviors that affirm the relationship as well as each individual and build solidarity in the marriage.

There is even a formula that tells you how you're doing. John Gottman, a marital researcher, has concluded that couples who remain in long-term committed relationships maintain a five-to-one ratio of positive to negative behavioral exchanges.[8] In other words, *they make five deposits for every withdrawal.* "You mean, in order to take inventory of our marital love bank, we could examine how many deposits (and the value of each) we make compared to how many withdrawals?" That's exactly right. For instance, for every act of selfishness, there needs to be:

- One act of kindness: politeness or basic consideration of the other's needs.
- One act of sacrifice: doing something on behalf of the other, putting your spouse first.
- Considerate conversation: you have to talk in ways that build up the other person and listen to his or her wants, needs, and desires. Also, the way you deal with conflict should bring you together instead of tearing you apart.
- Romantic expressions of affection and/or sexuality: holding hands, a card when it's not Valentine's Day, a neck or foot massage, cooking a favorite meal, creative sexuality.
- One deed of friendship:
  Thoughtfulness
  Loyalty to your spouse before others
  Compliments
  Sharing feelings, dreams, frustrations
  Support in times of crisis
  Showing honor toward your spouse

Putting the above into action is a vital investment in keeping the magical five-to-one ratio. But realize, no one is restricted to a five-to-one ratio. To have a terrific marriage, you can strive for ten-to-one!

Remember, no one but you puts money in your bank account, and if you don't invest you'll have nothing for the future. The same is true for your marriage. Besides, the dividends for you and your children are well worth the investment.

So what should couples do if their account is in the red or bankrupt? I have three suggestions to get you started. First, start slowly to make deposits. Stop focusing on how dry your account is and start making deposits *even though you don't feel like it.* This is reflective of John's commendation in Revelation 2:4–5 to the church at Ephesus. They had forgotten their first love for Christ and were told to "repent and do the things you did at first." Individuals who, for whatever reason, find themselves distant from their spouse should first of all repent, that is, renew their commitment and their attitude toward their marital first love. Then they should begin doing the things that brought them together in the first place. Knowing how to love someone is sometimes only as far away as our recent past. During courtship we easily display a selfless, sacrificial love, but frequently lose touch with our own efforts. Start making those same deposits again and reenergize your relationship.

Second, if you find yourself bankrupt with your spouse, start making deposits but realize they will probably be discounted at first. Resentment and hurt make it difficult to give a receipt of recognition for a deposit. Don't let that keep you from doing your part. And third, if necessary, find a qualified marriage and family therapist to help you address rebuilding the relationship. Not all counselors are created equal, so make sure it's someone who is trained in marital therapy and has special training in stepfamily dynamics. Above all, don't give up and don't file Chapter 13.

What's your current ratio of positive to negative behaviors? Take a minute to reflect and record your answers to this and the following exercise in a journal or your day planner.

Currently I believe our marriage has a ratio of _____ positive behaviors for every _____ negative behaviors.
Here are some things I can do in the next week to serve my spouse:_____

_____

Here are some things I can begin to do that will increase our positives and decrease our negative interaction:_____

_____

This may be a sobering and depressing exercise for you, or it may affirm your current efforts. Either way, approach your spouse (or dating partner) and share your thoughts about this aspect of your relationship. Do so openly, without defensiveness, so you can empathize with the other's perspective and renew your investment in each other. Remember, the dividends are well worth the investment.

Until now this chapter has discussed qualities of Christian marriage that apply to every couple. You still might be wondering why the divorce rate for remarried couples is higher than first-time marriages. I believe two key barriers to marital oneness in stepfamilies contribute to the higher divorce rate: parent-child allegiance and the ghost of marriage past. These barriers profoundly impact stepfamily couples in negative ways and must be addressed if the marriage is going to grow and mature.

PARENT-CHILD ALLEGIANCE: *REMARRIED WITH CHILDREN*

God's design for the family is that a man and a woman begin their marriage by emotionally separating from their family of origin. As the two "leave father and mother" and "cleave" to each other, a new foundation is laid for their home. The marriage relationship is established before children are born and continues throughout the child-rearing years. Scripture even affirms the necessity of a honeymoon period as the couple solidifies their relationship. "If a man has recently married, he must not be sent to war or have any other duty laid on him. For one year he is to be free to stay at home and bring happiness to the wife he has married" (Deuteronomy 24:5). But stepfamily couples don't have this bonding time. In fact, because parent-child relationships are bonded by blood and have more history, the marital relationship, instead of being the strongest bond in the home, is often the weakest.

The normal progression is for the couple's relationship to broaden from one characterized by romance before children to one of partnership after children. Without a honeymoon period, stepfamily couples are forced to negotiate their partnership at the same time they are solidifying their romance. Needless to say, the process is complicated, and frequently the couple's personal relationship gets lost in the stepfamily forest.

The challenge for stepfamily couples, then, is to make their relationship priority number one. "Wait a minute," said *Carrie*. "You mean I have to put my husband before my children? I understand your point, but they are my flesh and blood. He's just someone I picked up alongside the road somewhere." Her tongue in cheek meaning was evident, but so was her fear. "I can't do that to my kids. I don't ever want them to think I love him more than I love them."

Her statements call attention to a number of legitimate fears for biological parents that new spouses/stepparents must understand. First, children suffer significantly when a parent dies or their parents divorce, and biological parents feel guilty because of it. Guilt is a powerful emotion that can easily motivate parents to protect their children from future pain. This effort to protect children can take on many different forms. Shielding a stepparent from having an equal say in parenting decisions, monitoring the amount of contact between stepsiblings, and controlling money so that children don't go without are just a few examples. But behaviors that protect the parent-child relationship to the detriment of the marriage are dangerous to the long-term viability of the family. *Gary* and *Emily* know what I mean.

Gary's sixteen-year-old stepdaughter, Amy, walked into the kitchen while he was fixing dinner. He politely asked her to set the table while he finished the meal. She ignored him. A second time he asked, and this time all he got in return was a halfhearted, "I'll do it in a minute." Ten minutes later she showed no indication of helping, so he repeated his request, this time with tension in his voice. Amy's mother, Emily, walked into the room just as he was raising his voice. At first, Emily remembered how important it was to support Gary, so she gave Amy "the look." Amy grudgingly responded. Later, as the family sat down to eat, Gary made a snide comment about how Amy had forgotten the knives. Emily came unglued. "Why do you have to criticize her like that? Can't you just leave well enough alone?" Gary immediately felt that Emily was once again taking Amy's side and became resentful. In an instant Gary's conflict with Amy became Gary's conflict with Emily and ended when he slammed the front door and shouted something about divorce.

Stepfamily couples can learn two things from this story. First, Gary should not have criticized Amy's effort at the dinner table. He could have voiced his concern to his wife later (behind closed doors), and together they could have decided on a standard of conduct for the future. Later he confessed that his comment grew out of his frustration that she hadn't accepted him as her stepfather and because she refused to honor his authority. He should have settled for what I call the "little victory." Emily's initial support of Gary's request was a step in the right direction. But Gary, when he pushed for a big victory with a comment about her poor perform-ance, turned the situation into a big defeat. Little victories or big defeats.

Secondly, Emily's initial effort to support Gary was short-circuited by her need to protect Amy from more harm. Emily's divorce had been diffi-cult, and Amy got caught in the marital conflict often. Emily could have expressed her feelings about Gary's negative comment behind closed doors or done so at the table without attacking, but she lost her ability to respond appropriately when her allegiance to Amy took over.

Let me point out that conflict over loyalty to children is not unique to modern-day stepfamilies. In Genesis 16 and 21, we read how Abraham, on more than one occasion, got caught in the jealousy and competition of Sarah and Hagar. Sarah even approached Abraham and insisted he cut his son Ishmael out of the will because he was born to Hagar. "Get rid of that slave woman and her son, for that slave woman's son will never share in the inheritance with my son Isaac" (21:10). She was protecting Isaac's interests and insisted that Abraham put her first. But the decision wasn't so easy for him. The Scripture goes on to say that "the matter distressed Abraham greatly because it concerned his son" (21:11).

Stepfamily couples experience countless instances where the biological parents feel caught between their spouse and their children. Perhaps it a decision over what treat the family will pick up after Bible class. The kids want ice cream from Baskin Robbins, but your spouse wants pie from Per-kins. The decision may not appear to be significant, but it represents a choice of loyalty. If you choose to get pie for your spouse, your children may feel slighted and get angry. If you choose ice cream, your spouse may complain.

The real culprit driving the barrier of parent-child allegiance is when biological parents refuse to take whatever risks necessary in order to move their spouse into a place of priority. *Amber* was convinced that once *Ryan*, her husband's oldest son, moved out, she would once again enjoy her hus-band's favor. I checked in with her six months after Ryan left for the navy, and she had come to a different realization. "I really thought it was Ryan's fault. But my husband just switched his energies to his two other children. Now I'm third in line instead of fourth." It's up to biological parents to move the marriage to a place of priority. Otherwise, it won't happen.

How Stepparents Contribute to the Problem

But this dynamic coin has another side. Biological parents feel resentful when stepparents push them into having to make a choice. Like Sarah, stepparents often feel insecure when the biological spouse invests time and energy in the children and may try to force the issue. This is nothing but trouble. Stepparents cannot afford to put themselves in competition with their stepchildren. Besides, it's not a fair comparison.

Do you remember Carrie's comment, "I don't ever want them to think I love him more than I love them"? The love a parent feels for a child is qualitatively different than the love a spouse feels for his/her husband or wife. Carrie's fear is misguided because it assumes she has a certain number of love points to give away and once they're gone, everyone else will have to do without. This simply isn't true. God provides us with an endless supply of love. Children often feel insecure when their parent remarries and may even attempt to play the "you love him more" card to manipulate parents into choosing them. But biological parents who know they can love many people at once won't be manipulated. Likewise, stepparents shouldn't force their spouse into an either/or position to determine his or her dedication. They should, instead, acknowledge their personal worth in Jesus Christ, realize that during the Crockpot years children need reassurance of their parent's love, and work with their spouse to find time together. Stepparents cannot afford to be insecure. (Stepfamilies were not made for the emotionally fragile.)

So What's the Answer?

The answer to this significant barrier to marital oneness is unity. Stress in a stepfamily generally divides people along biological lines. When push comes to shove, the allegiance (or loyalty) between parents and children often wins out over the marriage unless the couple can form a unified position of leadership. If they cannot govern the family as a team, the household is headed for anger, jealousy, and unacceptance. Unity within the couple's relationship bridges the emotional gap between the stepparent and stepchildren and positions both adults to lead the family. If a biological parent is not willing to build such a bridge with the stepparent, the stepchildren will receive an unhealthy amount of power in the home. All they have to do is cry "unfair" and their parent protects them from the "mean, nasty" stepparent. This almost always results in marital tension, conflict, resentment, and isolation.

Stepfamilies are divided into "insiders and outsiders," that is, those who are biologically related and those who aren't.[9] Insiders have a strong bond that pulls them together in the face of stress or conflict. Outsiders often feel that they don't belong and frequently try to force their way in with insiders. The biological parent in stepfamilies maintains a relationship to both insiders (their children) and outsiders (new spouse and his or her children), and therefore must position the stepparent as his or her teammate. The couple should give time and energy to the marriage and not let their children keep them apart. Including the new spouse in parenting decisions (see chapter 7), setting a date night and keeping it, and taking a few minutes each day to connect as a couple without interruption are a few simple but significant ways to communicate the unity of the couple to the children. If the biological parent doesn't help the outsider stepparent into a leadership position, the stepparent is likely to try to force his or her way in. This almost always results in resentment and resistance from the insiders. Again, jealousy, rejection, and anger are common resulting emotions.

Now let me balance this truth by noting that biological parents must take a "both/and" stance with their children and new spouse. They must invest time and energy in both. Early in the remarriage, for example, it is especially important to stay connected with your children. But eventually the marriage must be made a priority, even in front of the children.

Returning to the ice cream or pie dilemma, I suggest that stepfamily couples purposefully choose ice cream for the kids' sake early on and privately enjoy pie together. If the stepparent is agreeable to this solution, the couple is unified in sacrificing for the children. As the Crockpot works over time, the biological parent can more overtly say no to the children while saying yes to the spouse. Such a transition almost always elicits anger and insecurity from at least one child, if not all. But a stepfamily in which the couple isn't working toward affirming the importance of their relationship before the children is one destined for mediocrity. A couple gradually moving their relationship to first priority is laying a foundation for the family that will last for all time.

Waiting for this to happen is difficult for many stepparents. Again, it is important that they are affirmed by the biological parent, and also that time and energy are put into the marriage. But instead of competing for time, stepparents need to encourage their spouse to be involved with his or her biological children. Stepparents who get in the way of the parent-child relationship are asking for trouble. Try to keep in mind that biological parents in two-parent nuclear homes frequently make marital sacrifices on behalf of their children. Your home must do the same. Be unified in your sacrifices for the children *and* find time to be alone.

Two-Step

As you can tell, the above advice requires a delicate balance of marital teamwork. It is a dance that takes harmony and practice. Now you know why I titled this smart step the "two-step." Couples in Texas are well aware of a dance they call the two-step. Like all dances, it requires that the couple work together to stay in balance. Striving to make your marriage priority one means balancing commitments to both children and spouse. As moving around the dance floor becomes more natural, greater harmony and enjoyment result. But sometimes learning to dance means fighting some battles.

Divide and Conquer

Not all stepfamilies struggle with the tug and pull of parent-child allegiance, but for most this developmental task is difficult. It takes some stepfamilies to the brink of divorce.

I had been working with *Jeff* and his new wife, *Kelly,* for a few sessions when they walked in with a worried look on their faces. I had been trying to help them make room for Jeff's fourteen-year-old daughter, *Lauren,* who had recently come to live with them. The transition had been difficult, to say the least. Prior to Lauren's moving in, the couple had integrated quite well. Kelly brought four-year-old Becky to the marriage, and she had warmly accepted her stepfather. The couple enjoyed three relatively hassle-free years together—until Lauren moved in.

"Lauren wrote me this letter after our last session," Jeff explained. Lauren was very jealous of her stepmother and had been cornering her father about his marriage. At my direction he had already talked with Lauren about how he could love her and Kelly without competition, and he reassured her that she didn't need to be concerned about losing him. "She's really forcing the issue now," he said. He showed me the letter. It started with a classic adolescent manipulative tool—a guilt trip.

> Dear Dad,
>
> Listen, I'm sorry I'm such a screw-up! But I really don't think I can do this anymore! I was thinking about what you said, it's (1) God; then (2) your spouse; then (3) your children! I can't live with you [believing] that if at the second Kelly and I get in a life or death situation that you would save Kelly over your own flesh-and-blood. . . . I can't live with you, knowing that would happen. I can't live here knowing that you love Kelly more than me. And Kelly loves Becky more than you. And don't tell me there are different kinds of love, 'cause you put her above me. I can't take this anymore. I knew this girl in school who gave herself up for adoption; I really think I want to do that! I don't want to, but it's the only option.
>
> Love,
> Lauren

Is it reasonable for a parent in this situation to be afraid? Absolutely. Everyone loses contact with someone when a family ends by death or divorce, and Lauren was threatening withdrawal from her father. His time with Lauren since his divorce had been very limited. The change of residence represented an opportunity for Jeff to enjoy his daughter, but now his relationship with Kelly apparently was threatening his chances.

Before we developed a game plan, I asked the couple to put themselves in Lauren's shoes for a moment. That was a stretch for Kelly who only saw a manipulative teenager systematically eroding her marriage. Kelly hadn't wanted Lauren to "invade" their home, but didn't have much choice due to difficulties with Lauren's mother. Kelly bristled when I suggested Lauren was frightened and simply trying to find her place in her daddy's heart. She found it even more difficult to hear me say that neither of them should take it personally. "Please understand, Lauren didn't ask for her parents to divorce, and she didn't ask for you to get married. She needs some reassurance." Kelly had to find some compassion for Lauren; the couple couldn't afford to be divided by this maneuver or Lauren would conquer. Not taking this personally and finding compassion was Kelly's task at this point. Jeff had to step up to bat and swing at the pitch Lauren had thrown.

And Jeff did just that. He took a "both/and" approach with Kelly and Lauren, giving personal time to each. He and Lauren spent exclusive time together and renewed their relationship. Jeff also made sure he and Kelly dated on a regular basis no matter how much Lauren complained. In addition, Jeff took a firm role in setting boundaries with Lauren and carried out the consequences even though he feared making her mad and "driving her away." At one point he let her know without question that if push came to shove, his loyalties were with Kelly. But somehow Lauren was able to hear that since her father had become so involved in her life as well; she knew she wouldn't be forgotten. Eventually, with time and constant effort, Lauren backed away from competing with her stepmom.

Kelly's role as stepparent in this situation was to avoid fighting fire with fire. It is tempting for stepparents who are being pushed out by the stepchildren to fight back by insisting their spouse choose them in all circumstances. Unfortunately, that kind of stepparent easily falls victim to insecurity and resentment if the biological parent doesn't do just that. Kelly needed to stand tall and support Jeff as he dealt with his daughter. She needed to give him space to spend time with Lauren and reassure her of his love. She also needed to express her fears to Jeff privately and appropriately instead of with accusation and contempt. Trusting that he was on her side and giving the Crockpot time to cook were critical. Together they made it through the sea of Lauren's oppositions. And so can you.

THE GHOST OF MARRIAGE PAST

The past has very little substance, but it stays close to your heels.
—Unknown

A cat that sits on a hot stove won't ever sit on a hot stove again; neither will it sit on a cold stove.
—Mark Twain

It is human nature to view new relationships in light of previous ones. It's like putting on sunglasses that are tinted yellow or black—everything you see has a yellow or black hue. We often view our current relationship through a previous marital lens (and family-of-origin lens) that sometimes leads to negative assumptions and expectations. Sometimes the meaning we ascribe to specific behaviors is also interpreted negatively. If these assumptions are not examined or the lens is not taken off, a new marriage can easily be colored by the experiences of the first (or second). That's why it's critical that divorced persons take time to resolve the ending of their marriage before jumping into another relationship. I recommend individuals wait at least three years before beginning a serious relationship. All too often, however, people rebound from one failed marriage into another and take their tinted glasses with them. When circumstances in the new marriage remind someone of negative events in a previous marriage, the person becomes frightened and reactive. This second barrier to marital oneness in the stepfamily is what I call being haunted by the ghost of marriage past.

Terri's first husband had an affair. She came home one day to discover he had packed his stuff and moved in with a woman half his age. The fallout from this rejection was almost more than she could handle. But with the help of a supportive church family, she and her eight-year-old son survived.

Bill made her feel good again. They met through a mutual friend and hit it off right from the start. He listened to her anger, supported her through the custody battle, and helped her son with his homework. Terri found herself trusting him with more and more of her life.

After the wedding, though, Terri would ask questions if Bill didn't come home on time. When they talked she shared her thoughts, but not quite everything. She often felt it wise to watch her step and not become too transparent. After all, look what happened last time. When they made love, Terri offered her body to Bill, but not her passion. In other words, she was willing to meet his basic sexual need, but guarding her heart meant never fully joining her soul to his. A year into the marriage she decided it wise to put money in a secret bank account, just in case anything ever went wrong. Finally, Terri invested much of her time in her son, "because his father hurt him so much." Terri was haunted, and her marriage was slowly being sabotaged.

Don's second wife misused money. She continually forgot to record checks in the ledger, maxed out their credit cards, and bounced numerous checks. Even before the divorce, Don's credit was ruined; he had to borrow money from his parents to buy a car for his third wife, *Judy*. The first time Judy forgot to record a check in the ledger, Don starting sweating bullets. Emotionally he withdrew, and financially he demanded control over the checkbook. Judy was granted an allowance, and all expenditures beyond that had to be pre-approved by him. Taking control seemed to be the only way to prevent another bad situation. But Judy's resentment over Don's controlling behavior created a new bad situation.

What's truly ironic about being haunted by the ghost of marriage past and responding out of fear is that you can systematically bring about a self-fulfilling prophecy. If you treat someone as untrustworthy long enough, he or she may give up trying to win your trust and begin to act untrustworthy. After all, you're going to respond as if he or she is anyway. What does the person have to lose?

I have a cartoon of a man shouting at his wife as she drives off with her luggage: "Marie, don't leave me. My ex-wife will think she's right when she says no one can live with me." That's a man who is married to one woman, but emotionally tied to another. In fact, his divided attention has left him unable to meet his current wife's needs and resulted in a self-fulfilling prophecy. No one can live with him.

Becoming a Ghost Buster

For most remarried partners, treating a current spouse fairly requires becoming a ghost buster. You must examine how you have been influenced by your previous relationships and strive to adjust your responses to similar circumstances. Recognizing your negative interpretations of the other's behavior is sometimes difficult. Often a husband or wife will say, "Why are you overreacting to this?" or "Wait a minute. I am not your ex!" When that happens, take some time to reflect. Examine whether your past is still part of your present. Then replace your reactive behavior with more appropriate responses. You may also have to struggle with matters of forgiveness as difficult emotions and memories come to the surface. We'll talk more about forgiveness in the next chapter, but for now work to take your ghosts to the throne of God and lay them down. You'll never regret leaving them behind. In addition, admit your ghosts to your spouse and enlist help as you fight to change your behavior. Ask your partner to pray for you and compassionately point out when he or she thinks you are being haunted. Talk to friends, grieve your past, and grow into your new marriage.

"But I don't know what else to do," someone might say. Then ask yourself, "If I had never been hurt before, how would I respond in this situation? If I were to treat you as if you are trustworthy, how would I act?" The answers to these questions are a great start toward how you should act and what you are trying to become.

CONCLUSION

Marriage is tough under any circumstance. Remarriages all too frequently fall prey to the common issues of escalating conflict over money, sex, and in-laws just like all other marriages. Yet some unique and unforeseen barriers do exist. That's why stepfamily couples must make their relationship a priority and must work harder—and smarter—at their marriage than anyone else.

The above barriers can quickly or subtly destroy a marriage, especially when they work in concert with one another and compound their impact. For example, why would a wife want to make her husband a priority and risk alienating her children when she is haunted by a ghost of mistrust? If she's not sure her husband will be there in two years, why not stick closer to her kids? After all, they're not going anywhere. Truly, the risk of marriage is vast. But so are the rewards for those who give it all they've got.

The challenges to remarriage are real. Gather all your resources, invest in marital enrichment programs, talk with other stepfamily couples, and keep God at the center of your relationship. Your stepfamily is depending on you.

Questions for Discussion

PRIORITY ONE CASE STUDY

Directions: Work through the following case study alone and then with your partner or small group. Share your responses and examine which aspects apply to you.

Read the statement and explore the questions. Record your answers in a journal or notebook.

The following statement was made by a man to his wife shortly after they were married. He brought two children to the marriage, while she had none: "Don't ever come between me and my children. They can't get another father, but you can always get another husband."

1. This statement communicates his priorities loud and clear. What are they?
2. How do you think she might feel in response to his statement? How might it lead her to walk on eggshells and doubt his commitment to her?
3. How do you suppose this would affect the relationship between the stepmother and children?
4. What fears are embedded in the man's statement, especially related to his children?
5. Even though stepfamily marriages start with a stronger bond between parents and children, the couple's bond must be given priority. While this sometimes generates insecurity and anger within the children, it eventually provides the stability the family must have to survive. What makes this statement difficult to accept?
6. What challenges have you faced in trying to make the previous statement a reality in your stepfamily?

FOR ALL COUPLES

1. Discuss your personal relationship with God and your ideas of what a faithful life would look like. In what ways do you need to grow spiritually?
2. How will your marriage be God-directed? What is your desire for spiritual intimacy?

3. What concerns do you have regarding your partner's commitment to Christ?

4. In what ways do you need to improve your understanding of God-esteem and your value in Christ? How could realizing this make a difference in your home?

5. What fears do you have for your children, and how do you most naturally protect them?

6. What barriers exist because of someone's allegiance to his or her children? Work to establish trust in a unified direction and plan for handling difficult situations. Don't put each other in a corner.

7. Identify and name the ghosts in your marriage (e.g., ghost of distrust, not-enough-space ghost). Make a contract to help each other exorcise them from your relationship.

8. How would you act differently if you had never been hurt before?

FOR PRE-REMARITAL COUPLES

While conducting pre-remarital counseling, I asked a couple what ghosts might be haunting them. They, like most before marriage, quickly dismissed the possibility. "I've got a decent relationship with my ex, and he just lets the stuff with his ex roll off his back," she said. He agreed, "Yeah. I just put things behind me and go on. I don't let it affect me much." I doubted that and was soon proven correct.

Within five minutes the couple was arguing about a current issue in which each felt the other was acting like someone from his or her past. The truth is this: We don't want to believe that previous relationships will impact our future ones, but they do—especially if we deny the ghosts that haunt us. Give careful attention to the following questions and honestly identify your ghosts:

1. Has it been three years since the ending of any prior significant relationships (whether to death or divorce)? Assuming you can keep your sexual passions in check, what are the benefits of slowing down your courtship?

2. To what degree have I/we achieved emotional divorce with a previous spouse(s) and healing from difficult emotions? (Rate yourself from 1 to 10.)

3. To what degree have I/we been able to renew self-esteem and accept my/our single identity? (Rate yourself from 1 to 10.)
4. Have I tried to reconnect with former lost relationships (children and/or extended family)? What has been the result?
5. How much did I need to be needed when we first began dating?
6. What scares you about committing again?

CHAPTER SIX

Smart Step Four: STEP in Line
(Part 1)

With the parenting team

"Parenthood is a partnership with God. You are not molding iron nor chiseling marble; you are working with the Creator of the universe in shaping human character and determining destiny." —Ruth Vaughn

"The greatest use of life is to spend it for something that will outlast it." —William James

Divorce doesn't end family life; it reorganizes it. This foundational truth first communicated in chapter 2 is nowhere more applicable than regarding the roles adults play in raising children in stepfamilies. You may have been reorganized into different households following divorce, but you still must act as a parental team. This is often called co-parenting. In fact, one of the great ironies of divorce is that you may have hated your ex-spouse at the time of divorce, but now you have to find a way to cooperate with him or her for the sake of your children.* After all, parenting is about your

---

*Not everyone in stepfamilies has been divorced, although most stepfamilies in America today are born from divorce or out-of-wedlock births. Many stepfamilies are born from the death of a spouse, and therefore do not have to negotiate co-parent issues. The first half of this chapter specifically deals with co-parenting. If this topic does not pertain to you, please turn to the discussion of stepparent roles found on page 140.

children's welfare, development, and spiritual nurturance. I like to say that parenting is "all about the kids." This means that your decisions, attitudes—including finding ways to deal with people you dislike—and goals need to be oriented around what will benefit your children and increase their desire for the Lord. Yet for most, putting aside selfish desires for the children is a terribly difficult task.

In Genesis 21, Sarah refused to consider Hagar or Ishmael as having a place in Abraham's life. Sarah showed great hostility and selfishness when she insisted that Abraham exclude Ishmael from the inheritance. She was looking out for her son and good old number one. In fact, her actions were driven by fear (of Isaac's not getting the full blessing from Abraham), anger (because Hagar and Ishmael were mocking Isaac), and jealousy (because Hagar had given Abraham the highly prized firstborn son). But why would she act that way? Didn't she know what was coming when she encouraged Abraham to give her a child through a union with Hagar (Genesis 16)?

No, she didn't. And neither do most adults realize what they must give up to successfully integrate a stepfamily. *Joan* thought she would find fulfillment in helping her husband raise his two girls. What she discovered were two confused girls who didn't want her around, a husband who forced her to cope with the girls because he didn't understand "female concerns," and very little time available (due to the girls' activities) to be with the man she fell in love with.

When *Mike* remarried, he thought his stepchildren would accept him fairly quickly. Their biological father was an irresponsible alcoholic who spent very little time with his children; Mike assumed his positive presence would be a welcome change for nine-year-old *Brad* and eleven-year-old *Rebecca*. What he experienced was hostility and resentment from Brad, who desperately wanted more time with his father and blamed Mike because he wasn't getting it. Both Brad and Rebecca defended their father, minimized his drinking problem, and took care of him whenever they could. Mike, despite his quality Christian character, received opposition and dirty looks.

Maintaining an attitude of "It's all about the children" is quite a challenge, especially when your needs and dreams are left unfulfilled. Yet that is exactly what it takes to make a stepfamily work—an attitude and willingness to sacrifice personal needs for others. Joan learned to let some of the negative jabs from her stepdaughters bounce off instead of penetrating her heart. She realized the comments were not personal and represented the girls' anger over their parents' divorce. Furthermore, she lowered her expectations for exclusive couple time and worked with her husband to take advantage of the time that was available. Mike refused to compete with his stepchildren's idealized father. He stopped criticizing him and pointing out to the children their father's faults (in hopes that they would draw closer to him). He learned his best influence would come by example over time. Mike dedicated himself to becoming a man of God and a good spiritual servant in his home, even though his stepchildren found it difficult to acknowledge his efforts.

STEP IN LINE—WITH WHOM?

I've never done it, but I've seen people line dance. I don't try it because I have very little dance coordination, and I would surely throw off the entire group. After all, if I can't fall in line with others and keep pace with the necessary movements, the effect is lost. The same is true for the adult caregivers in stepfamilies.

There was a time in America when parents had lots of children; today we say children have lots of parents. The parenting team is comprised of everyone who shares responsibility for child-rearing tasks. This primarily includes biological parents and stepparents, but might incorporate grandparents, ex-in-laws, stepgrandparents, and extended family members who aid in the child-care process. The more coordinated or unified they are the better team they become for the benefit of the children.

Parenting team cooperation is one of the most challenging aspects of stepfamily life. Leftover pain from previous relationships, broken promises, and envy often characterize how ex-spouses and new spouses feel about the adults in the other home. Walls of distrust are built as the bricks of painful emotions and experiences are stacked side by side. Tearing down those walls and setting aside personal agendas for the children's sake is no easy task. Yet adults in separate homes who successfully create a functional parenting team discover their individual homes blessed with increased harmony.

The two key relationships in the parenting team are the co-parenting relationship between the biological parents and the parent-stepparent relationship. The relationships between noncustodial parent and stepparent, both stepparents (when each ex-spouse is remarried), and grandparents are generally determined by the health of these two key relationships. Let's begin by looking at the ex-spouse co-parenting relationship.

CO-PARENTING—WHAT'S THE GOAL?

At a minimum, biological parents should contain their anger and conflict in order to cooperate and compromise on issues of the children's welfare. At a maximum, the co-parents can strive to enforce similar rules and standards of conduct in each of the children's homes. Most co-parents find it difficult to accomplish the former; only a few are able to achieve the latter. Nevertheless, co-parents should do everything they can to build cooperation between the two homes.

I cannot overemphasize the importance of this concept in regard to the well-being of children. Research clearly confirms that children successfully adjust to the ending of their parents' marriage and can fare reasonably well if: (1) parents are able to bring their marital relationship to an end *without excessive conflict*; (2) children are *not put into the middle* of whatever conflicts exist; and (3) there is a *commitment from parents to cooperate* on issues of the children's material, physical, educational, emotional, and spiritual welfare.[1] Bottom line—children need their parents to work together whether married, divorced, or married to other people.

A healthy co-parent relationship does not mean children will not experience emotional or psychological distress. "Numerous studies document that children who experience parental divorce exhibit more conduct problems, more symptoms of psychological maladjustment, lower academic achievement, more social difficulties, and poorer self-concepts compared with children living in intact, two-parent families."[2] Judith Wallerstein's longitudinal research discovered that the effects of divorce are often lifelong and traumatic for children.[3] Even Mavis Hetherington's research, which gives hope to parents by pointing out that 80 percent of children from divorced homes eventually adapt to their new life, acknowledges that 20 percent will continuously display impulsive, irresponsible, antisocial behavior, and depression.[4]

In addition, children face greater levels of family conflict while the stepfamily is integrating (compared to nuclear family children)[5] and are at increased risk for developmental behavioral problems, health problems, and substance abuse.[6] Stepfamily conflict and ex-spouse conflict have a number of negative effects on children and are contributing factors in all of the following statistics. Children in stepfamilies are less likely to complete high school,[7] have lower educational achievement,[8] leave home earlier,[9] and are more likely to cohabit before marriage.[10] Finally, it's worth noting that boys are more affected by divorce, but girls seem to be more affected by remarriage.[11]

Parents who want to reduce these negative effects on their children should strive to be effective co-parents because it reduces between-home conflict and increases cooperation. Taming your tongue, for example, is critical to cooperating. Scripture notes that the tongue is a small part of the body but that its impact can be severe. "Consider what a great forest is set on fire by a small spark" (James 3:5b). Conflict containment starts with controlling your speech. You cannot be an effective co-parent without doing so.

What Does a Co-parent Relationship Look Like?

As stated above, the goal of co-parenting (at a minimum) is to contain the anger and conflict with your ex-spouse in order to cooperate and compromise on issues of the children's welfare. I'll let the children explain what a functional co-parental relationship means in practical, everyday terms.

Julie, twelve, complained in a therapy session that she couldn't invite both her parents to her music recital. "If they both come they'll just scowl every chance they get. I tried inviting them both last year, and Mom wouldn't speak to me for two days because Dad brought *Amy* [stepmom] with him. She refuses to be in the same room with them." Julie has had to learn to take turns inviting her mom and dad. If one couldn't attend, she could invite the other. Unfortunately, this put her in constant turmoil, as she was forced to choose which parent she would invite to certain events. If the other wanted to come but couldn't, Julie heard that parent's disappointment and felt guilty. "Why can't they just put aside their differences and tolerate a couple of hours in the same room?" Good question.

Because *Terrance's* parents always ended up fighting on the phone, he became the middleman to their visitation arrangements. His mother stopped speaking to his father and asked Terrance, at age nine, to communicate her preferences for drop off and pick up. Terrance had no choice but to oblige, since he enjoyed spending time with his father on weekends.

In both these examples, children carried undue emotional anxiety and burden because their parents could not set aside their differences and be adults. An effective co-parent arrangement for Julie's parents would mean she could invite both parents to her recitals and not worry that they were fighting or anxious. An effective arrangement for Terrance's parents would include their finding a way to talk rationally about their schedules instead of triangulating Terrance. The bottom line is a system that allows children to be children and adults to be their parents.

Co-parenting does not mean sharing all decisions about the children or that either home is accountable to the other for their choices, rules, or standards. Each household should be autonomous, but share responsibility for the children. It also does not mean that rules or punishment from one home cross over to the other home.

Karen sought therapy in part because her ex-husband, *Ted*, refused to carry out the consequences she imposed on their children. In one instance, her teenage son lied about his homework, so she grounded him from weekend activities. The scheduled visitation meant her son would be going to his dad's house that weekend, so she called her ex to ask him to honor the punishment and keep their son home on Friday and Saturday nights. Ted refused, saying that was his only time with his son and he wasn't obligated to fulfill her decisions. That angered Karen, and she hoped the therapist could intervene and get Ted to cooperate. The therapist refused because to do so would be to cross an important boundary, taking control of Ted's home away from him. Karen's therapist explained that if her son was grounded, she should wait until he came back to her home to carry out the punishment. Her home is within her control. Ted's home is not.

You might be thinking, *But I thought you just said that co-parents should strive to enforce similar rules and cooperate regarding the children. Didn't that obligate Ted to honor her request?* Yes, I did say that between-home cooperation, even to the point of carrying out the other home's punishment, is a goal some co-parents obtain. However, that does not obligate either side to do so. If you can achieve this level of cooperation, terrific. If not, don't insist the other home follow your rules.

Incidentally, this control issue between Karen and Ted was nothing new. It was as old as their failed marriage. Remember, divorce doesn't end the dynamics of family relationships; it merely reorganizes them into separate households. Well into divorce most ex-spouses are still trying to change, control, or influence their ex in the same manner they did before they divorced. If it didn't work then, why should it work now? (Truly, this is one of the great insanities of divorce—trying to change someone from whom you are divorced even though you couldn't change him or her while married!) People who can't stop reacting to an ex-spouse in the same old ways haven't really obtained emotional divorce (sometimes called decoupling). They are still emotionally invested in what their ex does. Letting go of control is tough, but it helps co-parents respect one another's boundaries and work better as a team.

CHILDREN LIVING IN TWO "COUNTRIES"

Let's examine stepfamily life from the child's point of view. What do children in stepfamilies need from the parenting team? What factors help children adjust to a changing family composition over which they have no control? What are some healthy principles for managing between-home contact?

First, it is important for the parenting team to understand that children in stepfamilies live in two "countries."[12] They hold citizenship in each country and are, therefore, invested in the quality of life found in both. The parenting team should do everything they can to help children thrive and enjoy each of their two homes. But living in two countries does require some adjustments.

"What if the rules in my ex's home are different from the rules in our home?" is a question commonly asked. "It all depends on your diplomacy and how cooperative you are as an ambassador," I respond. Let me explain.

Shortly after my wife and I married, we went with my parents to Kenya for a brief missionary effort. My parents continued to lead an annual trip to Kenya for about seventeen years, coordinating volunteers' mission efforts in East Africa. I will never forget going on safari in the Masai Mara and seeing animals in the wild: lions, cheetahs, giraffes, and hundreds of other wild animals Americans can only see in a zoo. But what I remember most distinctly was the radical change in culture that we experienced. Clothing was different, social customs seemed odd, the economy and systems of government were unknown to us—we even had to learn to drive on the left side of the road. Despite all these shifts in customs, ritual behaviors, and rules of conduct, we learned to adapt quite quickly. Because my parents returned to Kenya year after year, the changes grew more predictable for them and, therefore, were not as traumatic as our first trip together. But they always experienced an adjustment period when traveling between countries. One year my father returned to the U.S. and began driving on the left side of the road. The oncoming traffic abruptly reminded him of the change in driving system! But generally speaking, my parents quickly adapted to their current living arrangement.

You can see the parallel with children living in two homes. At first, the fact that the two countries have different rules, customs, and expectations may require an extended adjustment. Later, when the territory is familiar, only a brief adjustment time is required, especially when the rules and expectations are predictable. Sometimes children need gentle reminders from their parents about what the rules are ("You may be able to play before homework at your mom's house, but here the rule is . . ."), but generally speaking children can adjust rather well.

Can you imagine what travel for my parents would have been like if Kenya and the United States had been at war? Getting on a plane and heading to the "other side," even to do mission work, would have been considered treason. And once they landed, they would have been met with anger and rage as co-workers protested how awful the other country was because of their wartime tactics. How would my parents function under that kind of stress? How would they cope with the external pressures to choose an allegiance to one side or the other? Every comment and criticism would be loaded with a battle for their loyalty, and trust would be defeated at every turn. And what if they decided to be ambassadors between the warring governments—would they have a voice? Depending on how suspicious the governments were and how convinced they were that the other side would never change, their attempts to bring peace would likely fail. What a losing position to be caught in.

An old African proverb says, "When two elephants fight, it is the grass that suffers." Biological parents who fight and refuse to cooperate are trampling on their most prized possession—their children. Elephants at war are totally unaware of what is happening to the grass, for they are far too consumed with the battle at hand. Little do they know how much damage is being done.

Researcher James Bray has confirmed what many therapists have believed for years. When one parent speaks negatively about a child's other biological parent, the child internalizes the comment. In other words, "a child who hears a parent attacked thinks, in some way, he is also being attacked."[13] A simple comment like, "Your father is late again. He can be so irresponsible," cuts the child as well as the parent. If the child is ever late for anything, she knows (or thinks she knows) how you feel about her. In addition, a negative comment subtly invites children to agree with the comment, which children hate to do. It implies they are choosing one parent over the other, and that brings guilt. Because of the internalized negativity and guilt over having to choose sides, Bray goes on to suggest that the child will eventually act out such hurt and anger in some destructive behavior. I say you can count on it.

Nine

I don't remember the exact day that it began.
Or the sweater I was wearing when my parents
"began their war against each other."
My sisters and I became the child hostages.
I was nine years old.
I remember my oldest sister,
Coaxing me to wake up to the screaming fight
of my parents in the kitchen.
She lovingly wrapped my Strawberry Shortcake blanket
around my shoulders as we ran barefoot
through the snow to take refuge with a neighbor.
I was nine years old.
My mother sat me down to tell me
all the reasons to hate my dad.
And she arranged more mother-daughter days,

to further preach her cause.
This is when I grew to hate my father.
When I was nine years old.
But then I thought for myself
and began to blame both my parents
for the hell that they've selfishly
dragged their children through.
This is when I grew to hate my parents.
And this is when I grew to hate men.
And this is when I grew to hate divorce.
And this is when I grew to hate love.
And this is when I grew to hate.
When I was nine years old.

—Jessica Dillon, age 17, New York[14]

Are you making a POW swap every other weekend? How often do you trample your children's loyalties to the other country in an effort to persuade them to remain faithful to you? How has your new stepfamily affected the amount of time children have with the other home? As citizens of two countries, your children should be privileged to all the rights, relationships, and responsibilities of each of those homes. Your job is to be at peace with the other country so your children can travel back and forth in security.

Caught in a Tug-of-War: The Matter of Loyalty

Stepfamilies and loyalty conflicts go hand in hand. In fact, successfully defusing the loyalty binds felt by children and adults within stepfamilies is one of the most significant steps toward integration. Loyalty speaks to where we put our allegiances and greatly determines insider/outsider positions.

When I was a boy, we played a game I call Lock Out. A group of kids would create a circle and lock arms. One person on the outside would try to infiltrate the circle and move to the inside. The battle was obvious. The more the outsider attempted to push, poke, or pry his way in, the more the circle banded together to keep him out. Stepfamilies have a similar dynamic. Outsiders are those not related by blood (e.g., stepparents and stepchildren), but whose natural desire is to become one of the insiders.

When tensions rise, splits along biological lines serve to keep out the pressuring outsider. In fact, the more the outsider demands or pries his or her way in, the more resistant the inner circle becomes, and the more resistant the inner circle, the more the outsider feels compelled to force a way in. And so it goes.

For example, stepparents often work very hard to belong and to be accepted. Biological parents want their children and the stepparent to get along, so they feel compelled to work the stepparent into the circle. A frequent and ironic dynamic is that the more a parent tries to orchestrate the acceptance of an outsider (the new spouse), the more resistance the group tends to take on ("lock out"). When insider children fuss or resist the additional group member, the biological parent can feel stuck between conflicting loyalties.

Again, the Crockpot mentality seems to work best. Don't try to force outsiders into the inside. Instead, move them to a place of nearness. Early on stepparents should metaphorically stand beside the circle of insiders and simply be a non-threatening presence. After some time, begin to physically touch the insiders and participate in conversation, yet not ask to be included or considered an insider. Eventually, with time and low heat, an outsider can move inward as the circle unlocks arms and makes space for the new member. At that point, outsiders can actually become "intimate outsiders," that is, closely connected family members, but not equal to blood relatives.[15] Stepparents, for example, should never expect to have the same type of bond that biological insiders have with one another. But some stepparents can become intimate family members as the circle of insiders opens and invites them to belong.

Loyalty Conflicts for Children

Understanding loyalty conflicts and striving as a co-parenting team to alleviate excessive loyalty concerns is important to children's emotional well-being after divorce. Even in the best of circumstances, children feel caught between their biological parents and often feel as though they are in an emotional tug-of-war. Loyalty conflicts seem unavoidable from the children's perspective. They simply want to love everyone—without strings attached and in such a way that others don't feel hurt. Little do parents realize how trampled children feel when they battle for the children's time or attention.

Which Limb Am I?

I have two sets of parents.
I'm lucky, you say.
Just try being in my shoes
Every other Friday.
"I love you!"
"I love you more!!"
Oh somebody, please somebody,
Get me out of this tug-of-war.
The lawyers and judges,
They all play a part
In creating a torn, shattered, and broken heart.
I know I'm not alone,
There are lots of kids like me
With a horribly complicated family tree.
—Colleen, age 11, Pennsylvania[16]

Parents implicitly ask their children to "choose" and, therefore, put children in a no-win tug-of-war when they

- badmouth the other parent or household;
- comment on or compare living conditions;
- cast blame on the other household for financial pressures or emotional pain;
- ask for the child's time when it takes time away from the other parent;
- coax the child into not visiting his/her other parent until child support payments are made or custody time is renegotiated;
- make children feel guilty for enjoying the people in the other home;
- refuse to listen to their happy stories of life in the other home.

All of these situations and many more teach children to take their emotions underground and train them to play the game of "keep everyone happy by making them think I love them most." Children who internalize this tug-of-war become depressed, discouraged, self-destructive, and unmotivated. Children who externalize their pain become angry, oppositional, have behavior problems, and may turn violent.

Children simply want to be connected to the people they love—no strings attached. The messages adults give children that attempt to gain their loyalty, in effect are strings. The goal of the string often is to mend the emotional wounds carried by parents. If your son seems to prefer you to his mother, it somehow affirms your wounded heart (not really, it just *feels* like it). This turns your son into an *emotional Band-Aid*. If his preference for you satisfies your deep desire for revenge against the woman who ended your marriage and broke your heart, your child has become a *toy soldier*, fighting your emotional war. Be careful not to let your wounded heart influence you to subtly and nonverbally elicit your son's allegiance. Children lose when they are made the caretakers of wounded parents. Parents should find ways to soothe their pain through their relationship with God and others. You may need help from a therapist, minister, or trusted friend, but never turn your child into your emotional healer.

The binds children feel sometimes create an unhealthy preference for one parent, usually the most distant or under-functioning parent. Boys, for example, often identify with an unavailable father to the dismay of their mother and stepfather. I've often had stable, responsible parents (and stepparents) ask why their child seems to prefer time with the noncustodial parent, who is an irresponsible drunk. Others wonder why their kids desire to be with a parent who shows no real desire to be with them. "We are good to my kids," one mother said. "My husband is good to them, we provide a financially stable home and a healthy environment. Why do they worry about their dad so much?"

Again, the caretaker dynamic applies. Children are often pulled into a helper role with a parent who needs help. Someone, it feels to the children, has to take care of Dad—even if he is a drunk—or he'll have no one. In effect, the irresponsible behavior of the father functions as an invitation to the children to be his emotional Band-Aid. Children are easily drawn into this protective role. Further, they may become harsh toward the high-functioning biological parent and frequently are harsh toward the stepparent. To enjoy time with a stepfather when your dad is alone and sad at home feels to some children to be disloyal. This struggle not to cause the under-functioning parent more pain is accentuated if he tells the children not to "call that man Daddy" or if he criticizes the stepdad in any way. The message is, "I can't stand for you to love him and care for him—take care of me by not honoring him." One five-year-old demonstrated his bind rather well when he asked his stepmother, "Can I love you when I'm here at Daddy's house and hate you when I'm at Mommy's house?"

There is something completely upside-down when parents rely on children to make themselves feel okay. If you find yourself guilty of placing your children in an emotional tug-of-war, please begin to alter your messages to them and take them out of the middle. *You can only trample grass so long before it ceases to grow.* Here are some suggestions:

- Acknowledge to your children your improper reliance on them. Communicate your desire to do better in the future.
- Make a list of ways you have inadvertently burdened your children. Then for each improper tactic, plan a more appropriate response. *For example:* Talking to the kids about your job frustrations and worries is improper. Focus conversations on their activities and interests; assure them of your competency; consult with a career counselor. (A chart on page 139 helps you develop your new responses.)
- Affirm your children for who they are, not how they care for you.
- Look to God for strength and wisdom as you discover how to heal the wounds of your heart. Remember that he is Jehovah-Rophe, the "God who heals you." (See Exodus 15:26.)
- Begin to connect with friends and counselors who can help you heal.
- Shy away from dating relationships that fill your emptiness. Remarriages that develop as two people rescue each other from painful pasts have difficulty long term. Get well before dating someone new.

Adolescents, Loyalty, and Living With the Other Parent

Stepping in line with the parenting team means understanding the developmental decisions adolescents often face. For many reasons teenagers usually do not welcome the birth of a stepfamily. One reason is the pressure that is put on them to bond with new family members at a time when they are trying to move away from the family.

Adolescence is a developmental passage in our society when children become young adults striving for increasing levels of autonomy and independence. It is a time of testing values and rules, of building a distinctive identity, and an opportunity to gain decision-making power. All of these developmental forces are moving teenagers away from parental control and away from the family.

When stepfamilies form, a nonverbal directive is given to bond with new family members. This demands spending time together and sharing conversation and activities. Teenagers, however, are trying to move away from the family, not toward it. This often creates a bind for teens, especially if adults take personally the teens' efforts to be away from the family. Eager stepparents who are bonding quite well with younger children sometimes complain that they don't have sufficient access to the adolescent children. The message teens hear is an expectation that rivals their efforts for independence. Parents and stepparents alike should, again, relax and not force a level of participation or acceptance from adolescent children. Realize they may be stepping back for many reasons. Maintain a Crockpot mentality and enjoy the bonding experience with younger children, while teens keep their main interests outside the family.

Striving for independence and identity formation is also expressed when teens begin wondering what it would be like to live with the other parent. Some 20 percent of adolescents will move in with their nonresidential parent during the teen years. What to them is further exploration into their history and family background can be easily taken as rejection by parents. Such a reaction, however, sometimes forces children to deny their own interests and take care of the parent by not voicing their desire to live in the other home. "I'm afraid of how Mom will react if I tell her I want to live with Dad," is a statement I've heard from numerous teenagers. "It's not that I don't like being with her, I just want to know my dad a little better." This is not a loyalty issue, nor is it necessarily a comment on the presence of the stepparent. But too many residential parents make it a personal issue and a statement of rejection.

Understanding this struggle for teens is important for parents because teens have been known to generate family conflict in order to be sent to the other home out of parent frustration. High conflict levels are not fun for anyone, but they seem to be less guilt inducing for teens than facing a parent who feels rejected after a request to live in the other home. Is conflict a good result? No. Is conflict the lesser of two evils for the adolescent? Yes. Show your children that you are emotionally strong enough to listen to their needs, even if it means a loss for you.

Unquestionably, some teens threaten to live in the other home as a way of gaining power. "Fine, I'll just go live with Mom," is a great trump card to a parent who fears losing another battle to an ex-spouse. (Notice: A lack of co-parental strength gives power to the adolescent's threat. That's why co-parenting is so crucial. The more united the co-parental team—the less manipulation children can achieve.) Parents cannot afford to be manipulated by a teen's threats. If you find yourself in this situation, seek outside help immediately. You will need help deciding how to respond.

In all the above circumstances, consider the individual growth needs of your teenagers. Be considerate of adolescents' strivings for independence and don't force them to give up their social life to bond with new family members. Be discerning about adolescents' desire to live in the other home and let them know that you would entertain a conversation about such a change if ever they desire it. Undoubtedly, watching them go will tear open your heart. But this isn't about you, remember? It's all about the kids.

SOME IMPORTANT REMINDERS FOR CO-PARENTS

1. You will never lose your children's affections. Blood is very, very thick and nearly impossible to erase. Your children will not forget about you just because they have a new, rich, and/or entertaining stepparent. You have to *intentionally* be a royal jerk before your children will consider leaving you behind. Don't worry or compete with the other household for loyalty; you already have it.

2. Never make children regret having affections for the other home. Remember that they have citizenship there, and forcing a loyalty battle only destroys them. Children need your permission to love their biological parent, and they need to see your psychological stability as they do so. Your permission helps to take them out of the emotional tug-of-war and relieves the pressure to take care of you. They also need your acceptance of the relationship they carve out with their stepparent. A stepparent cannot replace you, so don't force a competition. In fact, the more comfortable you are with the chil-

dren's relationships in the other home, the more likely it is that they will honor you (and *your* new spouse). Respect given is respect returned.

3. Relax and let your children open the circle of insiders to include your new spouse at their own pace. Some children will do so more quickly than others (more on this dynamic later), but don't try to push your spouse in or force your children to allow him or her in. You can find ways of getting along long before stepparents become "intimate outsiders."

4. If you have children who are protecting an under-functioning parent, do not try to force them away from the other parent. While your desire to remove your son's need to rescue is valid, coaching the child away from the other parent feels to the child like a betrayal. Your child may resent you for standing in the way of his relationship. Listen to his worries and affirm his concerns: "I can tell you are worried about your dad. You're afraid he is going to lose another job, huh? Tell me what you are thinking you should do." Express concern and gently *help them to decide* what their boundaries with the other parent should be.

Also, don't feel the need to protect the children from the other parent's actions. Many parents try to preserve the child's opinion of the other parent by covering or explaining negative behavior. This generally puts you in the middle of the child's angry feelings. Help your older children and adolescents to ask the other parent why he or she didn't keep a promise or to explain unhealthy decisions. This empowers children in their relationship. Protecting hides the truth. Children can cope with a parent's actions if they know what to expect, so try not to sugarcoat the truth.[17]

Guidelines for Co-Parents

The following are guidelines that will help you to help your children move back and forth between their two homes. All co-parents should seek to live according to these guidelines.[18] Consider how you might make each a reality in your situation. Remember that you are responsible for your contribution to how you and your ex interact. Change your part of the interaction even if you believe your ex-spouse is to blame for the negative exchanges that have occurred in the past.

1. Work hard to respect the other parent and his or her household. Agree that each parent has a right to privacy, and do not intrude in his or her life. Make space for different parenting styles and rules, as there are many healthy ways to raise children. Do not demean the other's living circumstances, activities, dates, or decisions, and give up the need to control your ex's parenting style. If you have concerns, speak directly to the other parent (see Borrow a Script and Stick to It, page 133).

2. Schedule a regular (weekly to monthly) "business" meeting to discuss co-parenting matters. You can address schedules, academic reports, behavioral training, and spiritual development. Do not discuss your personal life (or your ex's); that part of your relationship is no longer appropriate. If the conversation turns away from the children, simply redirect the topic or politely end the meeting. If you cannot talk with your ex face-to-face due to conflict, use e-mail or speak to their answering machine. Do what you can to make your meetings productive for the children.

3. Never ask your children to be spies or tattletales on the other home. This places them in a loyalty bind that brings great emotional distress. In fact, be happy when they enjoy the people in their new home. ("I'm glad you enjoy fishing with your stepdad.") If children offer information about life in the other home, listen and stay neutral in your judgment.

4. When children have confusing or angry feelings toward your ex, don't capitalize on their hurt and berate the other parent. Listen and help them to explore their feelings without trying to sway their opinions with your own. If you can't make positive statements about the other parent, strive for neutral ones.

5. Children should have everything they need in each home. Don't make them bring basic necessities back and forth. Special items, like clothes or a comforting teddy bear, can move back and forth as needed.

6. Try to release your hostility toward the other parent so that the children can't take advantage of your hard feelings. Manipulation is much easier when ex-spouses don't cooperate.

7. Do not disappoint your children with broken promises or by being unreliable. Do what you say, keep your visitation schedule as agreed, and stay active in their lives.

8. Make your custody structure work for your children even if you don't like the details of the arrangement. Update the other when changes need to be made to the visitation schedule. Also, inform the other parent of any change in job, living arrangements, etc. that may require an adjustment by the children.

9. If you plan to hire a baby-sitter for more than four hours while the children are in your home, give the other parent first right to that time.

10. Suggest that younger children take a favorite toy or game as a transitional object. This can help them make the transition and to feel more comfortable in the other home.

11. Regarding children who visit for short periods of time or spend time in another home:

    • Sometimes it is tempting to only do "special activities" when all of the children are with you for fear that some children may feel that they aren't as special as others. Do special things with differing combinations of children (it's all right if someone feels disappointed he or she wasn't able to go).

    • When other children come for visitation, let the lives of those living with you remain unaltered as much as possible.

    • Keep toys and possessions in a private spot, where they are not to be touched or borrowed unless the owner gives permission (even while they are in the other home).

12. Help children adjust when going to the other home:

    • If the children will go on vacation while in the other home, find out what's on the agenda. You can help your kids pack special items and needed clothing.

    • Provide the other home with information regarding your child's changes. A switch in preferences (regarding music, clothes, hair styles, foods, etc.) or physical/cognitive/emotional developments can be significant. Let the other home know what is different before the child arrives.

    • When receiving children, give them time to unpack, relax, and settle in. Try not to overwhelm them at first with plans, rules, or even special treatment. Let them work their way in at their own pace.[19]

13. If you and your ex cannot resolve a problem or change in custody or visitation, agree to problem-solving through mediation rather than litigation.

Tools for Helping Children Thrive Between Homes

I have learned a great deal from the stepfamilies that participate in my seminars. One group activity in particular is especially helpful in clarifying for adults what children need as they travel back and forth between homes. Without revealing any secrets as to how the activity is structured (you might want to come to a seminar someday), let me share the most helpful realizations parents have made through the years.

1. When children return from the other home, share what has been going on since they left. Upon return, it's very common for parents to ask what the child has done over the weekend or summer (not trying to make the child a spy, but simply taking interest in the child's life). However, rarely do parents take the time to tell their children what has been happening in their home while the child was away. This helps children to know the mood of the home and invites them to find their place in the flow. Remember that belonging can be an issue. Help children find their place.

2. Send lists of items to be returned. Children often forget items, such as their math book, and co-parents may assume it is being returned. Send a checklist of items that need to be returned so the child can be responsible (if old enough), or the co-parent can make sure it is returned.

3. Give children a little "grace space" as they adjust to your house and rules. Children can adjust to different rules in different homes. However, they may need gentle reminders of the rules in your home after spending time in the other. A simple reminder like "I know you can stay up till nine at your mom's house, but the rule in our house is eight-thirty. Off you go." Don't argue with the other house's rule or take issue with the rule-makers. Just manage your home and give the kids a break while they reorient themselves.

4. "Choosing sides stinks!" Try not to force loyalties as children move between homes. The transition from one house to the other is a natural time of comparison for kids. Don't ask them to make choices, and answer their questions regarding the other home with neutral, supportive statements. If you can't be supportive, don't expect your child to adopt your opinion and don't denigrate the other home.

5. "Who needs me the most?" When examining their fit in both homes, children will sometimes choose to invest themselves in the home where they are most needed. Parents need to be understanding about this. Try not to take personally the fact that a child is drawn to the other home; ask questions and listen to what pressures he faces. It may be that he can't fix the situation and needs to be relieved of the responsibility to do so. But it also may be that there is a legitimate reason for him to spend more time in the other home (e.g., a parent's illness that requires extra support from him).

BUILDING THE CO-PARENTAL RELATIONSHIP

"Now we know what we're trying to accomplish as co-parents, but how do we get there?" Obviously, a cooperative relationship with someone you used to fight with is not an easy task. In fact, this is where someone usually points out that conflict with his or her ex-spouse is not a thing of the past. "Sounds great to me—I'd love to have that kind of relationship with my children's parent. But he won't try. Everything I do always backfires or gets sabotaged. What can I do about that?" Believe me, I understand, it takes two to make any cooperative relationship work. Nevertheless, do what you can. (Notice: Rarely does someone admit that he or she contributes to a difficult co-parent relationship. Pointing the finger of blame is always easier, and we are usually blind to how we contribute to the difficulties.) This section will help you understand the emotional issues at play and provide practical ideas for building a better co-parental relationship.

Dissolving Marital Bonds/Retaining Parental Ones

As you attempt to build or strengthen your co-parent relationship, it may be helpful to understand the emotional tasks of ending your previous marital relationship while still maintaining your parental one. When a man and woman marry, they form a husband-wife relationship. Later, when children are brought into the marriage, the same two people form yet another relationship. This father-mother relationship is focused on the partnership of raising a child, while the husband-wife relationship is based on romantic love, companionship, and sexuality. The boundary between these two types of relationship is blurred and weak. For example, couples are well aware of how disagreements over discipline or which values to teach children can easily turn into marital rifts that pit husband against wife. What starts out as a parental issue quickly becomes a marital issue.

The challenge for couples after divorce is to dissolve their marital relationship and create a strong boundary between old marital issues and the current parental relationship. This is a terribly difficult task to accomplish for most people. In effect, the couple redefines their relationship to one of parents only (partners trying to raise a child), not lovers. This is especially difficult when old buttons get pushed, and past marital pain is resurrected through parental disagreement. Unless ex-spouses actively set aside their previous marital agendas, they will easily fall back into personal attacks and manipulative ploys. Again the elephants start fighting, and the grass gets trampled.

How many times have you heard of someone withholding visitation to a former spouse because the ex is a little behind with child-support payments? In effect, one parent holds a child hostage until the child-support ransom is paid. "But you don't understand. My ex was always irresponsible with money and is selfish even today. The only reason he doesn't pay is because he can't stand to part with material things." So you're going to change him by withholding his children? Does that sound like an old marital issue—that's supposed to be buried in a grave somewhere—or a parental one?

A second common example involves new boy/girlfriends or spouses. "My ex-wife left me for another man. Now they are living together. Since that is sinful, don't I have the right to insist that he be gone before the kids spend the weekend with her?" This is a tough question, because it involves a spiritual issue and a co-parental one. On a spiritual level, this man's ex-wife is violating God's law of sexual purity, but she remains the mother of his children and a critical part of their life. They need regular contact with their mom.

From a co-parental standpoint, this man's emotional pain from her affair and decision to end the marriage is skewing his parental decision-making. Again, withholding the children and trying to control her lifestyle, even "for the children's sake," is a decision made from personal pain. If the children have been taught God's principles for purity, they too will feel disdain for their mom's behavior. Nevertheless, the children should not be used as pawns of revenge or attempts to change the mother's behavior. This father should enlist the help of spiritual leaders who might compassionately reach out to this woman and draw her back into holy living. In addition, he needs to talk with his children about their feelings and spiritual concerns for their mother (without berating or criticizing her in a personal manner) and equip them for unwanted interaction with her lover. Reminding them to be Christ to their "enemies," to "overcome evil with good" (Romans 12:21), and to actively pray for their mother's repentance, would be good spiritual leadership. The bottom line—barring legal abuse, the more spiritually upright parent does not have the "right" to control the other parent, his or her lifestyle, or access to the children.

This loss of spiritual influence over your children's other parent is one of the most unfortunate results of divorce. God's spiritual buddy system of marriage does generate a level of spiritual accountability that single life cannot sustain. Being married keeps many people from pursuing selfish or addictive behaviors and promotes godly living. But divorce severs that accountability cord and may result in one parent turning away from a previous Christian life. This may leave you solely responsible for faith shaping and often battling the values of the other home. I'll return to this issue with more specific help in chapter 9.

One final example of ex-spouses who have not adequately dissolved their marital bonds involves too much contact. *Dave* and his new stepfamily came for therapy when his eight-year-old son became unmanageable. Like most stepfamilies, they struggled with many integration issues. One particular dynamic caught my attention. It involved his frequent calls to his ex-wife to discuss their son's difficulties at school. This was a problem for his new wife, because Dave seemed very controlled by his ex during their marriage, and she feared he was letting her have too much power even now. I asked Dave to help me understand the reason for his daily phone calls. He shared that during the marriage his ex-wife had been very critical of his parenting and now frequently threatened to take custody of their son due to his "parental incompetence." Dave was fearful of losing his son. Even more important, however, was Dave's ongoing effort to earn his ex-wife's approval (which was easily withheld). They hadn't been married for three years, but he was still emotionally starving for her approval. This need was leading to too much contact with his ex-wife, which debilitated him even further.

The impact was subtle, but very critical to his son's misbehavior. Dave parented out of fear and anxiety of how his ex would evaluate him, which stole his ability to effectively manage his son. He was easily overrun by the boy and manipulated by his ex-wife. Once he began acting out of strength instead of fear and set appropriate communication boundaries with his ex-wife, his competency increased dramatically and his son's misbehavior diminished.

Putting to death the old marital bond with all its pain, power, and privilege is difficult. Yet it is just what the doctor ordered for effective co-parenting to begin. Your ex may have been inattentive to your marital needs, but you and your children have different needs. Many parents who were poor marriage partners are good parents, and children enjoy them very much. Men in particular often improve their parenting activity after divorce, yet their ex-wives assume they haven't changed and don't give them the respect they deserve. Give your ex-spouse the opportunity to be wonderful with the kids, even if he wasn't wonderful with you. Separate your marital past from your parental present and do everything you can to make the co-parental relationship work.

Ex-Spouses: What's Your Type?

In her book *The Good Divorce*, family researcher Constance Ahrons identified five types of ex-spouse relationships. Consider her descriptions and see where you and your ex fit.

- *Perfect Pals*: These couples are high interactors/high communicators, and comprised just 12 percent of her research sample. Even though these couples were divorced, their friendship behaviors continued.

They still considered themselves good friends, spoke once or twice a week, and were interested in each other's lives. They remained connected with family and old friends. Not many of these couples remained in this category, but moved on to less cooperative relationships. Also, five years after their divorce they had not recoupled with new partners. (Indeed, it's difficult to establish a new relationship while holding on to a former spouse.)

- *Cooperative Colleagues*: These moderate interactors/high communicators represented 38 percent of the research sample. While not considering each other best friends, these couples did cooperate quite well around issues that concerned the children. Some talked frequently, others minimally. For the most part, they were able to compromise when it came to dividing up time with the children. In handling conflict, they usually didn't end up in vicious battles, but resolved issues or avoided them. A common denominator for these couples was the ability to compartmentalize their relationship; that is, they separated out issues related to their marital relationship from those related to their parenting relationship. Their desire to provide the best situation for their children took precedence over their personal issues.[20]

- *Angry Associates*: These moderate interactors/low communicators (25 percent of sample) communicated only to make plans for their children and usually got angry doing so. Conflict was the major issue for these couples. Unlike cooperative colleagues, they were not able to compartmentalize their anger, but found it spreading to most aspects of their interaction.

- *Fiery Foes*: These low interactors/low communicators made up about 25 percent of the sample. "These ex-spouses rarely interact, and when they do talk they usually end up fighting. Their divorces tended to be highly litigious, and their legal battles often continued for many years after the divorce. Each change brings further anger: they were not able to work out arrangements for the children without arguing. Many relied on a third party (i.e., a lawyer, friend, or child) to settle their disagreements over each issue as it arose."[21]

- *Dissolved Duos*: These ex-spouse pairs stop contact entirely. It was common for one ex-spouse to move away and leave little or no contact. There is no two-household arrangement here, truly a single-parent family.[22]

Did you find your type or the one that most aptly describes your current ex-spouse relationship? What type is your new spouse and his or her ex? Which of these types should co-parents strive for? Cooperative Colleagues works best. If you look closely at the description, you can see why: they have the ability to compartmentalize personal issues relating to their marriage from parenting issues relating to their children. They are able to dissolve their marital issues while continuing to work together as parents. They simply don't allow old marital junk to spoil their ability to cooperate.

What if you find yourself an Angry Associate or a Fiery Foe? Take control of yourself and make changes to your part of the relationship. Improving your ex-spouse relationship, even if you have an "impossible" ex, is not completely out of your control. You can always—and God expects you to—control yourself and not give in to anger or pain. Yet the obstacles for some are many. Let me offer some tools to help you to be a Cooperative Colleague.

Spoiled Leftovers From the Past: Coping With Anger, Hurt, and Guilt

Relational attachments come in many shapes and sizes. The highest attachment is, of course, selfless covenant love. What surprises most people is the realization that hurt, anger, and guilt can tie two people together as tightly as love.[23] The root of such attachments is pain; it binds people together in disharmony. Even more surprising is the realization that conflict, bitterness, and control are the umbilical cords through which anger and guilt stay alive. As criticism and defensiveness pass back and forth between ex-spouses, hurt and the bond of disharmony are kept alive. One of the greatest ironies of bitterness is that it imprisons you with the person who hurt you. Over time you actually contribute to your own pain and misery.

If you are the leavee (your ex left you), you probably feel more anger, rejection, and hurt. If you cannot set this aside and compartmentalize your feelings, you can easily spoil the co-parental relationship. If you were the leaver (you initiated the divorce) you may feel a great deal of guilt, especially when you see your children's pain. You may find it difficult to separate from your decision and fully invest in your present stepfamily situation. Your new spouse may feel insecure with your commitment, and your stepchildren may feel rejected by you. Your guilt may even lead you to keep your ex-spouse from being angry with you. For example, some feel obligated to their ex and go out of their way to accommodate him/her regarding money, time schedules, or taking care of maintenance tasks for their ex-spouse's home. For both the leavee and the leaver, whether you feel rejection or guilt, your pain is dictating your responses. You are locked in a prison cell of pain, and your continued negative interaction is keeping the key beyond your reach.

Learning to Forgive

So what do you do? Let it go with forgiveness. I know this is where I'll lose some of you. Your back is already bowed, your blood pressure is going up, and you want to close the book. "After what he did to me, how dare you suggest I forgive?" One woman heard me discussing the necessity of forgiveness as a tool to improve co-parent relationships, and she was offended. She called to say, "My ex left me for another woman and now she is my kids' stepmother. There's no way I can forgive him for that and I won't accept her place with *my* children. In fact, I'm doing everything I can to sabotage her authority." She went on to explain how she was telling her children to disobey their stepmother, since she broke up their family.

Please understand, I don't take the suggestion to forgive lightly, nor do I believe it an easy task. I was a crisis counselor after the Westside School shooting here in Jonesboro, Arkansas, and worked with a number of the families who were so painfully impacted by that event. Never have I seen such pain or crying out to God. Never have I felt so inadequate as a therapist. And my passion for those who lost so much on March 24, 1998, would not allow me to flippantly urge them to "forgive and move on." To discount the value of lives lost in such a way would be reprehensible. Yet acknowledgment of a loving God, who reigns supreme even in the midst of agony, and the ability to offer forgiveness, eventually became the backbone of healing for those I worked with.

Your pain is real too, and your anger may be completely justified. Yet you can't be for your stepfamily everything God calls you to be if you're carrying around a burden of anger, hurt, and guilt. The woman caller mentioned above used her children to seek revenge and threw her children into the middle of a war. Such a misguided solution generates pain for innocent people and keeps your pain alive and well. How can that be considered Christian?

Forgiveness is an unnatural act of a will that has been shaped and molded by a forgiving God. There is nothing human about it. Forgiveness doesn't restore the broken relationship or repair the emotional damage done. It simply writes it off. And it only becomes practically possible to us when we realize what God has forgiven us. Even after having his debt canceled by his master, the unmerciful servant of Matthew 18:21–35 was not able to cancel the debt owed him by a fellow servant because he didn't fully appreciate his gift of forgiveness. Paul reminds us in Colossians 2:13–14 that while we were dead in our sins, God made us alive with Christ. "He forgave us all our sins, having canceled the written code, with its regulations, that was against us and that stood opposed to us; he took it away, nailing it to the cross." Only when we realize what stood between us and God (our sinfulness) and how God removed that through the cross, can we ever realistically apply forgiveness to that which stands between us and another person. Be humbled by the magnitude of your forgiven debt and you'll discover that the unnatural act of forgiving is possible.

Some Practical Observations About Forgiveness[24]

- Forgiveness begins with a decision. The process of forgiveness begins with our intellect. Saying the words "I forgive Lisa for abandoning me and our family" starts a process of forgiveness. The challenge, then, becomes living that choice. Please know that emotional release—a letting go of pain and hurt—follows the intellectual decision to forgive, not the other way around. Until emotional release is achieved, peace comes in the form of trust. Trust that God knows what's best for us, and that his way will work. The feeling of peace may occur immediately or gradually; until then it is the promise of peace that keeps us going.
- Choose to forgive one offense at a time. All too often we face a mountain of hurt that cannot be overcome. Make a list of the boulders that

comprise that mountain and strive to forgive them individually. Take it in manageable pieces.

- Communicating your forgiveness is optional. For some, relief comes just by having made a personal decision to forgive. Others need to communicate their decision to bring closure to the process. Do what is best in your situation.

- Forgiveness and accountability are not mutually exclusive. We can forgive someone and still hold him or her accountable for his or her actions (not for revenge or personal gain). For example, you can forgive an ex-spouse for driving drunk with your children in the car, but you don't have to then subject your children to future possible harm. Work with your ex and/or the court system to ensure safety (e.g., another person must be present when driving) until your ex demonstrates more responsible behavior.

- Forgiveness takes one; trust and reconciliation takes two. Mercy can be extended to someone without reestablishing trust. Many resist forgiveness because they believe they will be forced into making themselves vulnerable to the other person again. If a bank employee steals from a bank, he can be forgiven and still not be given his job back. There is nothing wrong with learning from your past experience with someone and protecting yourself or others from hurt. Just check your motives.

- Forgiveness is empowering. Holding on to hurt and pain enslaves us to the person who hurt us. Conflict and bitterness keep alive our hurt. The result is a helpless victim. Have you ever been guilty of constantly blaming your poor life circumstances on someone else? That's what victims do—constantly complain about how others have ruined their life. In doing so, victims alleviate themselves from personal responsibility for the condition of their life.

Forgiveness moves us from victim to empowered victor. It breaks the chains of imprisonment and severs the umbilical cord that gave life to the pain. When you forgive, you no longer have to react to the other out of pain, but have free choice to decide the best course of action. For example, an ex-spouse might continue to act as a Fiery Foe, but you do not have to return fire (as in the past). Forgiveness is the key that opens your prison cell door. Ex-concentration camp victim Corrie ten Boom said, "To forgive is to set a prisoner free and discover the prisoner was you."

While forgiveness is fresh on your mind, take a moment and complete this action point: Write a brief answer to the following.

1. What offenses or leftovers from the past do I have before me? (Make a list.)

2. Which of these can I decide to forgive today?

3. Decide how you will continue to struggle with forgiving the remaining items.

4. What personal acts do I need to repent of, release to God, or seek forgiveness for?

Keep the Goal in Mind

Working with an uncooperative ex-spouse is difficult, especially when the ghost of marriage past begs you not to give the other any credit for change. On some level many ex-spouses need to view the other as incapable of change. This leads us to look for evidence that the ex is still the same and can't be trusted; we might also discount evidence to the contrary. Keeping the goal in mind means doing everything you can to be a Cooperative Colleague and remaining open to the possibility that your ex-spouse might change along the way. When treating children who are members of a post-divorce family or stepfamily, a standard part of my clinical work is to call ex-spouses for a consultation. I generally find them to be much less disagreeable than the other parent assumes they will be. In fact, they are often eager to improve the living conditions for their children. Remember, if you can grow up and change, so can they.

Learn How to Invite Cooperation

Some parents, after reading this material, can simply call their ex-spouse, share this book, and have a rational meeting to discuss how they might better implement the Guidelines for Co-Parents (page 117). If that is within your power, by all means set up the meeting soon. Angry Associates and Fiery Foes, however, will fear a face-to-face meeting, believing it will erupt into World War III.

"You just don't understand. My ex is a jerk and won't listen to anything I say. If I mail her a copy of your book she'll throw it away. I have no control over her attitude." True, you have no control over your ex's attitude, but you may have some influence. Years ago I wrote "An Open Letter to Parents Who Are Divorced" (see next page). It was designed to remind parents of their vital role and invite ex-spouses to consider how they might better cooperate. I had no idea how useful and productive the letter would be to angry, fiery co-parents.

Here's the plan. Copy the letter and mail it to your ex-spouse with this written or verbal message: "I have been reading a book on stepfamily life and co-parenting. The author of the book recommended that I share this letter with you; otherwise, I wouldn't impose. I also want you to know that I've realized I have been violating a few of these principles and am committing myself to do better. Specifically, I've noticed that I am guilty of [provide two examples of mistakes you have made and what you intend to do next time. For example, you could say, "I shouldn't cut into your visitation time by bringing the kids over past five P.M. I'm sorry. My new goal is to be on time, every time. Also, I'm going to stop saying negative things about your new husband. I now see that that puts the kids in a tight spot."] I appreciate your time. [your name]"

There are, of course, no guarantees that sending the letter will change anything; you are simply trying to open the door to change. You must not send a copy of the letter with a message like "Boy, do you need to read this. You're a terrible co-parent and it's tearing up our kids." Obviously, this attempt to control your ex will re-ignite your battles and close the door to

An Open Letter to Parents Who Are Divorced

This letter is about your children and the invaluable role you will play in bringing healing to their lives. You see, since the moment you and your ex-spouse informed them of your impending divorce, your children have been in a transitional crisis. How well they recover from that crisis has a lot to do with you, that is, your continuing role as a parent. Whether you are the custodial parent or the noncustodial parent, you play a vital role in the emotional adjustment of your children. Consider, for example, the following empirical data:

Children successfully adjust to the ending of their parents' marriage and can fare reasonably well if (1) the parents are able to bring their marital relationship to an end *without excessive conflict*; (2) children are *not put into the middle* of whatever conflicts exist; and (3) there is a commitment from parents to *cooperate* on issues of the children's material, physical, educational, and emotional welfare.

It is this last point that I am emphasizing here. Please understand that I am not necessarily asking you to reconcile with your former spouse. However, it is very important that you and your ex-spouse separate the dissolution of your marriage from the parental responsibilities that remain. In other words, while your marriage has ended, your role as a parent has not. This notion is sometimes referred to as *co-parenting* and involves the cooperation of both biological parents even while living in separate households.

I do realize, however, that many ex-spouses have great difficulty cooperating about anything, let alone the nurture and discipline of their children. But that does not absolve you of the responsibility to try—perhaps even harder than you did on your marriage. After all, your children deserve *your* best effort.

If necessary, perhaps a trained family therapist can help you and your ex-spouse negotiate your co-parental arrangement. Whatever the case, please, for their sake, assume the responsibility of being involved in the lives of your children.

Please understand, this letter is not about casting blame, nor is it intended to add to your level of guilt. It is simply an earnest plea that you offer your children the most valuable resource you have—*yourself.*

Sincerely,
Ron L. Deal, M.MFT.
Author, *The Smart Stepfamily*
Licensed Marriage and Family Therapist

change. Furthermore, admit your mistakes without asking your ex to evaluate his or her parenting. The influence comes when you admit your failings with no strings attached. This quietly invites the other parent to consider his or her own behavior without pressure from you. Above all, keep the goal in mind, do your part, and pray that the Lord will soften your ex-spouse's heart.

Be Businesslike If Necessary

Many co-parents have learned how to handle difficult ex-spouse relationships. Some use note cards while speaking on the phone to help keep them on task. Others avoid personal contact altogether, relying on answering machines, letters, and e-mail. No matter what your avenue of communication, treat the contact as you would a business deal. Don't get personal, seek the win/win solution, and stick to discussing the kids. Having a business mentality may help you to avoid being sidetracked when your buttons get pushed. For example, one good business principle that applies in many circumstances is to try to find the common ground. Whenever possible, agree with some aspect of what your ex is saying, even if you disagree with the main point. "You're right, every teenager wants the independence a car provides; I'm just wondering if he should be rewarded with one right now given his poor grades." If you can't "close the deal" because of personal pain or attacks, politely take a time-out from negotiations. Return to the table later when you have gathered yourself.

Borrow a Script and Stick to It

Patricia Papernow has designed some scripts to help co-parents deal with one another and the differences between their homes in a constructive manner.[25] Before calling your ex, for example, have a written script in your hands to guide your responses. This will help you manage yourself during the conversation.

Here are some of Dr. Papernow's scripts to help you communicate.

1. Letting the Bullet Bounce

After answering the phone, you hear your ex say, "I can't believe you forgot to send Jennifer's Halloween costume. We're going to be late, she's crying, and once again you are irresponsible! When are you going to grow up?"

Your response: [Take a deep breath and gather yourself] "I know it's a pain. I'm sorry. Do you want me to bring it over, or do you want to pick it up?"

Note: I call this letting the bullet bounce, because your ex is attacking you, and if you let the bullet penetrate, you will react defensively. Putting on thick skin is a premium in stepfamilies. Don't respond to the accusation; get to a behavioral solution. And next time remember to send the Halloween costume.

2. Mom's House Rules/Dad's House Rules

You say to your son: "Homework *before* watching TV."

He says, "Dad lets me watch TV before doing my homework."

Take a deep breath and say, "That may be true in your dad's house. And in this house, the rule is homework *before* TV."

Note: It's okay to have differing rules and expectations. The temptation is to argue with Dad's rule or judge his motives by saying, "That's because your dad likes to watch TV all the time himself." Don't worry about Dad's rule. Stick to yours. Also, notice the use of the word *and* instead of *but* preceding "in this house . . ." The latter creates defensiveness; *and* is much more conciliatory.

3. The "Looking for Information" Phone Call

Sometimes situations like the one above require further information from the other parent. The biological parent should make the call; how you make that call is important to maintaining a cooperative relationship.

If you call and say the following, you are igniting a battle: "I can't believe you let Johnny watch TV before doing his homework."

Rather, call and say, "Hi. I'm calling for some information. Johnny and I had a little run-in, and he says that in your house it's okay to watch TV before getting his homework done. I'm wondering if that's true, or if he's trying to get away with something."

If you are Cooperative Colleagues, the response may sound like this: "Yeah. I figure he needs to unwind a little bit after basketball practice."

You say, "Okay. I can understand that. That's what I needed to know. Thank you."

If you are Angry Associates, the response may sound more like "He comes home tired from basketball practice, and he's just a kid. Why should he have to do it anyway—homework isn't that important right now."

You say, [take a deep breath] "Okay. Thank you."

Note: This second response is by far the most difficult. However, it is likely that arguing is not going to convince the other parent to change (has it ever worked before?), and you don't need to try to control them anyway. You got the information you were seeking, and it wasn't pretty. Hang up and work with your son within your home.

Say to your son: "Moms and dads are different. I have lots of rules about chores in the house; your father has more rules about manners at the table. I'm concerned about your grades and wonder what you can do here to improve them. [Discuss the possibilities.] What might you do while in your dad's house to get your homework done?"

4. Off the Hook and Out of the Middle

Parents can sometimes tell when kids are getting caught in negative battles between adults. However, many times children themselves are not aware of a loyalty bind nor can they articulate it, so parents may not know their child is caught. Here are some possible ways to respond when you notice your child is in the tug-of-war.

To your children: "It seems to me that you are kind of caught in the middle between your mother and I. I know that is a tough place to be. I'm wondering how you feel about it? [Listen and affirm.] When do you feel stuck the most? I'm sorry you have to hear negative things. I want you to know if you hear me say something about the other home that makes you feel bad, you can ask me to stop. And you can ask your mom to stop too. If not, you'll be in a bad spot between us. Do you want to talk about it? [Listen and validate feelings.] By the way, I know you know this, but you have my permission to love your mom and respect or love your stepdad. That's important for you, and I'm okay with it."

If your child responds, "Come on, Dad. You know Mom won't stop even if I ask her to. Once she gets started, she can't stop." Reply by saying, "You may be right. But I think it's worth saying out loud to her that it makes you feel bad."

To your ex-spouse: "I know you would never mean to hurt the kids. But your comments like [give specific examples] are putting them between us. Please stop. I'm learning not to say negative things in front of the kids, and I hope you will do the same. Thank you for your time."

If your ex isn't convinced that negative comments hurt the children, don't try to defend yourself to the children. That only forces them into the middle again. The children will form their own opinions as they grow, and they tend to finally respect the parent who manages their tongue (see James 3).

5. Reconnecting

When noncustodial parents have been disconnected from their children for an extended period of time, many wounds are created. If you have been absent from your child's life and now want to reconnect, understand that it won't be easy. As children grow into adolescence and adulthood, they can develop emotional walls that have protected them from feeling your rejection. Your ex-spouse may have great anger toward you for disappointing the children and being unavailable to help raise them. Consider the following script as you hope to reconnect.

Communicate to your ex-spouse: "I apologize for not being involved like I should have been. I know I have cheated you and our children out of a lot. And I'm sorry. I am hoping to reconnect with the kids but will not force myself on them. I will just let them know I'm changing, and they can contact me when they are ready."

Write a letter to your child: "I know this is tough to hear from me after I've been away for so long. I can see you are loyal to your mother right now. That is as it should be. Sometime I hope things change enough that you feel you can reconnect with me. I love you. When you're ready to call, I'll be happy to talk to you."

Note: Once you have stated your desire to reconnect, don't make it tough for kids to reach back and find you waiting. Send birthday and holiday gifts with short, friendly messages. Don't induce guilt by saying, "Happy birthday. Why haven't you called?" Short e-mails can also help you stay at a safe distance until your children decide to step closer.

Reconnecting Following Blocked Relationships

Unfortunately, parents are sometimes prohibited from seeing their children because their ex-spouse has cut off contact between them. Children are confused by all the mixed messages and often hesitant about reconnecting.

Say to your child: "I know we haven't been able to have any contact for some time. I know your mom said a lot of bad things about me. I am not sure why she did that. Sometimes when people are in pain it is hard for them to do the right thing. You and I are going to have a lot of sorting out to do. I hope, as you are ready, that you'll ask me about the things she said. I will tell you honestly which ones are true and which ones are not. Sometimes I think we will both be really sad or mad about the time we have missed together. I hope you'll talk to me when you feel that way. Meanwhile, I'm really glad we're talking again."[26]

Stepping in Line

This chapter and the next suggest that a key step in stepfamily success is taken when all the adults on the parenting team put their needs aside and consider the children. Remembering that it is "all about the children" keeps the focus of adult interaction where it should be. The first key relationship in the parenting team is the co-parent relationship. The next chapter will discuss the second key aspect: the parent/stepparent relationship and their roles as caregivers.

Questions for Discussion

FOR ALL COUPLES

1. On a scale of 1 to 10 rate your co-parental relationship on your ability to contain anger and conflict in order to cooperate and compromise on issues regarding the children's welfare.
2. List two or three things you might do to improve this rating.
3. During the first year after remarriage, disruptions in the visitation schedule can be quite problematic for children. Regularity of contact is critical to children's self-esteem and reduces more feelings of loss. When a remarriage takes place, the visitation routine is often disturbed. Indeed, fathers on average drop their visits to noncustodial children by half within the first year of their ex-wife's remarriage. What disruptions in access to both parents have your children experienced? What can you do to improve the access and regularity (predictability) of this contact?
4. Consider whether your children have your permission to care for others in their two homes. If not, what needs to change within you in order to grant that permission?

5. What fears do you have about losing touch with your teenagers? If they wanted to live in the other home, how would you react?

6. Review the Guidelines for Co-Parents on page 117 and create a checklist of items you need to develop or work toward. Affirm yourself and your ex for the things you are currently doing well.

7. Consider each point in Helping the Children Thrive Between Homes (page 120). Which have you already implemented and which could you adopt now?

8. On a scale of 1–10 how well are you able to compartmentalize old marital issues from current co-parental ones? What triggers are you most susceptible to?

9. Share some of the forgiveness issues you have had to face or are currently struggling to release.

10. Which scripts might be helpful to you in the future? Why?

FOR PRE-REMARITAL COUPLES

1. Openly discuss your present co-parent relationships. How cooperative have you been in the past with your ex? What issues are problematic? How well are you able to contain your anger and responses with your children's other parent?

2. With whom do you need to step in line prior to your remarriage?

3. What are your hopes regarding how quickly your children will accept their new stepparent? What do you think is reality in this?

4. How did you contribute to the breakup or divorce of your last relationship?

5. To what degree have you emotionally resolved the ending of your first marriage?

6. To what degree have you resolved what happened to your future spouse in his or her previous relationship?

7. The presence of moderate to severe anger and/or guilt is a good indication that you have not emotionally de-coupled from your former love relationship. How de-coupled are you and your ex-spouse?

Burdens My Children Face

Make a list on the left side of unhealthy co-parenting patterns. On the right, list your new plan and how you will respond. Consider, for example:

- Ways I put them in an emotional tug-of-war
- Expectations put on them to take care of others or of me

Unhealthy Burden	My New Plan
1.	1.
2.	2.
3.	3.
4.	4.
5.	5.

CHAPTER SEVEN

Smart Step Four: STEP in Line (Part 2)

Parent and stepparent roles

"But Sarah saw that the son whom Hagar the Egyptian had borne to Abraham was mocking, and she said to Abraham, 'Get rid of that slave woman and her son, for that slave woman's son will never share in the inheritance with my son Isaac.' The matter distressed Abraham greatly because it concerned his son" (Genesis 21:9–11).

Parenting in stepfamilies is a two-, three-, or four-person (sometimes more!) dance. Parent-stepparent harmony is the crux of successful parenting within your home—whatever the condition of your co-parental relationship(s). The two most critical relationships in any stepfamily home are the marriage and the stepparent-stepchildren relationships. The marriage must be strong to endure the many pressures stepfamily couples face and provide the backbone to stepfamily stability. Marriage, we might say, is the Crockpot itself; without the pot, nothing gets cooked. Almost as important is the stepparent-stepchildren relationship. The stepparent's role in the family is critical because it dramatically affects the level of stress in children. Less stress in children equals more harmony with stepparents; that in turn leads to more harmony in the marriage.

Many people assume incorrectly that stepparenting is the sole responsibility of the stepparent. This assumption pits husband and wife against each other when the stepparent flounders or upsets the children. Lest there be any confusion, let me say very clearly that stepparenting is a two-person task. Biological parents and stepparents must work out roles that complement one another and play to each other's strengths. Just as in two-biological-parent homes, parents and stepparents must be unified in goals and work together as a team. Stepparents who are struggling need biological parents who will step up to the plate. Stepparents and biological parents do not function in a vacuum, isolated from one another. In fact, what is needed most is a working alliance between the parent and stepparent that helps to clarify the stepparent's role. Stepping in line means planning and parenting together.

JUST IN CASE YOU THINK YOU'VE GOT IT ALL TOGETHER . . .

I'm convinced that children are God's tool for humbling adults. We could pretty well sail through life in control of almost everything if we didn't have children. But competent, self-assured, capable people can be reduced to Jell-O when face-to-face with a typical two-year-old. Throughout the child-rearing years humility comes to parents in many forms: the helplessness of trying to help a six-month-old infant to stop crying at three in the morning; the powerlessness of struggling with a sixteen-year-old daughter who keeps breaking the rules; the inadequacy you feel when your nine-year-old son says, "So do you and Mom have sex?" And nothing can embarrass us more than the surprises kids throw at us at the most inconvenient times. I'll never forget carrying a constipated three-year-old out of worship (during the quiet, reflective time of communion, no less), only to have him announce at the top of his lungs why we were leaving: "Poo-poo!" Once you have kids, your life will never be the same.

Yet the only challenge more humbling than raising children is raising stepchildren! There is no doubt that throughout the years of integration stepparents are often the most rejected, least affirmed, and most vulnerable adults in stepfamilies. At any given moment stepparents may have all the responsibility for daily childcare that biological parents have but may have very little authority to manage the child's behavior. They are expected to make the same sacrifices as biological parents but reap very few rewards. ("Thanks for washing my clothes for school today" doesn't come often enough.)

Stepmothers are at an even greater disadvantage than stepfathers for a number of reasons. First, children tend to maintain more frequent contact with their noncustodial mothers. Second, children's attachment to their biological mother is believed to be stronger than their attachment to their father, making the acceptance and bonding with a stepmother even more difficult. Third, because society expects women to achieve a higher relational standard than men, stepmothers feel greater pressure to build a strong attachment with stepchildren. Despite changing roles in America, women still bear the primary responsibility for childcare, maintenance, and nurturing of children. Stepmothers are not excused from these responsibilities and try to fulfill society's expectations by working hard at building a relationship—only to discover a strong loyalty to the biological mom standing in the way. No wonder stepmothers report greater dissatisfaction with their role and exhibit higher levels of stress.

"Unguided by norms, role clarity, or realistic expectations, the stepmother works to 'make up for the past' experiences of the stepchildren, only to come to the awareness that she is overwhelmed, frustrated, and less committed to them than she believes she should be. . . . The lack of role models for women who become stepmothers means that women have nowhere to turn for meaningful advice."[1] Truly the job of a stepmother is a challenging one. Family therapist and stepfamily educator Jean McBride says one woman described it well: "Being a stepmother is like setting your hair on fire and then trying to put it out with a hammer!"[2] You get it coming and going.

Because of the awesome task stepparents face, I've taken the liberty of modifying the Serenity Prayer by Reinhold Niebuhr to articulate the Stepparents' Serenity Prayer. Perhaps you can relate:

> Lord, grant me the serenity to accept the things I cannot change,
> the courage to change the things I can,
> the wisdom to make my mate's ex-spouse vanish into thin air,
> and the power to force my stepchildren to love and honor me,
> so that my mate and I will live happily ever after.

If only it were so.

REWARDS AND CHALLENGES

No one ever dreams of growing up and becoming a stepparent. It's just not part of our "and they lived happily ever after" fantasy. Nor does society teach us an effective stepparent role. We make it up as we go. Even those who had stepparents as children don't study their technique because they don't assume they'll become one. This leaves stepparents and parents with an ambiguous definition of their role and a lot of questions. When things don't go well it is easy to blame oneself and think about returning to Egypt.

> *"I feel more like a maid than a mother."*
>
> *"After two years, I still sometimes feel like an outsider, like my wife and stepchildren are a group that I'll never be part of."*
>
> *"I feel that every time I try to set some rules it's like a declaration of war with my stepchildren."*[3]

But not all children feel negatively toward stepparents.

> *"When I was four years old my father died, and two years later my mother met my stepdad. There were six of us kids to raise, plus he had three from his previous marriage. When they got married, he helped her raise us and treated us like his very own kids. I never knew my father; Ted is the only real father I ever knew. Though we have had our ups and downs, I would never trade him for any other father in the world."*
>
> *—Stepdaughter*

> *"He's only been my father for about six years. He seems like my real father. He takes me fishing, hunting, and four-wheeler riding. I think the only thing we haven't done is skate and golf. If I want something and he can afford it, he gets it for me. He shows me love and discipline. Even when he disciplines me, I can tell he still loves me."*
>
> *—Stepson, age 9*

Children nominating their fathers for our church's "Father of the Year" award wrote these last two quotes. The respect and appreciation of these stepchildren is evident. I share it with you as a reminder that there is a Promised Land. All the hard work and discomfort of stepparenting can pay off. It probably won't live up to the fantasy you have created, but it can be pretty good.

So how do stepparents and parents work together to generate this type of recognition? What are some common pitfalls, and how can stepparents avoid them? Let's begin by examining some mistaken assumptions of ineffective stepparents.

"It takes five years to learn how to parent a five-year-old. I just got one yesterday, and no matter what I do, I am five years behind."
—David Mills, therapist

Our assumptions or expectations of what is good for our children and stepchildren guide many of the decisions we make as parents. The parenting team (parent and stepparent) is frequently confused about the stepparent's role and makes assumptions as to what should happen. Many of those assumptions are misguided and lead to ineffective stepparenting. However, research is giving us practical help to follow. Here are some common assumptions of out-of-step stepparents and practical advice for getting back in step.

Ineffective Stepparents Make Becoming an Insider Their Goal

It's perfectly understandable to want to be considered a part of the family, but stepparents who make it their goal to become insiders often end up terribly disappointed. It is one thing to find ways of getting along or to be respected by stepchildren as an adult with moderate authority; it is another to want stepchildren to want you in their innermost family circle. This desire leads stepparents to force their way in, orchestrate bonding experiences, and put pressure on the biological parent to help bring them in. Simply put, these stepparents try too hard, rather than accept the relationship that develops.

Effective Stepparents Enjoy the Relationship They Have Now. The cardinal rule for stepparent bonding is to let the children set the pace for their relationship with you. If they welcome or seek affection, then go for it. If they remain distant and cordial, honor that as well. If they follow your rules and respect your decisions, continue to assert your given authority. If they challenge your authority, find ways to live on borrowed power from the biological parent (see below). Effective stepparents know that building a connection with stepchildren takes time, yet they don't emphasize "deepening the bond" to the point that they miss the relationship they currently have. Learn to find the nuggets of good in the relationship you have now. Be patient and keep seeking to grow with your stepchildren, but don't add too much pressure.

Ineffective Stepparents (and Their Spouses) Expect Too Much of Themselves

Parents and stepparents tend to assume that children want a close, warm relationship with the stepparent. Biological parents want their children to be happy with their choice of mate, and stepparents assume they need to be someone special to the children. Kids say otherwise.

When asked how the stepparent role *should be performed,* parents and stepparents generally envision the role in similar ways. In one study, close to half of them said the ideal stepparent role should be one of "parent" as opposed to "stepparent" or "friend." In contrast, 40 percent of stepchildren identified "friend" as the ideal role. Far fewer children thought a "parent" role was ideal.[4] "Parents" give hugs and expect obedience to their rules; "friends" offer support and encourage positive values in a child's life.

Effective Stepparents Have Realistic Expectations for Their Role. Stepparents need to learn to relax into their role and not expect too much of themselves. To expect too much is to set themselves up for disappointment and frustration. Parents also need to relax and let stepparents and stepchildren carve out their relationship. This will eventually happen as a result of the Crockpot's low heat.

James Bray discovered that most stepchildren in the early years of stepfamily life view the stepparent like a coach or camp counselor.[5] Such people have limited authority with children and provide instruction, but they are not "parents." However, just because your stepchildren don't give you unsolicited hugs does not mean you don't have a decent relationship. Having stepchildren who only talk to you when they want something is not an indication that you are a poor stepparent. It represents where you are today. Relax and trust the Crockpot.

Ineffective Stepparents Rush Into Parenting

You may be familiar with what parent educators call *authoritative parenting*, identified as the most effective parenting style. The authoritative parent seeks to maintain firmness with respect for the child, boundaries, while providing limited choices, and rules with stated, consistent consequences that are balanced by nurture and love. Authoritative parenting at its best is a mirror of the parenting God gives us. Love and grace stand side by side with law and discipline.

Authoritarian parenting, by contrast, is characterized by high rules, harsh discipline, and excessive control. This strict parent essentially says, "You do it because I said so."

Permissive parents represent the other end of the parenting continuum. They provide very few limits or rules and give children unlimited choices. These parents make excuses for their child's behavior and assume the child will find his or her own way in life.

The authoritarian and permissive parenting styles have consistently been shown to produce children who lack self-control, have poor decision-making abilities, and who struggle with value-centered living. Stepparents don't want to adopt either of these styles. So one would naturally assume that since authoritative parenting is best for children, stepparents would need to begin there. Surprisingly, research suggests this is not so. It is a matter of timing.

Effective Stepparents Grow Into Their Role. Stepparenting changes as relationships grow. Authoritative stepparenting, especially within the first six months after remarriage, does not have the same positive outcome that authoritative parenting does in biological families, at least with most children.[6] Authoritative parenting requires stepparents to set rules and determine structure for children's lives, as well as display high levels of affection. This kind of parenting is based on a bonded relationship, which does not exist for stepparents until the Crockpot has had time to help the stepfamily integrate.

"Early in remarriage, the most successful stepparent-stepchild relationships are those where the stepparent focuses first on the development of a warm, friendly interaction style with the stepchild. Once a foundation of mutual respect and affection is established, stepparents who then attempt to assume a disciplinarian role are less likely to meet with resentment from the stepchild."[7] Closeness and the authority to discipline develop over time, and neither should be rushed. For example, stepparents are often eager to build a relationship and commonly seek one-on-one activities with stepchildren. Bray discovered that stepchildren were usually uncomfortable being alone with a stepparent. [8] They preferred family group activities to intense one-on-one experiences. After a period of time, one-on-one opportunities are received more openly. The length of time required for stepchildren to build a relationship with their stepparent depends on a number of factors that will be discussed later in this chapter.

The research evidence suggests that the best stepparent initially works through and with the children's parent. Initially, maintaining an emotionally non-threatening, distant relationship is best. After a couple of years, stepparents can begin to spend more time in direct childcare and rule setting. Agreement between the spouses as to the timing of this role shift is important. Marital consensus and mutual support always provide the strength a stepparent needs to become more authoritative. (A more complete discussion of effective stepparenting can be found in "A Prescription for Evolving Parent and Stepparent Roles," page 155.)

I should note here that there are exceptions to this guideline based on age and gender of the stepchild. Stepfathers of young stepsons who move into authoritative parenting fairly quickly have positive outcomes. Instead of being disengaged, stepfathers can move more rapidly into leadership with young stepsons. This is not, however, the case with stepdaughters. Relationships between stepfathers and stepdaughters became more conflicted over time, regardless of the parenting styles used by the stepfather. Even if early stepfather-stepdaughter conflict is minimal, it seems to erupt around adolescence.[9] In addition, it seems that stepmothers and stepdaughters have the most difficult time bonding their relationship, in part due to strong mother-daughter bonds and competing female gender roles in the home.[10]

The point is this: Stepparent-stepchild relationships vary widely given a number of factors. You won't be able to discern every factor, so remember to listen to each child's cues and read his or her openness to you. If you let the child set the pace—and you honor the need for space—the Crockpot may eventually bring you closer together. But keep in mind—it also may not. Accept what you have, make the most of it, and be open to a deepening relationship over time.

Ineffective Stepparents Attempt Punishment Before Having Relationship

By my estimation, this is the most common and one of the most destructive mistakes stepparents make. We've established that parental authority comes through relationship. If you want to test my assertion, just go to a neighbor's house and try to punish his children. Just because you live next door doesn't mean you have any say over those children. You can claim authority, but the level of authority the neighbor's kids grant to you will be much less than what you claim. Likewise, stepparents earn authority by building relationship.

Susan Gamache calls this *parental status*, that is, the degree that stepfamily members consider the stepparent a parent to stepchildren.[11] Parents can expect stepchildren to accept discipline from their stepparent, and stepparents can *claim* to have as much authority as the biological parent, but the only thing that counts is how much authority children will accept from the stepparent.

I've heard stepdads fall back on Scripture and claim that "since I am the man of the house I should have the power of a father." Nothing could be further from the truth. They have a father—and you're not it! If you want to exasperate your stepchildren (see Ephesians 6:4), just try to live out your claim of authority. The ability to lead and influence children comes the old-fashioned way—you earn it. Trust, respect, and honor grow out of a relational history, and there is no quick way to establish that. Stepparents must be dedicated to building a relationship over time. Give your Crockpot time to bring you together.

Effective Stepparents Gradually Move Into Disciplinary Roles. Power comes with relationship and grows over time. Let's look at three positive relationship styles that give way to parental authority.

1. The baby-sitter role: Baby-sitters have power to manage children only if parents give them power. When our favorite baby-sitter, Amy, comes to watch our three boys, I remind them in front of her that she is in charge while we're away. "She knows the rules, and if you disobey her, you are disobeying me. She has my permission to enforce the consequences. Plus, she'll tell me about it later, and you'll have to deal with me, too." After saying this before a number of date nights, my kids now finish the sentence before me. "We know, we know. Amy's in charge."

Biological parents must pass power to stepparents shortly after remarriage so that children will understand that stepparents are not acting on their own authority, but the parent's authority.[12] You might say, "I know Sarah is not your mother. However, when I am not here, she will be enforcing the rules we have all agreed on. I expect you to be courteous and respect her as you would a teacher or coach."

Parents and stepparents negotiate rules *together* behind closed doors and must seek unity in their decisions. The biological parent then communicates the rules to the children with the stepparent standing in support. If a rule is broken, as far as the children are concerned it is the parent's rule, not the stepparent's. If a consequence is to be enforced by the stepparent, to the children it is the parent's consequence. Baby-sitting stepparents, then, are extensions of biological parents.

In a classic example, a ten-year-old girl scowls at her stepfather when he asks her to begin her Saturday chore of cleaning the garage. She barks, "I don't have to do what you say. You're not my dad," and then walks toward a friend's house. His response: "You're right, I'm not your dad. But I am the adult here right now, and this is the rule we agreed to at our family meeting last month, remember? It's your choice. You can clean the garage by three o'clock or pay your brother to do it from your allowance." She may grunt and groan the whole way to the garage. If she keeps walking to her friend's house, the stepfather arranges to have her little brother clean the garage for extra pay. When Mom returns home later that afternoon, she should support the action taken. "I expect you to obey the rules even when I am not here. Your decision to leave cost you ten bucks. Tell me what you plan to do next time."

Complex stepfamilies, where both parents bring children to the stepfamily, still negotiate rules together, but each takes the lead role with their own children. Simultaneously they are the primary parent to their children and the "baby-sitter" to the other's children. It is important to note that this arrangement will not work if the couple does not adopt consistent rules. You cannot afford to have one set of rules for his kids and another standard for hers. Consistency without favoritism is key.

The stepparent/"baby-sitter" system maintains the pre-stepfamily parenting arrangement with the biological parent acting as the primary nurturer and disciplinarian. Most critically, it allows the stepparent time and emotional space to focus on relationship development with the stepchildren. The stepparent can learn about the child's interests, share talents and skills, and engage in family group activities without having to worry about negative confrontations with the children.[13] James Bray says one of the most important stepparenting skills after remarriage is *monitoring the children's activities.*[14] This involves knowing their daily routine, where the children are, who they are with, and what extracurricular activities they are involved in, but does not necessarily include being involved in the child's emotional life. Monitoring stepparents check homework and daily chores and befriend stepchildren, yet refrain from emotional closeness that is unwelcomed by the child.

Still, many stepparents complain that this model prohibits them from having power with the children. Actually, I would argue, it gives them power they otherwise would not have. The baby-sitter role doesn't mean that you don't have any say about rules or consequences. Your say simply occurs behind closed doors. Before a parent communicates rules to her children, she and the stepfather must be in agreement. Initially, then, your power or influence in parenting comes in the negotiation process.

"But what if she won't listen to me? She's very protective of her kids," someone typically responds. Biological parents do have difficulty adjusting their parenting to make room for the stepparent's influence. Parents may have many established rules and rituals (ways of getting things done), especially if they had a number of single-parent years before the remarriage. Single parents often dislike having to make all decisions by themselves, but they frequently enjoy not having to ask anyone else, either. Upon remarriage, they may have a difficult time opening their parenting style up to criticism or input from the stepparent. Nevertheless, the process of integrating a stepfamily demands that couples find ways of talking, listening, negotiating, and deciding on rules. Initially they should strive for few changes. This can be particularly difficult for structured, rule-oriented stepparents who marry flexible, permissive parents. However, stability for the children should be sought; stepparents may have to make adjustments until new bonds are developed. Over time, changes in rules and rituals may be necessary.

When changes do occur, children likely will complain, especially if the rules are getting tighter. "You never made us do chores before you married him. He's just bossing you around." Kids are great with manipulation! At a time of change, parents and stepparents must stand together. If there are any chinks in your armor, children will divide and conquer (they think that is their mission in life). Thus, the age-old principle of unity is still critical to effective parenting—even in stepfamilies.

2. The "uncle/aunt" role: After a moderate relationship has developed, stepparents can move into the "uncle or aunt" stepparenting role. If my sister comes to my house, and Nan and I are away for a few hours, she carries some authority with my children simply because she's their aunt. She is not a full-fledged parent, but carries power through her extended family kinship. Stepparents can gradually gain a basic level of respect that allows children to accept them as extended family members by marriage. Stepparents can become more authoritative, clearly communicating limits and encouraging family discussion of rules. Furthermore, as personal bonds deepen, shows of affection and appreciation can become more common. One-on-one activities can become more frequent and personal connections increase.

3. The "parent" or stepparent role: Eventually, *some* stepparents will gain "parental" status with *some* stepchildren. Younger children tend to grant stepparents parental status much more quickly than adolescents. It is quite common to be considered a baby-sitter by an older child, an aunt by a middle child, and a parent by the youngest child. These roles can be confusing, so be sure you and your spouse are a solid parenting team. Discuss circumstances often and work together to make changes over time.

It is important that stepparents not consider themselves failures if they do not achieve parental status with every child. Again, the length of time required to move into this role depends on a number of factors, most of which are beyond the stepparent's control. Enjoy the relationship you have now and trust the integration process.

Ineffective Stepparents Try to Replace the Noncustodial Biological Parent[15]

When stepparents feel insecure about their place in the family and have high expectations for their relationship with stepchildren, they commonly feel as if they must compete with the noncustodial biological parent. This competition for the children's love may be fueled by insecure noncustodial parents who try to belittle and hamper the stepparent's acceptance. However, efforts to "move out" the other parent almost always backfire.

Cassie, Sheryl, and *Amanda* were furious when they came to see me. Their stepfather made every effort to block their relationship with their biological dad, and they resented him for doing so. Passive-aggressive games were his favorite tools to seek revenge on the man who made his wife's former life so miserable. He dropped the kids off late when it was their father's visitation and conveniently forgot to convey their dad's phone messages. He tried to control every part of their life—and at the same time, wondered why the girls weren't receiving of his kindness.

Effective Stepparents Encourage Stepchildren to Maintain Contact With Noncustodial Parents.[16] Healthy stepparents not only respect a child's right to be with his or her parent, they encourage such a relationship. Stepparents who acknowledge the losses children face will work to keep contact alive and regular. They allow pictures, mementos, and special items to be kept and cherished by the children (especially if a parent has died). They invite noncustodial parents to important ceremonies and events, encourage the children to write, phone, or e-mail their parent on a regular basis, and listen to children's joyful stories about the other household and their past.

Noncustodial parents are not the enemy, nor do stepparents have to compete with them. Effective stepparents recognize their role as an additional parent figure rather than a replacement parent. Telling stepchildren of your role and intentions to honor their relationship with their parent is very helpful. It can be even more helpful to noncustodial parents.

One of the most common reasons noncustodial parents criticize and coach their children away from a relationship with a stepparent is fear. Noncustodial parents have lost contact with their kids and may resent a stepparent for having more time with the children than they have. Loss creates the fear of more loss. In this case, losing contact with your children is tough, but watching them begin to give their love to a stepparent is even more painful. Thus, noncustodial parents may find themselves trying to sabotage the stepparent's relationship with their children. If stepparents will articulate a supportive message to noncustodial parents and then live up to it, fears can be diminished and criticism and sabotage may decline as well.

Call or e-mail the noncustodial parent and say, "Bob, I want you to know that you don't have to worry about me getting between you and your kids. I respect you as their father, and I will never intentionally do anything to keep you from them. I will expect them to speak respectfully about you when in our home and will do my part to make sure the visitation schedule stays on track. If I inadvertently cause a problem, please let me know, and I'll rectify the situation. You are important to your kids." This informal non-aggression pact helps the noncustodial parent know what to expect from you. If negative comments about you continue from the noncustodial parent, stay in control of yourself and take the high road of righteousness. "Heap burning coals" of kindness on their head, even in the face of their critical words, until your good cannot be ignored (Romans 12:20).

Ineffective Stepparents Take on the Peacemaker Role[17]

All remarital couples want their stepfamilies to be successful. To this point I've detailed how a Crockpot mentality keeps you from expecting too much too soon. But despite that awareness, when problems arise, everyone wants peace in the home. Biological parents are notorious for wanting everyone to be happy and work hard to keep peace. Sometimes stepparents take on the peacemaker role, especially when they themselves have been through a previous marriage. They know what a family breakup does to people, and they don't want more loss in their life either. The temptation to deny problems, shut out negative emotions, and discount other people's feelings can be high.

Effective Stepparents Accept Difficulties and Face Them. Stress and painful emotions are not signs of stepfamily failure, but they should not be minimized. Pain is a sign of growth and the need for change. To deny pain or anxiety in ourselves or others is to shut off the warning light without paying attention to what's not working. Effective stepparents accept that problems exist and allow a full expression of pleasant and painful emotions.

A few years ago I developed a chart to visually demonstrate the changing roles of parents and stepparents over time (opposite page). This chart summarizes many of the principles I have laid out in this chapter. The research evidence supports this general model but acknowledges that there is no one universal best way to stepparent. Some may discover that they broke all the rules yet still managed to experience low levels of family conflict. Others may find that they need to retreat from their current system and begin working this model immediately. Parents and stepparents should not lock themselves into one "right way" to manage their family. The keys are to be unified and work together as a team. Continually ask God's guidance as you strive to lead your home.

Parental Status. The vertical axis on the left of the chart is labeled Degree of Authority to Discipline and represents a person's parental status. The higher you go, the more authority you have. Notice that biological parents have parental authority from the beginning of stepfamily life. After all, you're Dad and always will be. Stepparents, however, in most cases begin only with as much authority as a coach, teacher, or camp counselor. Biological parents, even after remarriage, continue their role of single parent, only now they have a live-in baby-sitter to help. Biological parents remain the primary nurturer and disciplinarian and should spend special time with each child. Stepparents initially focus on building relationships with their stepchildren and monitoring their activities and interests. Over time some stepparents move to higher levels of authority. Note the jagged line representing a multitude of up and down experiences with stepchildren. The variables impacting increasing authority vary widely, and many are beyond your control. Ride the waves with faith and hope.

As stepparents develop a greater bond with stepchildren and move up the vertical axis, parents will have to release control to stepparents. This is difficult for many parents who have been their children's primary provider for a long time; they don't know how to let go. Indeed, some parents block the stepparents' increasing authority, even after they've pushed for it. Giving up control is difficult.

Some parents decide not to make room for the stepparent, while some stepparents don't desire to have a close relationship with their step-

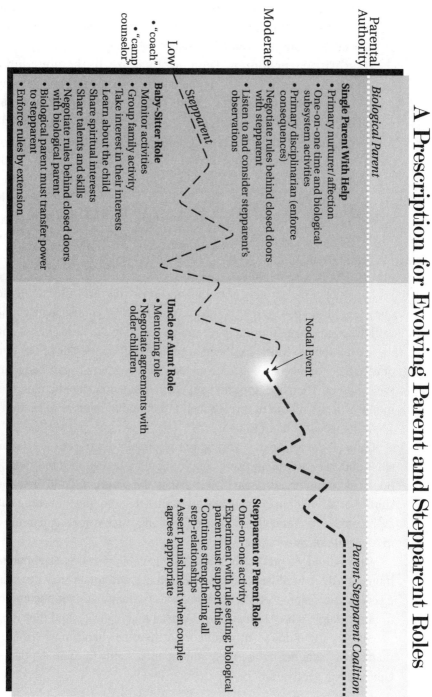

DEGREE OF AUTHORITY TO DISCIPLINE[18]

Interface between "asserted authority" by the stepparent and "accepted authority" by the stepchildren.

A Prescription for Evolving Parent and Stepparent Roles

Parental Authority

Biological Parent .... *Parent-Stepparent Coalition*

Single Parent With Help
- Primary nurturer/affection
- One-on-one time and biological subsystem activities
- Primary disciplinarian (enforce consequences)
- Negotiate rules behind closed doors with stepparent
- Listen to and consider stepparent's observations

Moderate

Stepparent

Baby-Sitter Role
- Monitor activities
- Group family activity
- Take interest in their interests
- Learn about the child
- Share spiritual interests
- Share talents and skills
- Negotiate rules behind closed doors with biological parent
- Biological parent must transfer power to stepparent
- Enforce rules by extension

Low
- "coach"
- "camp counselor"

Nodal Event

Uncle or Aunt Role
- Mentoring role
- Negotiate agreements with older children

Stepparent or Parent Role
- One-on-one activity
- Experiment with rule setting; biological parent must support this
- Continue strengthening all step-relationships
- Assert punishment when couple agrees appropriate

TIME WITH STEPCHILDREN

Length of time required to increase parental authority will vary according to age of child, previous family experiences, relationship with noncustodial parents, child's temperament/personality, parenting style variations, and child's overall stepfamily satisfaction level.

children. Don't assume you as a couple have the same expectation for closeness with the children. Talk about your relational preferences and periodically evaluate your changing goals.

Time With Stepchildren. The horizontal axis of the prescription focuses on the amount of time stepparents have had with their stepchildren. Many people wonder if this begins with dating or the actual remarriage. Dating is important, but true stepfamily relationships start with the wedding. During courtship children can be tolerant, even encouraging, of their parent's new romance because "she's happier while with him." While the couple dates, however, the children are usually out of the picture, spending time at Dad's house. The dating partner stays friendly with the children, and everything seems to go along fine. However, after remarriage, when everyone is thrown into the same pot, roles change, the intensity of relationships increases dramatically, and nearly everyone experiences unexpected anxious emotions.

Mike called me the day after he and *Carrie* married. After dating for two years, they spent three months in pre-remarital counseling trying to work through issues from the past and anticipating the needs of her children. Even though much had been accomplished, on the day of the wedding, Carrie's nineteen- and sixteen-year-old daughters began badgering their mother. They had appeared supportive, but now they berated their mother's decision both to divorce their father and to remarry Mike. Carrie spent her wedding night in tears.

Dating for at least two years and pre-stepfamily discussions of relationships and roles are things every couple should do. Keep in mind that the bonds of commitment qualitatively change the nature of family relationships. Not all children change their tune after the wedding, but some will.

A number of variables influence how long it takes for stepparents to move from one role to another.[19]

Age of Child. As previously stated, younger children accept stepparents more quickly than older children. Children five and under may need just a year or two before viewing stepparents as "parents." It's not uncommon to find children who call their noncustodial parent "Dad" and their stepparent "Daddy." Adolescent children, on the other hand, may require a number of years before ascribing full parental status to their stepparent. Others never get that far.

Experts speculate that in the best-case scenario stepchildren need just a couple years to bond with stepparents and grant them full parental status. The worst-case scenario suggests it may take as many years as the age of the child at remarriage. If the child is eight, it may take eight years or more for the stepparent to achieve full parental status. If the child is fourteen, it may take fourteen years. Realistically, a teenager will be out of the house in four to six years. Therefore, the relationship may not ever develop beyond a friendly bond.

A child's openness to a stepparent, of course, has a major influence on the success of the marriage. In fact, it seems that "the best time to remarry is before a child's tenth birthday and after his or her sixteenth; couples who marry in between often find themselves on a collision course with the teen's developmental agenda."[20] A small window of attachment and feeling their close parent-child bond threatened (especially pre-adolescent girls and their mothers) just doesn't make for quick acceptance of the stepparent.

In the end, remember that no one can predict how long it will take to build a working relationship with your stepchildren. Accept what you have and make the best of it.

Previous Family Experiences. The family you grew up in (called "family of origin") has had dramatic effects on you, your choice of mate, and your marital behaviors—whether you know it or not. Similarly, previous family experiences impact children and their willingness to trust, honor, or open themselves to new relationships. Spend some time reflecting on what your children and stepchildren have experienced, and talk with your spouse about how it has impacted the children. Learn to be sensitive to their wounds and needs.

Relationship With Noncustodial Parents. Loyalty issues come into play here. As mentioned earlier, children whose other parent is "poisoning" them against a stepparent are caught in a trap. To love the stepparent is to "harm" their parent; to begrudge the stepparent is to please the insecure parent. If this is the case, stepparents should avoid further complicating the stepchild's loyalty conflicts. Taking the unfair, short end of the stick is a tremendous sacrifice, but one that will help the children through their turmoil.

If stepchildren have a positive relationship with the other parent, that too can generate resistance to the stepparent. Ultimately, what is needed is for the other parent to give the child permission to bond with the stepparent. This helps children make space in their heart for stepparents.

Child's Temperament and Personality. Some children are outgoing, some more reserved. Variations in personality between siblings can play a significant role in their willingness to open themselves to new relationships with a stepparent and/or stepsiblings. In addition, a child's interests in sports, music, art, computers, etc. may create an immediate connection with a stepparent that can help bring them together in a non-threatening way.

Parenting Style Variations. Stepparents who have more structured rules and are more demanding than either of a child's parents make bonding difficult. Julie's stepchildren complained that since moving into "her house," she always made them take off their shoes. They never had to do that before their father married Julie. "Yeah," said the youngest, "and she won't let me drink my milk in the living room."

This is not to say that stepparents cannot assert their preferences for household rules. Not drinking milk in the living room is a reasonable rule, and children can adjust to the change. Stepparents should simply understand that pulling the rein a little tighter slows the bonding process; choose your battles carefully.

Child's Overall Stepfamily Satisfaction Level. How much transition and loss has the new stepfamily brought to children? What is the level of conflict within the home and between homes? How well are stepsiblings getting along? How well are personalities within the stepfamily mixing—do people have a lot in common or are they strangers under one roof? Are noncustodial parents involved and secure with the amount of contact with their children? If most of stepfamily life is positive for stepchildren, the likelihood of accepting a stepparent increases. If most of stepfamily life is tense and stress-producing, stepparent acceptance decreases.

Summary of Points to Remember

- This model of parent-stepparent roles seems to work for most stepfamilies. There is no universal way to work out your parent-stepparent roles. Be sure you are unified in evaluating your approach.

- Early in remarriage biological parents need to remain primary care-givers and disciplinarians. Handing off the children to the new step-parent sabotages his or her ability to build a relationship.

- Early in remarriage parents should empower stepparents by commu-nicating to the children their expectation of obedience. Later, even if you disagree with what the stepparent has done in your absence, sup-port their position with the children. Then take your disagreement behind closed doors and work out a unified plan and consequences for the next offense.

- Stepparents need to grow into their relationship with stepchildren. Be friendly and support the house rules. Seek to be adaptable to your stepchildren and enjoy the relationship you have.

- Encourage and insist that children maintain regular, consistent con-tact with the parent living in the other home. Do your best to have a functional co-parent relationship.

- Let children set the pace for their relationship with the stepparent. Consider each child individually. Give and expect affection, nurtur-ance, and emotional sharing only to the degree children appear open to it.

- Parents should consider stepparents' input into child rearing. It is easy for parents who are used to having complete control over their children to discount the stepparent's perspective. Keep in mind that, as outsiders, stepparents can see things your blind spots prevent you from seeing. Listen and consider their input.

- Stepparents need to learn to be a nonjudgmental sounding board for parents. When parents get frustrated with their own children, they may confide in the stepparent. However, stepparents who begin to agree and add their own frustration may find their spouse reversing position to defend the child. The parent-child bond is indeed a pro-tective one. Stepparents would do well to listen and affirm without criticizing the child. "I can see you are angry at Jane for lying to us. What do you suggest we do?"

- Finally, but most important, effective parent-stepparent teams begin with healthy marriages. Take time to nurture your relationship, date on a regular basis, learn to communicate and resolve conflict, and enjoy a healthy sexual relationship. Make your marriage a priority!

"But We're Already Stuck. What Do We Do Now?"

You've done the best you could, proceeded with what you thought best, but have now discovered you've made a number of mistakes. Perhaps you are facing some resistance or open defiance from an angry child. So what do you do now?

First Step: Evaluate Yourselves As a Parenting Team. Together with your spouse, examine the interaction between you as a parenting team.

- Are you cooperating poorly?
- Do you frequently disagree about rules and consequences?
- Does one of you feel sabotaged by the other?
- Does the biological parent frequently feel caught between his or her children and the stepparent?
- Do the same conflicts repeat because they aren't getting resolved?

If you answered *yes* to two or more of the above, the root of the problem is not the children (but may be complicated by the emotional condition of the children). You have a weak parental alliance, and you must work out a mutual plan to act as a team.

The failure to function as a team is key to child behavioral problems in nuclear families and in stepfamilies. Roles for two-parent homes are different from roles for parent-stepparent homes, but the task of teamwork is the same. Plan a time together or with your support group and decide what aspects of your parenting need to change. You may also decide to seek outside help as you work through some difficult circumstances. Remember that there are lots of ways to parent kids well. The critical element is your ability to do it together.

Second Step: What If the Stepparent Has Overstepped His or Her Bounds? If this chapter has helped you to see that you as a stepparent moved into punishment too quickly, and it has hampered your relationship with your stepchildren, consider these points of action:

- Pull back from punishment and your high expectations. Let the biological parent take over being the heavy while you refocus on relationship healing and development.

- Ask your stepchildren for forgiveness and admit your misguided attempt to join the family. Seeking forgiveness displays character and models commitment to your family. Say something like, "Hey kids. I want you to know I'm learning how to be a better stepparent. In fact, I've learned that I've been making some mistakes, like not letting you talk to your dad each night before bedtime and being a little too bossy. Can you forgive me? I really want to do better. Here's what you can expect at this point. . . ."
- Biological parents may also need to seek forgiveness for being under-involved and abdicating their primary role to the stepparent. Together you can tell the kids how each of your roles is going to change and what they can expect.
- Implement the changes slowly. Stepparents must realize that forgiveness may be slow in coming, and even then, children may have hard feelings from the past. Don't drop your boundaries to win them back. Continue to seek relationship and model respect. Remain flexible with your new plan, as you may need to make adjustments along the way.
- If necessary, consult a Christian family therapist who is knowledgeable in stepfamily therapy. (It is important to ask any therapist what specific training they have had regarding stepfamilies. Many therapists have no specialized training and utilize a first-family model of treatment. That will only make matters worse. An article that addresses this matter is available for download at my Web site: *www.SuccessfulStepfamilies.com.*)

I often tell parents that raising children is a work in progress. No one ever has all the right answers, and all parents and stepparents yell, scream, plead, and lose their cool at some point. None of us is perfect. That's why we must rely on a perfect God for wisdom and guidance. I cannot emphasize enough the necessity for parents to study the Scriptures on a daily basis. The more we are transformed into the likeness of Christ, the greater chance we will become who our children and stepchildren need us to be. We must be filled with the Holy Spirit and guided by God's nature. Only then will we be able to set an example for our children that leads them to the Father. Press on with your work in progress.

Questions for Discussion

FOR ALL COUPLES

1. Stepparents, what are your most common frustrations? Now share the rewards you've experienced so far.
2. What part of you would like to frame the Stepparent's Serenity Prayer and put it over the mantel?
3. Review the descriptions of ineffective vs. effective stepparents on pages 144–151. Rate yourself using the following scales and discuss what you'll be doing differently when you improve in each area.

Becoming an insider is my goal.	1 ———— 7	*Enjoying the relationship I have now.*
Expect too much of myself.	1 ———— 7	*Have realistic expectations for myself.*
Rush into parenting.	1 ———— 7	*Growing into my role.*
Attempt to punish before I have relationship.	1 ———— 7	*Moving gradually into discipline.*
Trying to replace the noncustodial parent.	1 ———— 7	*Encouraging noncustodial parental contact.*
Taking on the peacemaker role.	1 ———— 7	*Accepting difficulties and facing them.*

4. Look again at the chart on Evolving Parent and Stepparent Roles (page 155). How well are you working together as a couple? What role is most suitable for the stepparent at this point in your integration?
5. What is the stepparent currently doing to build a relationship with each child?
6. In what way does the biological parent need to be more supportive of the stepparent or more involved with the children?

7. Review the Summary Points to Remember on pages 158–159. Commend yourself for what you are currently doing well and challenge yourself with areas that need improvement.

FOR PRE-REMARITAL COUPLES

1. In what way have you been assuming the children will be the same (or better) with the stepparent after the wedding?
2. How does it frighten you to read that emotional shifts after the wedding can complicate the stepparent-stepchildren relationship?
3. How can you protect yourself from getting drawn into the out-of-step stepparent's ineffective behaviors?
4. Look again at the chart on Evolving Parent and Stepparent Roles (page 155). What principles do you agree or disagree with? Discuss how you might implement the "baby-sitter" role even now.
5. Share your expectations for your role as parent/stepparent and the other's role. Begin developing a plan for what role each of you will play with each child. Be aware that you will likely need to adjust your plan after marriage.

CHAPTER EIGHT

Smart Step Five: Side STEP

The pitfalls common to stepfamilies

"Was it because there were no graves in Egypt that you brought us to the desert to die? What have you done to us by bringing us out of Egypt?" (Exodus 14:11).

"When they came to Marah, they could not drink its water because it was bitter. . . . So the people grumbled against Moses, saying, 'What are we to drink?' " (Exodus 15: 23–24).

The journey from Egypt to the Promised Land was very long. Repeatedly throughout the trip the Israelites lost sight of God's faithfulness and protective hand. Grumbling and complaining, they voiced their lack of faith and fear of dying in the wilderness. From a human standpoint, even with God in control, the journey was challenging, filled with pitfalls and uncertainty. They had to cross the Red Sea, walk day after day without knowing where they would be when the day was done, and once they crossed the Jordan River, had to fight battles against fierce enemy nations.

From a spiritual standpoint, however, the journey was ultimately in God's hands. God did all the hard work; they just had to believe and act according to their confidence in God. That task proved to be the most difficult of all. And it continues to be the most difficult for us today.

A great many pitfalls threaten the stepfamily's journey to the Promised Land. We've already encountered some of the most strenuous:

- Adults who are disconnected from God and his church body due to personal shame and guilt or judgment from friends and church leaders.
- Unrealistic expectations that bring about unhealthy attempts to "blend" family members quickly instead of relaxing in a Crockpot-cooking style.
- A weak marital relationship eroded by pre-existing loyalties to children, ghosts of previous relationships, and unpacked emotional baggage.
- Couples who don't function as a team because they have poor communication skills, don't nurture their relationship as they should, or focus all their energies on the children.
- Battles with ex-spouses that make children prisoners of war.
- A lack of clear boundaries with ex-spouses and poor co-parent relationships.
- A poor parental team resulting from misguided parent and stepparent roles and ineffective parenting skills.

The previous chapters have addressed these pitfalls to help you avoid being tripped up by them. Yet the journey is long, and we all get caught in the pressures of life once in a while. The secret to perseverance is continuing to look to the One who delivered you in the first place. From a human perspective, stepfamily life is full of pitfalls and uncertainty. From a spiritual standpoint, however, God is still doing the hard work on your behalf. You must continue to believe and act according to your confidence in him.

In addition to the pitfalls listed above, a number of other significant pitfalls must be sidestepped, including:

- Unrecognized loss and unexpressed grief,
- Being driven by menacing emotions,
- Combining holiday and family traditions,
- Birth order changes, and
- Money matters.

Let's consider them one at a time, beginning with the most hidden and menacing of all.

UNRECOGNIZED LOSS AND UNEXPRESSED GRIEF

Marriage is supposed to be a time when a new relationship and family is born. Hollywood tells us that marriage is just the beginning of "and they lived happily ever after." But for a stepfamily, a wedding is not the beginning, it is the middle. Stepfamilies are born out of the loss of previous family relationships; that is, they are created when a marriage follows death, divorce, or the lack of marital bond when children are born out of wedlock. This loss creates a paradox of emotions for the new stepfamily—hand in hand with joy and hope lingers sadness and grief.

If you are currently married, think back to your wedding day. Do you recall any mixed feelings? Joy and anxiety? Optimism and fear? Happiness and sadness? Love and anger? Do you remember trying to decide whether to invite your ex-spouse's parents and how to break the news of the engagement to your children? If your spouse died, do you remember wondering if up in heaven he or she somehow knew what you were doing? Did you feel your spouse's blessing to "move on," or would your partner be troubled by your decision? What concerns did you have for your children, and how did they voice their pleasure or disdain with your remarriage?

Many adults readily acknowledge their conflicting emotions but are surprised to consider that their children probably felt a mixed bag as well. If you're courageous, spend some one-on-one time with each of your children and ask how they felt at the time of the wedding. Open the door to some honest conversation about mixed emotions, and be open to affirming the difficulties those created for you and your children. After all, everyone experiences loss in stepfamilies.

As you continue reading, note the typical losses experienced by everyone in your stepfamily (even those in the other home). Your losses are easy to identify. The challenge of understanding involves stepping into the shoes of others to experience what troubles them. Make a list of your realizations—it just might help you to relate better to someone in your home.

Spouses Have Lost a Partner

Whether by death or divorce, the loss of a marital relationship is very difficult. Even if you initiated your divorce, you probably have felt a roller coaster of emotions.

The grief cycle after divorce is often assumed to parallel the grief cycle most persons experience after the death of a loved one. There are, however, some distinct differences. After death people tend to experience grief stages one after another (denial, anger, bargaining, depression, acceptance). After divorce, however, persons experience a cycle of love, anger, and sadness.[1] Feelings of love, which include a fondness and longing to be with the person lost, the hope of reconciliation, and guilt over what has been lost, cycle periodically through a person's heart. Close behind this wave of emotion is anger, characterized by frustration over what was lost, resentment, rage, and hurt. The third wave of emotion to follow is sadness. After missing the person or the idea of what the marriage was supposed to be and becoming angry over the loss, sadness comes in the form of loneliness, depression, despair, pain, and grief. At first, feelings of love, anger, and sadness are experienced with great intensity. Eventually the feelings become less intense and less problematic.

Couples often begin new relationships out of these intense emotions. The new relationship rescues them from negative feelings, hurt, and depression. Forming relationships on the rebound is common and very dangerous. I have worked with numerous stepfamily couples who after ten or more years of marriage are suffering, believing themselves to be in a relationship that was never meant to be. "I was hurting when I met him, and he made me feel good again. On the wedding day, I had second thoughts but didn't want to disappoint everyone. I just thought I was scared. Looking back, I don't think I ever really loved him."

It is important to be aware of this cycle of emotion, because depending on how quickly someone remarries, the cycle may continue at intense levels well into remarriage. To some degree, grief is never something we get over; it is a journey, not a destination. Not giving yourself sufficient time to grieve a loss may result in problems later. Persons who remarry in less than three years, for example, are likely to experience longing, anger, and sadness at substantial levels. New spouses may become insecure if they catch their mate fondly reminiscing over the lost relationship, yet this is normal to some degree (be sure not to act on these feelings). Anger at a former spouse is expected and understandable, but so should be sadness and grief over what has been lost.

The task for new couples, then, is to set appropriate boundaries with former spouses that reflect the ending of a committed relationship, yet make space for sadness over what has been lost. Preferably couples would give each other plenty of time to resolve the ending of former relationships. For many, however, the wisdom of waiting before remarriage is difficult to accept.

A second task is giving each other permission to struggle with grief. The story is told of a widow who married a widower and soon found herself challenged by a friend, "I suppose, like all men who have been married before, your husband sometimes talks about his first wife?" "Oh, not any more, he doesn't," the newly married woman replied. "What stopped him?" the friend asked. "I started talking about my next husband." The underlying message of the wife's response could be said this way: "I feel insecure about us when you speak about her. Don't admit you ever enjoyed her, or I'll back away from you." Obviously no one should ever hold up an ex-spouse so as to intimidate a current spouse. But neither should his past be completely off limits. This woman was withholding permission for her husband to feel sad.

Michael's first wife, *Sara*, was killed in a tragic incident, leaving him behind with a seven-year-old son. After one year Michael married *Debbie*, who brought her own child to the marriage. Debbie has continuously allowed her husband and his son to talk in her presence about Sara's death. Even when they express admiration for Sara, she is not threatened by their fond memories. To many people, allowing a spouse to express sadness over a loss feels like moving yourself out of the family portrait. "If she hadn't died, I wouldn't be here right now." But Debbie's identity is not based on being the only focus of Michael's life. She acknowledges that everyone has special attachments in life, and her identity is firm in her relationship with Christ. This empowers her not to be threatened by Michael's former bond to Sara. By the way, acknowledging her husband and stepson's grief is an incredible gift to her stepson. He is able to hold on to Mom in a meaningful way and isn't forced to move on without her.

Other losses for spouses after death or divorce include the loss of social status, financial stability (this is especially true for women and their children), friendships and family connections, and social shifts within a religious community. For example, many people find themselves socially out of place after the ending of a marriage, cast-off, or mistreated by people who didn't agree with the divorce. As a result, many lose their support system and connection with God.

One final significant loss worth mentioning is the loss of contact with children. Many noncustodial parents are hammered by the impact of seeing their children only two weekends a month. The emotional and mental strain this adds can be quite debilitating. So much so, it leads some noncustodial parents to reduce contact even more because the process of saying good-bye is agonizing for them and for their children. "It is just easier not to put myself or them through the pain of leaving." This, however, is never recommended, as it inadvertently communicates a lack of care to the children.

In addition, after remarriage, a noncustodial parent may feel the loss of contact with his own children when stepchildren enter the picture. I've heard many fathers, for instance, say they feel guilty spending time with a stepchild or sharing special moments when they can't experience the same things with their own children. On visitation weekends, noncustodial parents frequently minimize time with stepchildren and focus their energies on biological children. This mini-family activity is understandable, yet it may hurt their spouse's feelings when stepchildren are neglected. Adults should strive to understand one another's losses and how they impact the decisions parents and noncustodial parents make. Giving each other space to take advantage of time with children and opportunities to voice sadness over time lost is important.

Loss After Death

A common myth is that stepfamilies formed after a death are easier than stepfamilies formed after divorce. While it does appear, statistically speaking, that remarriages following the death of a spouse have a better chance of lasting, they do have some unique struggles. John and Emily Visher have identified four major challenges.[2]

Giving yourself and your children enough time to mourn the loss. Time doesn't heal all wounds, but it allows for a decrease in the intensity of grief. Both adults and children need time, as do grandparents and extended family members. If a parent remarries too quickly, acceptance of the stepparent becomes more difficult. In addition, parents may find themselves holding on to material possessions and rituals (ways of doing things) because they haven't fully said their good-byes.

As stated earlier, most grief experts recommend waiting two to three years before beginning to date seriously or making a decision to remarry. Unexpressed grief clouds judgment about intimate relationships and leads people to step into relationships out of need, not choice. During a therapy session, *James* reflected on his now floundering remarriage after the death of his first wife to cancer. "I was lonely," he said. "I felt inadequate to provide for my daughter. I guess I needed a partner, and I wanted a mother for my daughter." This need and emptiness led him to look past his second wife's personality distortions and rush into a new marriage that was ending after just one year. Relationships that rescue people from grief are relationships of convenience. The problems come when the conveniences wear off.

Making the dead person into a saint. Memories of a deceased spouse or parent tend to be positive and interpreted through rose-colored glasses. It's easy to forget or minimize the frailties and failures of the person we love.

A second wife may find herself intimidated each Christmas, for example, when her adult stepchildren gather and share stories of "Mom's unbelievable blueberry pie." Even if the remark is not intended to offend their stepmother, she may find it difficult not to feel compared.

Attempting to replace the spouse who died. If a couple had a good relationship prior to death, it is natural for the remaining spouse to seek out someone with similar qualities and characteristics. This sets up the new spouse not to feel accepted for who he or she is and the bereaved spouse to be disappointed when the new partner doesn't match the other entirely.

Money and inheritance. Possessions and promised inheritances are particularly meaningful to children who have lost a parent to death. The presence of a stepparent may bring out the fear of losing those items if their other biological parent were to die before the stepparent. Giving children (adult or minor children) "first choice" over family possessions shows honor to the one who has died. One couple saw to it that each of their adult children took possession of whatever items they needed prior to their wedding. This made sure that "Mom's dishes" stayed in the family and that grandchildren grew up hearing stories of Grandpa when they used his golf clubs. Drawing up a new will that details the distribution of sentimental and monetary assets is also a good idea.

Losses for New Spouses/Stepparents

No one grows up with the fantasy of someday getting married and having two or three stepchildren competing for the time, energy, and love of his or her spouse. The marriage fantasy Hollywood sells us is that of a man and woman riding off into the sunset together—perhaps on a horse or in a BMW—but never with children all around them. New spouses in stepfamilies experience the loss of privacy and exclusive access to their spouse they dreamed marriage would bring. In addition, the experience of being an outsider to the history and bond between their stepchildren and spouse is quite a shock for many.

Another significant loss for stepparents is the early bonding time that biological parents have had with their children. Stepparents are thrown into parenting with no owner's manual and very little working knowledge of the likes, preferences, personality quirks, and motivating attributes of their stepchildren. It is on-the-job training at best. If the stepparent has not had children as old as the stepchildren, it may be difficult to fit into the "flow of parenting" with a particular child. This leads to frustration and possible conflict with the child and/or spouse.

If stepparents have not had children of their own, pre-marriage fantasies may have led them to believe their need to nurture a child would be met by helping to raise a stepchild. When *Randy* married *Judy*, he was sure that living with her two children would satisfy his desire for children. Judy was relieved to hear his expressed enthusiasm because she didn't want any more children. After a difficult three years, Randy realized that the strained relationship he experienced with his stepdaughters would never fill the emptiness he felt. When he began asking Judy for an "ours baby" she became angry. "He's going back on his promise," she complained. "I thought this was settled before we got married." Unfortunately, it was settled on a fantasy. Reality brought an unexpected loss to Randy and a complication to the marriage.

Losses for Grandparents

The losses of grandparents are numerous but often unnoticed. When a son or daughter divorces or dies, contact with grandchildren usually diminishes. Later, remarriage may again reduce the amount of contact, especially when grandchildren live with an ex-daughter-in-law. After her daughter's divorce, *Lana* cherished holiday visits with her grandchildren. But when her daughter remarried and the children began to spend some holidays with their stepgrandparents, her time with the kids was cut in half. Parents and stepparents should be sensitive to the loss of contact between children and grandparents (and extended family) and attempt, when possible, to bring the two together.

Two distinct patterns seem to emerge over time after a remarriage. Grandparents and stepgrandparents seem to either *replace* their former children-in-law or *expand* their family connections.[3] I believe that God would have Christian grandparents expand their connections, keeping alive supportive relationships with ex-children-in-law and developing new relationships with new spouses and stepgrandchildren. This is not to say that equal amounts of time and energy will be spent with all parties, but children should not suffer for the choices of their parents. Furthermore, God calls us to love our enemies (even your child's ex-spouse) and extend to them his hand of love. Resentment over the past should be forgiven and respect be the basis for ongoing relations.

Losses for Children

No one in stepfamilies experiences more loss than children. This truth is difficult for most adults to recognize simply because they are consumed with their own losses. It's human nature to notice our own wounds more than someone else's. Yet children, because of a lack of maturity and coping skills, need more help processing their grief than adults.

The death of a parent or a parental divorce means children lose *control* of their lives, *contact* with parents, grandparents, and siblings, and lose *continuity* to living arrangements and routines.[4] Life in a single-parent family and stepfamily is full of transition and change. Here are just a few changes that bring loss to children: not wanting parents to divorce; not wanting to change residences or move between two homes; a new stepparent they didn't ask for and the death of the dream of parental reconciliation; new stepsiblings; having to share a room with a sibling or stepsibling; loss of a role in the family when remarriage brings other people to the household; loss of familiarity with a school, teachers, neighborhood, friends, activities, and traditions; financial pressures; and changes in rules and expectations from their parent and stepparent. This list doesn't begin to capture the kinds of changes (losses) forced upon children when families end and begin. And some changes have greater impact than others.

It's not uncommon for single parents and children, for example, to develop a close bond due to the "stick together and survive" mentality they share. Persons pull together and make life work the best they can. That's why the announcement of a new marriage often brings more loss for children because it threatens the closeness they have with their custodial parent. I once worked with *Jessey*, a seven-year-old whose mom had been single Jessey's entire life. Mother and child had a very tight bond, and now her mother was planning to marry. I asked Jessey how she felt about her mom's decision to marry: "You know when you're playing with someone on the playground and they push you down and run off without you—that's what it feels like." Wow! *Well said*, I thought. Another child, a four-year-old, told her mom why she was acting so angrily toward her mom's fiancé. "Me thinks it in my heart if you get married you'll have this much love for him [holding her hands apart] and only this much [holding her fingers close together] left for me."

This important truth—that remarriage often disrupts the parent-child bond and produces insecurity in children—is not intended to make you feel guilty. If you are a parent, you need to understand the impact loss has on your children. If you are a stepparent, you need to empathize with—not resent—your stepchildren's grief. Remember the stepping-stone of *understanding* in chapter 2? I suggested that the experience of other members of your stepfamily is often dramatically different from yours and that you must strive to empathize with their perspective. That is nowhere more important than in regard to the losses children experience.

I believe that one of the hardest things children in stepfamilies must learn is to share a parent with a stepparent or stepsiblings. They've lost so much already, it's understandable why they would resist "losing" another parent. To protect their relationships, children may push away the outsiders and block their involvement in the family. This brings about competition and insecurity, especially if a stepparent takes the threat personally. I wish I could count the number of stepparents who have described their stepchildren as "jealous" and "trying to be manipulative." I respond with, "I know that's what it looks like on the outside, but what they are on the inside is hurt. These children have experienced a great deal of loss in the past and that makes them scared of more hurt. One of the things they fear most is losing their parent to you. Don't get hooked into competing for time. You're the adult. Back away every once in a while and give them exclusive time with their parent so they don't fear you quite so much. Someday, when they allow you in, you can share time with their parent more equitably." Respecting the significance of the parent-child relationship is important for stepparents, just as is being aware of how previous losses create fear in children. But then again, it is not just children that become fearful after loss.

Fear: The By-Product of Loss

How does loss impact your family's integration process? It slows it down. Imagine if someone walked up to you and firmly slapped your face. Do you suppose you might blink the next time he lifted his hand—even if it wasn't near you? Loss brings pain, and the experience of pain leads adults and children alike to "blink" when faced with the potential for more hurt. The fear of more pain powerfully leads people to build relational walls that protect them from further harm. These walls can be built with many emotional bricks, but the most common are guardedness, distance, and anger.

Tim learned this the hard way. Shortly after his remarriage he began to sense his second wife, *Lisa*, pulling away and his stepchildren's growing resentment. Prior to their mother's marriage, Lisa's children had a nightly ritual of lying in bed and waiting for Mom's good-night kiss. Lisa would lie with each child for a while and talk with her about the day's events. They shared stories, warm affections, and plans for the week ahead. It was a special and comforting time for the children and for Lisa.

Tim's fantasies of being with his new wife and building their marriage were quickly squashed by the realities of a busy stepfamily. Tim grew increasingly possessive of the time he and Lisa had together after the children went to bed. But because he felt cheated by her time with the children, Tim began to stand outside the children's bedrooms and monitor the amount of time she spent talking with them. If he felt it was too much, he would stick in his head and say, "Is she asleep yet? When are you going to come in here with me?" In effect, Tim was saying, "Hey, don't you think it's time you chose me over the kids?"

Little did Tim realize how he was sabotaging his marriage and relationship with his stepchildren. Losses throughout the divorce process and Mom's marriage to Tim had made the nighttime ritual even more important to Lisa and her children. Tim's whining led them to fear the loss of time together and the love it communicated. Tim's wife also grew resentful of his jealousy and began to distance herself from any expectation that she would choose him over her children. This, of course, complicated Tim's fears, and he escalated his attempts to gain her loyalty. The children remained guarded with their new stepfather and angrily refused over time to grant him parental status. In the end, a vicious negative cycle of fear and resentment resulted.

Anger: The By-Product of Fear

When we fear losing contact with someone we love, we naturally develop anger toward the person or persons we believe are responsible for that potential loss. The above example is a perfect illustration. Notice how each person makes sense of the other's behavior. Tim became increasingly angry toward his wife "because she babies her children." Anger toward his stepchildren took the form of a label—"they are spoiled rotten." His wife was angry with him for "forcing her to choose." His stepchildren were angry that he "was so selfish" he would invade their special time with Mom. (Notice that the stepparent is the recipient of more anger than anyone else. The insiders can hold on to one another, but stepparents are forced back to the outside when anger builds. I told you it is tough being a stepparent!) Each explained the other's behavior in very negative terms instead of acknowledging the losses and fears each was communicating through his or her insecurity.

Consider how this situation might be different if Tim was empathic with his stepchildren for all they had lost and was willing to sacrifice his couple time in order to ensure their bonding time with Mom. He would not have stood outside the bedroom door nor watched the clock. He would have backed away from intruding on the nighttime ritual, yet still expressed his need for couple time with his wife. Couple time is very important, but not at the expense of valued parent-child touch points. How much better it would have been if Tim and his wife had compartmentalized their relationship and found some exclusive time together during weekends. Likewise, Tim's wife would be sensitive to his loss of a marital dream and may have tried to carve out some valuable time for their growing marriage—perhaps ten minutes of coffee-talk each night after dinner—even while unashamedly continuing to spend time with her children each night.

Coping with loss is not an easy task for anyone. Adults must set the example for how losses will be handled. Here are some tips to help.

Practical Strategies for Coping With Unrecognized Loss and Unexpressed Grief[5]

Identify painful losses for each family member. Grief is an emotion that will not be denied. If it is not expressed, it will seep out in resentment, anger, bitterness, fear, and blocked stepfamily relationships. Give permission to sadness and don't demand that others finish grieving on your timetable.

Make a list of each family member and the losses you believe he or she has experienced. Imagine what it has been like to be that person at each point along the way: pre-divorce or death, after the divorce/death, during the single-parent years, after the remarriage was announced, since the wedding. You may be stunned by the number of losses you can identify.

Look behind surface emotions to identify how loss is playing a role. For example, children often display sad emotions with mad responses ("mad is really sad"). Also, spouses maintain a guarded distance from their mate through distrust in order to prevent further hurt from another loss. Be sympathetic to what's under the surface instead of reacting to what you see in front of you.

Help persons express sadness and grief. One wise stepparent said, "I'm wondering if your refusal to go to the game with me is because you'd rather be with your dad than me right now. You miss him, huh?" He was right. Acknowledge loss when you see or hear it. "I can see you're hurting right now. Tell me what you're sad about."

Talk about *your* losses. This helps children and teens know how to think about loss and gives permission to talk openly.

Take advantage of the windows of opportunity kids give you. One boy who had a brother living in the other household said, "I'm missing watching my brother grow up." That's a window into his grief. Peer through and become inquisitive. Respond with questions and statements like, "Tell me more. What else do you miss?"

Realize that grief cannot be "fixed." You can't say something to make it go away, so don't try. Besides, that inadvertently stifles more conversation later. Listen, acknowledge, and reflect with concern what you hear them say.

If your child seems to be "doing just fine with this," keep monitoring. Children grieve in spurts, and the pain may resurface later, or they could be hiding it to relieve you of the burden of worrying about them.

Some children will express their feelings with art or play. Use whatever allows them to express their loss.

Make changes in your stepfamily slowly. Try to keep as much stability in the new home as possible. Remember, more change equals more loss.

Biological parents should compartmentalize their life to spend exclusive time with children without the stepparent. Regular noncustodial parent access is also a must.

Keep alive the "touch points" you have with your children. Important rituals between parents and children, like a wink, holding hands in the park, or bedtime stories, communicate love and commitment to children. If the transition to a new family has made you lose some of them, try to reestablish this valuable form of communication.

Help build connections between multiple generations. Acknowledge the losses grandparents have experienced with grandchildren (and stepgrandchildren). You as an adult child can talk to your parents—the grandparents—and make suggestions as to what their role might be in the new stepfamily.

DRIVEN BY MENACING EMOTIONS

> But now you must rid yourselves of all such things as these: anger, rage, malice, slander, and filthy language from your lips. Do not lie to each other, since you have taken off your old self with its practices and have put on the new self, which is being renewed in knowledge in the image of its Creator. . . . Therefore, as God's chosen people, holy and dearly loved, clothe yourselves with compassion, kindness, humility, gentleness, and patience. Bear with each other and forgive whatever grievances you may have against one another. Forgive as the Lord forgave you. And over all these virtues put on love, which binds them all together in perfect unity. (Colossians 3: 8–10, 12–14)

In the above Scripture, God declares that his children cannot afford to be driven by negative emotions. We are the reflection of Christ, since we have been clothed with him. I shudder to consider how Jesus would have responded on the day he was to go to the cross had he given in to his emotions. He was fearful of being crucified, yet he "endured the cross, scorning its shame" for our sake (Hebrews 12:2). Everyone's emotions get the best of them at some point in time, but you can't afford to be dictated by them; if you are, you can be driven to destructive behavior toward yourself and your stepfamily.

Resentment led *Larry* to envy the material possessions his ex-wife was provided with after her remarriage. She had left Larry and her children after having an affair with a wealthy businessman in their community. Larry was left to raise the children and manage on a moderate income; she was driving a new car, taking tennis lessons with a private instructor, and living without concern for the future. Bitterness, anger, and revenge are close cousins of resentment, so it was no surprise when Larry started using his custody rights to the children for leverage in his legal battles with his ex-spouse. Needless to say, Larry was a terrible co-parent and was responsible for generating a great deal of pain for himself and his children.

Guilt is another menacing emotion. Whether it relates to decisions you made or circumstances your children have been forced to endure through no fault of your own, guilt is debilitating if we allow it to be. For example, parents who think their children "have suffered enough" frequently loosen their discipline and lower their expectations for proper behavior. This simply teaches children that acting mad, depressed, or hurt gives them license to get their way. While we must be sensitive to children's emotions, we should not fall victim to them. Boundaries need to be firm and expectations maintained.

The prescription for these difficult emotions is forgiveness and releasing the burdens to God. For a full discussion of the forgiveness process, go back to chapter 6, but let this section remind you of the need for managing your pain. Turning over to God what you cannot control relieves your burden and brings back the choice of holiness, compassion, kindness, humility, gentleness, and patience. Be in the Word each and every day so you can more closely imitate your Savior in daily life. Our humanness will never allow us to completely escape our emotions. But with the Spirit's help we do not have to be subject to them either.

COMBINING HOLIDAY AND FAMILY TRADITIONS

The stepping-stone that applies most to the area of traditions is flexibility. Traditions—sometimes called rituals—refer to the activities and patterns of interaction that we repeat on a daily, weekly, or even annual basis. How you greet one another at the end of the day is a valuable ritual and just as important over time as your twenty-year tradition of eating Thanksgiving dinner at Grandma's house. Traditions are important because they communicate our identity as family, and their predictability provides security to our lives. When traditions are broken or changed—even if the change is preferred—something dies inside us. Most people have no idea how important traditions are to them until they can't do them anymore. Oh, how we'll fight to keep our traditions alive.

The issue of belonging and family identity is very much tied to traditions. During the integration years, stepfamilies discover a good bit of positioning taking place between the insiders and outsiders as individuals try to keep their traditions alive. Persons who don't share in a given tradition feel like outsiders and a divided family identity is obvious. But that's to be expected, since the Crockpot has not had time to bring people together. Finding common ground for traditions over time requires a great deal of flexibility, particularly from adults. When parents and stepparents refuse to be flexible, battle lines are drawn, pitting insiders against outsiders.

Holiday traditions in particular put co-parent relationships to the test. If you find yourself in a Fiery Foe or Angry Associate relationship with an ex-spouse, don't expect the holidays to work out just as you hoped. Yet even the best co-parent relationship, characterized by considerate negotiation regarding time with the children, still can't erase sadness over traditions lost and memories from previous family holidays. Getting used to new traditions, different food, and being with strangers in unfamiliar homes is awkward at best.

Holiday experiences open the underlying, hidden dynamics of stepfamily life. Ongoing silent battles between co-parents, for example, often become open battles as parents pressure children regarding how much time they will have together and how travel plans will be made. Loyalty conflicts and issues of loss can easily spoil the joy of the season for children if parents are not careful.

David, an eleven-year-old whom I was counseling, decided it was just easier not to visit his dad at Christmas one year for a number of reasons. First, his parents maintained a low-grade battle for control that demonstrated itself in proposals and counter-proposals of how David would get to his father's house and for how long. A second reason related to his stepmother, who "wants me to be part of her family. I don't want to be with her or my stepbrother when I visit Dad. I just want to be with my dad. Why can't she just leave us alone?" As usual, my conversations with the adults in each household revealed their belief that the other parent was responsible for David's not wanting to visit his dad. Mom blamed Dad; Dad and Stepmom blamed Mom. In truth, it was David who thought it best to keep the peace, not make his parents negotiate (which he knew they couldn't do), and avoid feeling intruded upon by his stepmother when he was with his dad. He just stayed home.

Practical Strategies for Combining Holiday and Family Traditions

Be flexible and make sacrifices. You cannot make everyone happy all the time. Accepting this truth immediately takes away the pressure to give everyone what they want. Being flexible means realizing you can combine, modify, or sacrifice old traditions during a given year in order to give your stepfamily opportunity to develop new ones. Set the tone for negotiation by showing a willingness to sacrifice. If you won't, why should your children or stepchildren?

Plan, plan, plan. As a couple, be proactive in discussing upcoming holiday plans. Determine your preferences and wishes and what sacrifices you will make on behalf of the other home. Then contact the adults in the other home and start negotiating. If you have three or four homes involved in the equation, start planning very early.

Complex stepfamilies may have to be really creative. Maintaining a Crockpot mentality may help you find solutions to seemingly impossible situations. Stepfamilies that have children from both adults (complex stepfamilies) often find themselves pulled in multiple directions during the holidays. One creative approach is to let each parent and children spend the holidays with the extended family members of their choosing. This may lead them to be in different homes for Easter dinner, yet acknowledges their differing family connections and honors family traditions. This may be particularly useful to new stepfamilies. As the stepfamily integrates over time, the decision to combine holiday activities may be met with less resistance.

Do what you can do and accept what you cannot change. Work on your co-parental relationship throughout the year so as to improve your chances of respectful negotiation during the holidays. But realize that ultimately you cannot control the other household and you may have to grin and bear it. When stuck in awkward or tough situations, appeal to difficult family members with "For your dad's sake, let's try to put our differences aside."[6] Hopefully this will be motivation enough. In the end, lay what you cannot change at God's feet and go on.

Maintain the stepping-stone of patience as individual family members grow to accept new traditions.

Live and learn. One stepfather found himself disappointed year after year because his stepson had to be rushed off to his father's house in the middle of Christmas Day. He was never able to fully enjoy the day with his wife and stepson, because everyone was watching the clock. Eventually he and his wife proposed a change to her ex. As it turned out, her ex-husband was also discouraged each Christmas and was open to changing the visitation agreement. They settled on an alternating arrangement that gave each home an undisturbed Christmas holiday while the other home had an undisturbed Thanksgiving holiday. The loss of togetherness experienced during a given holiday was moderated by the joy they received during the other.

Be compassionate regarding your child's preferences during the holidays. At the same time, teach children that sacrifices sometimes have to be made to make the new stepfamily a priority.

Daily rituals of connection are important to the integration process. The small, simple behaviors that families repeat on a regular basis communicate care and commitment. Hugs before leaving for school, a special note in a lunch box, Friday night pizza and a family video, and Sunday dinner with Grandma are rituals that keep people connected. Biological parents should strive to keep alive pre-stepfamily rituals of connection, while stepparents work to create new comfortable ones. For example, a parent will hug children before leaving for work, and the stepparent may touch them briefly on the arm. A parent may write an "I love you" note and hide it in a backpack while the stepparent's note notifies the child of a raise in allowance. Take advantage of repeated behaviors to communicate care and develop trust in steprelationships.

BIRTH ORDER CHANGES

From a developmental standpoint, shifts in birth order can be problematic for children.[7] This common shift in role and position for children is often unrecognized by adults, but it has a potent impact on children. Nine-year-old *Tara* was the oldest in her family until Mom remarried a man with a thirteen-year-old son, *Josh*. During the single-parent years Tara gained special status with her mother by learning to set the dinner table and changing her younger brother's diaper. She became Mom's helper in many ways, and her efforts were rewarded with a special mother-daughter bond. Once Josh entered the family, Tara's mom thought having him help her in the kitchen would give them a chance to bond. Without realizing it, Tara soon became overlooked and lost a significant role in the family.

Have you ever been displaced at work? Perhaps a new employee has stepped in and captured the boss's attention. Or a competing salesperson has subtly pushed you out and taken your place. How would you feel if your boss decided to move someone alongside him who, despite your laying the groundwork for a project, got to reap the rewards? Or perhaps you've been in a work situation where the new employee didn't pull her weight and the burden of training her or cleaning up after her mistakes fell on you. Can you feel your stomach tightening?

Not all shifts in birth order are this extreme, but they all represent change. Let me remind you that change brings more loss, and loss added to substantial previous losses generates weariness and insecurity. It is the continual process of change that disheartens children, and that is what parents need to be sensitive to. *LeAnn* was just five when her father remarried. She had two older brothers, eleven and fourteen, who picked on her from time to time, but who mostly joined their father in protecting their "baby-doll" sister. LeAnn didn't know, of course, that she was coddled and catered to, she just knew she didn't like what happened when her father remarried a woman with two children, a boy age eight and a girl age three. The queen had been dethroned. Her displaced position and importance resulted in fits of anger in Wal-Mart and cutting her stepsibling's hair when no one was looking. Only when her father and stepmother stopped to notice the loss of status in LeAnn's life did they find the energy to return some of her significance. They did not cater to her to the exclusion of others but sought a healthy balance between special times with Dad and punishment when she acted out. The loss of birth order position was not, of course, the only loss she was dealing with. But her father and stepmother's sensitivity to this particular loss was helpful over time.

In order to consider how shifts in birth order have impacted your children, try one of the following ideas:

- If your children are old enough to articulate their feelings (and you are courageous enough), sit down with them and ask how their role in the family has changed since adding stepsiblings. Discuss with them how you treat them differently now and what responsibilities they have lost or gained in the new family. Give them permission to be sad or angry over what has changed, but don't promise to restore the past (having a new family requires change from everyone). Empathize and feel sorry for their losses, but support them with a vote of confidence that they can manage the change in role or position.

- Whether you can speak with your children or not, make a list of each child's roles before and after the changes occurred. Strive to be sensitive to old roles and restore jobs or tasks when possible or replace them with new jobs. This builds a sense of importance as the child contributes to the home and receives your approval for doing so.
- During the early years, spend time with each child away from stepsiblings so as to affirm their uniqueness.

MONEY MATTERS

A good writer knows when to ask for help. The finances of stepfamilies are incredibly confusing and diverse, so I asked for help. I have turned to trusted friend and expert on stepfamily finances, Margorie Engel, Ph.D., to write this section. Dr. Engel is currently president of the Stepfamily Association of America, an author and media consultant, and a frequent writer on stepfamily finances. She graciously shares the following suggestions regarding money matters for the stepfamily home:

Money does not have a neutral connotation in stepfamilies. Money will always be a major issue for remarried couples because trust, commitment, and the guarantee of permanence are the underlying issues. As a result, it is hard to put together the perfect money management package. However, because of previous life experiences, these couples are typically ready to search for creative solutions to new challenges. Stepfamilies often have a combination of three money pots: yours, mine, and ours.

Some remarried couples cannot fathom pooling all of their financial resources, while other couples can't imagine not doing it. Each side is convinced their philosophy is the secret stepfamily strategy to a happy financial relationship.[8]

Separate Accounts: "Yours" and "Mine"

Husbands and wives may be embarrassed to initiate a discussion about ways to keep stepfamily finances separate. Feeling the need for separate money seems to evolve from circumstance as much as temperament. When couples desire separate finances, they are acknowledging that they have separate or different interests and that they want to make certain financial choices as an adult without needing to ask "permission."

Even though they love each other deeply, the effort to avoid potential hassles prompts many remarried couples to keep their money as separate as possible. "Avoiding dependency" is another reason for choosing to keep separate stepfamily money. Divorce laws have sent a clear message to married women that financial dependency is not, and will not be, rewarded. Stepfamily couples may deliberately arrange their finances to preserve individual autonomy in routine money matters, even though most of them have not negotiated a formal financial contract.

Two separate families living under the same roof tend to be created when each remarried parent pays for herself or himself and her or his children's expenses. These "separate pot" couples strongly believe that each partner must contribute an equal share toward stepfamily household expenses, which is seldom fair. Most wives do not earn as much as their husbands, and incoming child-support payments don't often make up the difference. Therefore, her 50 percent of the family's expenses will be a much larger percentage of her income than her husband's 50 percent share of the expenses. When this equal concept doesn't work out, the wife winds up feeling dependent and the husband feels he is paying too much. The old model of men providing all financial support for the family doesn't fit for stepfamilies; neither does the newer idea of a fifty/fifty split.

A completely separate system also tends to fall apart in a stepfamily financial crisis. Two particularly decisive moments: A can't-turn-down career opportunity for one partner and a corporate downsizing causing job loss for another. Out of necessity, these couples find themselves financially merged—at least until the crisis is resolved.

Mixed Accounts: "Yours," "Mine," and "Ours"

Even when remarried couples begin a relationship with the intention of keeping money separate, they tend to drift into at least some pooling of funds. Because they are married, couples cannot legally escape responsibility for one another's economic decisions. From a practical standpoint, individual preferences for separate stepfamily accounts often begin to take a backseat to convenience.

It appears that the best of all worlds for many remarried couples may be one of two variations on the "three pots—yours, mine, ours" system:

- Small separate accounts and a large joint account, or
- Large separate accounts and a minimal joint account.

Joint accounts are funded equally or, more often, in proportion to each spouse's income. Stepfamily couples will compromise on issues that are joint financial responsibilities and handle their own accounts independently.

For most stepfamily couples, each spouse comes to the remarriage with a credit history, credit cards, and individual bank accounts. They may also have brokerage accounts and/or retirement accounts. Couples typically continue to maintain their own accounts. Remarried couples often agree to pay for ordinary expenses related to their biological children (residential and child-support payments), insurance premiums, repairs and maintenance of property individually owned (cars, rental property), and personal expenses for clothing, business costs, medical expenses, hobbies, and gifts. Joint expenses such as rent/mortgage, groceries, entertainment, and family/couple vacations are paid for in a flexible manner according to ability to pay. Most remarried couples also struggle valiantly to accumulate savings for emergency funds and investments.

Financial advisors suggest keeping cash flow separate from investments. It is preferable to fund joint accounts for children and household with the income stream from employment and/or child support collection. This avoids the typical situation wherein wives spend most of their money for consumables (family food, clothing, vacations, treats for the children) and husbands put most of their money into appreciable assets (mortgage, stocks, retirement funds).

One Big "Ours" Account

Stepfamilies often find themselves easing into pooling their finances. This pool drift frequently starts by establishing a joint vacation fund, purchasing a replacement household appliance, or having an "ours" child. Sometimes there's a purely psychological transition.

When all of the money is put into a common pot, couple decision-making is critical to successful money management. Confrontation may arise regarding one spouse dominating financial decisions or non-recognition of the pooling—and that is usually what the remarried couple is trying to avoid.

It is important to make basic decisions about management of step-family money in the common pot. These include:

- A record-keeping system (running totals or monthly tallies)
- Who will be responsible for bill-paying from the account
- What will be paid for out of the joint account
- How much each spouse can withdraw without discussing it with the other

The joint bank account needs to be set up where it is convenient for each spouse to deposit and withdraw money. As with most team efforts, husbands and wives typically handle different financial activities according to their ability to get the job done. Sometimes, especially after a bad financial experience in a prior marriage, couples need to earn each other's trust.

However Money Is Handled . . .

Stepfamily money—separate accounts, pooled accounts, or a his-hers-ours accounts system. There's no absolute right or wrong way to handle the finances in a remarriage. The comfortable balance will change with the amount of money available, the length of the marriage, and changing needs. The initial stepfamily money management system needs to be flexible, not carved in stone.

Talk about each of the options. During this discussion, consider how you will treat each other if the initial choice proves wrong after a trial period. Once the foundation of your new financial system has been laid, schedule regular review periods. Ask yourself, "Is it broken? Should we fix it?" Something is always working and something is always failing. Keep the choices that are working well and replace the duds with new options. It's an ongoing process that requires compromise and renegotiation.[9]

Keys to Financial Harmony

- For couples to share the relationship spirit, each partner should have a reasonable amount of discretionary money to meet personal needs.
- All wives must have credit in their own name. It is too important a commodity in our society not to be protected (in case of spousal death).

- It's very important for each spouse to keep some readily available money for emergencies.
- Marriages need nurturing. All couples need financial plans that provide money for private time and enjoyment together. One of the essential elements of any healthy financial plan is periodic celebration of its achievements.

Good Reasons to Share Financial Management:

- It's fair.
- A lifestyle is determined by spending decisions, so both partners deserve a voice in making decisions.
- It's effective.
- Sharing makes for better decisions, actions, and further reason to trust your spouse.
- It's successful.
- People who share in decisions have a reason for making them work.

Decisions, Decisions:

1. When money is separate:

   - What money is to be separate (checking/savings/investment accounts)?
   - How much will each partner contribute to the household?

2. When money is pooled:

   - What money, if any, is to be personal?
   - What money is to be shared?
   - What expense categories are most important?
   - Will yearly expense plans be created? By whom? How closely will they be followed?

3. Who will manage the books?

   - How will they be kept?
   - How often: weekly or monthly?
   - How accurately?

4. How much discussion is appropriate (and whose opinion prevails) when purchases are made?
5. Whether money is kept separate or shared:

- How will financial emergencies and unexpected expenses be handled?
- When will credit be used?[10]

FAMILY MEETINGS: A TOOL FOR PROBLEM SOLVING

Throughout this chapter I've offered specific strategies for dealing with each of the pitfalls discussed. In addition, one general strategy for managing issues and pitfalls is the family meeting. This tool is one of the most effective you can add to your stepfamily toolbox; make use of it in a variety of circumstances.

Corporations have strategy meetings on a regular basis. Department heads, supervisors, and managers join together to discuss current production goals, sales reports, and marketing efforts. The purpose behind such meetings is to generate teamwork and improve efficiency and profit as the whole works toward a common goal. Family meetings help stepfamilies do the same. The goals are different (integration, spiritual formation, and generating unconditional love and respect), but the process is similar.

Weekly or biweekly family meetings are the perfect time to process emotions and negotiate preferences, rule changes, discipline consequences, and roles in the home. Vacation plans can be made, rituals for the holidays worked out, and feelings of loss and hurt shared. But perhaps the most unexpected result for many stepfamilies that make use of this tool is the sense of identity that comes from a new tradition. The meeting itself becomes a unique tradition that helps family members listen, spend time with each other, and experience their family being together. Not all stepfamilies have the discipline to have a regular family meeting, but those that do appreciate its impact.

What is a family meeting?

- Time set aside to promote meaningful communication and to provide for family discussion, decision-making, problem solving, encouragement, and cooperation.

- Family meetings can be structured and formal or flexible and informal.
- Everyone has a part and something to contribute. Meetings are democratic; that is, everyone has a voice, but not the same decision-making power. Parents have the final say but should empower children to contribute whenever possible.
- Ultimately, family meetings build much needed family traditions, create memories, and establish a working family identity.

How do we get started?

- The process is easier if meetings begin when children are young (age four or five). Older children may have negative reactions at first, but most come to value the process once they experience the benefits.
- Simply make a decision to start, have a plan of action, and begin.

General guidelines for effective family meetings:

- Make meetings a priority. They should happen at regular, predictable times (e.g., each Thursday night). Don't allow distractions to diminish your commitment to the process. Establish and stick to time limits.
- Begin each meeting with compliments and words of appreciation when they can be offered genuinely. Encouragement facilitates integration but shouldn't be offered if not sincere.
- Post an "agenda board" (perhaps on the refrigerator) and encourage everyone to contribute to the list. Be sure each item is discussed and equal consideration given to each concern.
- Rotate leaders so that children have a turn (your teenagers will love being in charge!).
- Honor one another's feelings and opinions. Use your listening skills and speak with respect. Don't permit meetings to become gripe sessions. Seek first to understand, then to be understood.
- Work to find solutions to problem situations. Brainstorm possible solutions and consequences if agreements are not kept. This helps each person take ownership of the problem and its solution. This also clarifies expectations and allows each to experience the stepfamily working together.

- End the meeting with an enjoyable activity. You all may be together or break into mini-family groups, but have ice cream, play mini-golf, or play board games. Make it fun.

Summary:

Stepfamilies have a number of pitfalls that can be avoided, if not entirely, at least partially. The pitfalls discussed in this chapter, if not addressed, can easily add stress and conflict to your marriage and home. Be proactive as you work to address these and other issues, and seek God's wisdom as you look for solutions.

Questions for Discussion

FOR ALL COUPLES

1. When could you begin having family meetings? Try it for a few weeks and decide if it works for you. Share your experiences with your support group.
2. For each person in your home, make a list of the losses he or she has likely experienced. How does this list help you to understand each person's behavior?
3. What losses has this chapter made you aware of that you hadn't considered before?
4. Do a case study in stepfamily loss, fear, and anger. Review the comments made by the Thomas family in chapter 1 (page 18).

    - How are their losses evident in their current fears?
    - List the fears for each person. Discuss the possible similarities in your home.
    - Notice how fear and anger are expressed, especially by John, Susan, and Frank.

5. Review the Practical Strategies for Coping With Unrecognized Loss and Unexpressed Grief on page 176. Which strategies are you already doing, and which could be improved?
6. Identify and list some of your menacing emotions. What are you doing to lay them at the throne of God?

7. What traditions have you yet to sort out? What successes have you had? Share some of your creative solutions.
8. Stepparents—what rituals of connection have you developed thus far with your stepchildren?
9. Review and share your thoughts regarding questions addressing birth order on pages 182–184.
10. What has been your system of money management so far? Share whatever changes you believe necessary at this point in time.

FOR PRE-REMARITAL COUPLES

1. The time to begin formal family meetings is after the wedding. However, you can implement some informal meetings during the engagement. How might you use the time to decide on rules, relationships, and what the kids will call their stepparent after the wedding?
2. Has this current relationship grown during a time of intense grief? Did you wait two to three years before deepening this relationship? If not, slow down your dating and give yourself time to grieve former losses.
3. Share how you would feel if your dating partner were to admit to feelings of fondness for his or her previous mate.
4. What are your desires for more children?
5. Consider the birth order of each child. How will the child's role, position, and relationships change once you marry?
6. Schedule a time to discuss your ideas about money management in the new family. Review Money Matters (page 184) and develop a tentative plan as you work through the Decisions, Decisions questions (pages 188–189).

CHAPTER NINE

Smart Step Six: STEP Through

The wilderness: overcoming special challenges

"Every craftsman makes excellent use of his tools. The craft of building a strong family requires a variety of tools—and the skill to use them."

The journey for stepfamilies to the Promised Land can be long or relatively short, but one thing is certain: the journey will bring challenges. This chapter discusses special challenges in the Christian stepfamily home and gives strategies for managing their impact. Special challenges include managing sexuality, how Scripture applies to the stepfamily, and spiritual formation in stepfamily children.

SEXUALITY

A mother once asked me, "We really don't have to talk about this, do we?" Unfortunately, yes, we do. The matter of sexuality in the stepfamily is important (it's important in any home), whether you want it to be or not. Educating children about healthy sexuality is an important part of all Christian parenting. Protecting children from the sexual abuses and myths of the world is another. Stepfamily couples, like biological parents, must keep both of these objectives in mind as they raise their children and stepchildren. But the stepfamily has an added challenge that must be addressed.

While the research on stepfamily sexual exchanges is still coming in, it does seem that children not living with both their biological parents run higher risks of child sexual abuse from both family members and others.[1] This finding is not limited to stepfamilies but pertains to children living in single-parent and cohabiting homes as well. Don't assume, however, that this is due to the "less than ideal" structure of a stepfamily. Family structure itself, that is, the composition of a home (single parent, biological, or stepfamily), is not as responsible for this increased risk of sexual abuse as is the process of interactions within the home. When there is poor adult psychological functioning, new relationships with unclear roles and boundaries, poorly defined values, and stress that leads to a lack of proper parental monitoring, there is vulnerability that can lead to sexual abuse.[2] In other words, sexual boundaries are not going to be crossed just because you live in a stepfamily. But there is increased risk, and you need to protect your home from the potential devastating impact of sexual abuse.

Karen and *Frank* learned something that would shake the foundations of their stepfamily. For a period of two years, Karen's fifteen-year-old son had been entering his fourteen-year-old stepsister's room to fondle her genitals. "How could this happen?" asked Karen. "Frank and I have been married for ten years. The kids have known each other since they were five and four. They've grown up together. How could something like this happen now?" Her shock and pain were quite evident. The discovery of sexually violating behavior is both traumatic and baffling. How could something like this happen?

The Command for Closeness

When two families come together, there is an assumption that people will do just that—"come together." This creates an unspoken expectation that relationships develop and bonding occurs. Displays of affection, warmth, and hugs of endearment are non-sexual ways of communicating this coming together. However, these non-sexual touches can take on sexual implications for people whose psychological boundaries are not strong.

For example, biological fathers sometimes report a growing discomfort with their daughter's physical changes during adolescence. A sweet little girl begins to look like a beautiful woman within a short period of time. Fathers, who don't want their daughters in any way to feel that their dad is thinking of them in sexual ways, often pull away from physical contact. Unfortunately, this may be interpreted by an adolescent girl as a rejection, instead of an acknowledgment of her increasing femininity.

Stepfathers, as well, often find themselves confused about the physical relationship they have with their stepdaughter. Hugs from a little girl take on a strange new meaning from a blossoming stepdaughter. A conscientious stepfather may, too, pull away from physical contact. However, even that can be seen as a comment on sexuality and result in a shift in how persons view one another. Biological fathers must remember to keep hugging and physically connecting with their daughters during adolescence (it helps to confirm an insecure girl of her worth and value as a woman). Stepfathers should seek to present clear non-sexual intentions to their touch and restrain the temptation to view a stepdaughter's touch as having any sexual connotation.

In addition, a stepfather who works to create a happy marriage with an adolescent girl's mother helps to reduce sexual anxiety. "As they mature, girls begin to view a good marriage in a stepfamily as a kind of sexual insurance policy. The girl thinks that the closer the stepfather is to her mother, the less likely will be his real or imagined advances toward her. Once the sexual threat is tabled, often a girl becomes more accepting and open."[3]

A Sexually Charged Environment

In addition to an expectation of closeness, stepfamilies have a sexually charged environment. This occurs for a number of reasons. First, children watch their parent go through a period of dating and developing romance. Children may even coach their parent on how to act, talk, or what perfume to wear on a date. In addition, a child is often witness to the increasing physical affections and touches that couples share as romance deepens. One father shared how this impacted his children. "While dating, I kissed my future bride in front of the house before saying good-night. My youngest son poked his head around the corner and yelled, 'Goooooo, Daddy!'" Children can't help but witness these romantic affections and hear discussions of where the couple will go on their honeymoon. And then there's Uncle Roger's "1001 Erotic Nights" gag gift at the wedding reception.

But romance doesn't stop there. A second reason for a sexually charged environment is what happens after the wedding. The first year of marriage is frequently speckled with romantic gestures and snuggling on the couch before bedtime. All of which communicates the message that "sexuality is alive and well in this household."

Bob recalled, "When my wife and I were first married, my stepdaughter came into our room in the morning and said, 'What's he doing in here? And where are your pajamas, Mom?'" *Connie* said her five children and stepchildren saw her and her husband kiss a lot during their first year of marriage. One of her daughters was uncomfortable with it and always tried to pull them apart. His daughter, on the other hand, would say "Ooo-la-la," while the boys teased them about "tongue twisting." While these examples are embarrassing, to say the least, some observations by children, if not handled well, can be debilitating to the family.

Shortly after *Judy*'s remarriage to *Tony*, her nine-year-old daughter, *Lisa*, started walking into her mother's bedroom at night to see if they were having sex. At times, Lisa would sit outside their bedroom door to see if she could hear them making love. Lisa's curiosity in the sexual aspects of her mother's marriage was brought on when Judy started closing the bedroom door. Prior to remarriage, Judy had an open-door policy with her children. As a single parent, she felt it important to be available to her children, especially at night. She slept with her door open so her children could reach her if they had any need. It was her way of reassuring her children after her husband's death.

Upon remarriage, Judy began to close her door so as to have some privacy with her husband. Making love was just a part of that time, but closing the bedroom door was, for Lisa, an unmistakable nonverbal comment on the couple's sexuality. This fed Lisa's curiosity. "Why didn't Judy and Tony just lock their door?" someone might wonder. Because they didn't have a lock on the door. Pay attention, everyone, here comes Ron's big tip for improving your sex life—get a lock on your bedroom door!

On one occasion, Lisa was successful. She burst through the door at two in the morning to discover her mother and stepfather having intercourse. She went running through the house, screaming, "They're having sex! They're having sex!" Tony and Judy were embarrassed beyond belief. And because their embarrassment paralyzed them, they did nothing. They simply couldn't talk about it with Lisa. After that night, whenever the couple closed their door, even for nonsexual reasons, Lisa would later accuse them of going in their room "just because you want to have sex." The couple's shame deepened, and they began accommodating their marriage to avoid any accusation from nine-year-old Lisa. Quickly Lisa had more power over their sexual and marital intimacy than did Tony or Judy.

A natural result of good sex education is curiosity. We cannot fault Lisa for that. However, the first time she burst into her mother's bedroom and accused them of "just wanting to have sex," two things should have happened. First, the couple should have put a lock on their bedroom door and begun educating all the children on respecting one another's privacy. Secondly, Judy could have used the situation as a springboard into discussions of sexuality. Whether Judy and Lisa had talked about sex before or not, this was a perfect opportunity to teach about God's gift of sex to married couples. The content and frequency of Judy and Tony's sexuality is off limits, but the acknowledgment of God's gift is not. Tony's participation in this conversation is up to the couple and should be based on his level of connection with Lisa. Beyond this initial response, Judy would need to assign a behavioral consequence to further misbehavior, accusations, or inappropriate questions about their sexual practices. "It's none of your business whether we went into our bedroom to have sex. If you want to talk about sexuality, we can do that tomorrow evening, but I don't want to hear questions about our intimacy. The next time you ask, you will be grounded for three days. And that includes gymnastics practice. Your choice."

A third reason for a sexually charged environment in stepfamilies is developing teenage sexuality. Our society is obsessed with sex. It pervades the movies, music, and conversation of the average adolescent. Sex is everywhere—even inside the bodies of teens. Changes in hormones and physical appearance also lead to many confusing thoughts and feelings for teenagers. It is imperative that parents present a godly view of sexuality—its purpose and promise—throughout the life of a child. But the guidance parents give during adolescence is the most critical. If parents begin early to discuss God's design for our bodies and sexuality, important conversations with confused adolescents will be easier. Easy or difficult, they must take place.

In summary, children in stepfamilies, and adolescents in particular, are surrounded by a number of dynamics that call attention to sexuality. Biologically related relationships contain a natural taboo against sexual exchanges that step-relationships do not have. To make up for this natural genetic protection, stepfamilies need to set behavioral boundaries that discourage intentional and unconscious sexual attractions.

Boundaries That Honor

The goal is to set boundaries (rules governing behavior) that teach family members to honor one another. Respecting privacy and valuing the specialness of each family member is an important message for everyone to learn. Here are some suggestions to help you get there.

Set rules that honor privacy. It may feel totally unnecessary, but consider having a dress code. Teenagers, in particular, can overlook how their dress invites others to see them in sexual ways or consider them a symbol of sexuality. Girls, for example, who sleep in their underwear and a long T-shirt may be comfortable walking around the house dressed for bed. Little do some girls realize how that arouses a natural curiosity within boys about their body shape.[4] Boys can easily entertain thoughts that cross from non-sexual curiosities to sexual ones. To counter this possibility, set a dress code and explain why it is necessary. The dress code teens would naturally assume if on a church youth retreat would work well. Make sure you discuss as a couple what the standard should be. Get on the same page and stick together. Then call a family meeting and invite your elementary-age and teenage children to give their input and determine the rule.

Other rules you might implement include knocking before entering bedrooms and how persons will share the bathroom. It always amazed me how the children on *The Brady Bunch*, who were similar in age but unrelated, never showed any embarrassment or sexual tension while sharing a bathroom. Again, Hollywood's version of family life doesn't even come close to reality. Help your children work out a respectful system for shower schedules and sharing bathrooms.

These boundaries are particularly important when a stepsibling from another home moves into your home. Children and teens who have known each other for years, but never have lived together full time, need clear rules of conduct. Finally, be sure not to turn a blind eye to any signs that someone is uncomfortable. If you perceive a child withdrawing or showing signs of stress, calmly approach the child to investigate the situation. Err on the side of caution.

Have frank discussions with teens and pre-teens (separately) about sexual boundaries and healthy sexual attitudes. Setting rules that honor sexuality and privacy is sure to create opportunities for adults to speak with children and teens about sexuality. Take advantage of such opportunities to teach God's purpose for sexuality and the protection his statutes provide. The message parents give children in stepfamilies is the same fundamental message any parent would give—it just applies to people both inside and outside the home. The message is this: Your sexuality and the sexuality of others is a gift from God that is to be honored and protected. Healthy sexuality between two married people helps build their relationship to each other and to God. Sexuality outside God's boundaries erodes relationships and creates a sin barrier between God and us.

Unfortunately, some parents rely on scare tactics to encourage sexual purity before marriage. In an effort to keep their children from having sexual thoughts or urges, they scare them with the consequences of premarital sex. I believe we should be honest with children and teens about the potential emotional and physical consequences of premarital sex. However, the scare method doesn't present sex as a gift from God to be honored. It turns it into a curse to be avoided. When children grow to be married adults, switching the messages in their brain to see sex as something to be embraced and pursued is often difficult. It is much better for parents to teach sex as a gift to be protected and honored. God's law that sex be kept until marriage is meant to protect us from harm and provide for our sexual pleasure in marriage. We can teach our children to protect one another's honor and their own so that the gift of sexuality can be enjoyed later in its proper marital context.

Talk about sexual attractions in a matter-of-fact manner. Having healthy and honest conversations about the sexual truths of life normalizes them for children. For example, explaining menstruation to a pre-adolescent girl or wet dreams to a boy before they occur prepares the child for the onset of such experiences. Preparing and normalizing such experiences is important because, in addition to teaching children proper hygiene, it gives the child a God-perspective on the event ("You're becoming a woman!" or "There is no reason to be ashamed of having a sexual dream that results in ejaculation or to think that you've sinned.").

In the same way, acknowledging that sexual attractions between stepsiblings can occur normalizes them for the child. This is not to give permission to them but to teach a proper perspective. The alternative is to say nothing and leave the child to determine the meaning of such an attraction (not a good idea) or to give negative messages that needlessly shame children ("How could you think something like that about her? That's disgusting.").

Instead, a parent might say something like this to his son: "You know, son, as we talk about sharing the bathroom with your stepsisters, it occurs to me that some kids in a stepfamily like ours sometimes have passing sexual thoughts about their stepsiblings. If that ever happens to you, it doesn't mean you are bad or a disappointment to God. There will be lots of times in life that you have sexual thoughts or feelings toward other people, but it would be inappropriate for you to act on them or keep thinking about the person in that way. So if it happens, ask God to help you to stop thinking about your stepsibling in that way. And make sure you don't dishonor the other person by acting on the attraction or thoughts. If the thoughts keep happening and you get concerned about it, feel free to talk to me. I won't be angry. We'll find a way to handle it. Any questions?"

HOW DOES SCRIPTURE APPLY TO STEPFAMILIES?

Throughout this book we've applied a number of Scripture passages to stepfamily life. God presents his standard for the family throughout Scripture, so how do passages about the "ideal family" apply to stepfamilies? Let's look at some examples.

> Discipline your son, and he will give you peace; he will bring delight to your soul. (Proverbs 29:17)

> Fathers, do not exasperate your children; instead, bring them up in the training and instruction of the Lord. (Ephesians 6:4)

These passages obviously apply to biological parents and children, but do they apply to stepchildren and stepfathers? If children have two men trying to take responsibility for their moral development, does the child get confused? What if they are teaching similar but different things? What if a biological father is not fulfilling his obligation; does that mean the stepfather should take his place?

> Children, obey your parents in the Lord, for this is right. "Honor your father and mother"—which is the first commandment with a promise—"that it may go well with you and that you may enjoy long life on the earth" (Ephesians 6:1–3).

This text for children lays the foundation for hierarchy in the home. Fathers and mothers are to guide children and be respected as leaders by children. But are stepchildren under the same obligation to stepparents? In what ways might stepchildren show honor to a stepparent?

It is quite clear that we do not have Scripture passages that specifically address stepparents and stepchildren. There are many stories of what I have referred to as "expanded families," whose family dynamics mirror those of the modern day stepfamily. However, we don't find God giving specific relational directives to stepparents or stepchildren.

However, I would suggest that *in principle, all Scripture applies to the individuals in stepfamilies and the relationships in stepfamily homes, just as it does to people of every culture, race, and family structure. However, the process of applying the scriptural principle to life may be different.* Let's consider two examples.

"Fathers, do not exasperate your children; instead, bring them up in the training and instruction of the Lord" (Ephesians 6:4). This passage charges fathers not to exasperate their children. To be exasperated means to have one's spirit broken or to be discouraged or disheartened. We know that discouraged children are more likely to misbehave, be uncooperative, withdrawn, and oppositional. Without a solid relationship, it is very easy to discourage children; they take criticism more personally and receive training with more resistance. Stepfathers need to understand that early in their stepfamily's development, it is much easier for them to exasperate their stepchildren due to a lack of relationship. If anything, stepfathers should be cautious not to increase resistance in their stepchildren or to discourage them, because this makes spiritual training all the more difficult. A stepfather who claims authority just because he is the "man of the house" is likely to lose respect from his stepchildren and reduce his spiritual influence.

In addition, the biblical role for husbands as the "head of the wife" (Ephesians 5:23) is not license to claim anything for personal gain. Men are challenged by Paul to love their wives "as Christ loved the church and gave himself up for her" (Ephesians 5:25). That sounds like sacrifice to me. When did Christ insist that others care for him? When did he use his authority and power for personal gain? He didn't. Christ served others for their benefit. He selflessly sought to bring them into relationship with God.

Bryan Chapell, in his book *Each for the Other: Marriage As It's Meant to Be*, says that "authority is not the right to order others around for personal benefit; it is the responsibility to arrange for a family's well-being. Biblical authority seeks the good of others and, therefore, serves their best interests. In this sense, the head of a home sacrifices himself for the good of his family and surrenders his desires to the needs of others in the home."[5] Stepfathers who try to insist on a position of authority are confused into thinking they can't lead without direct authority. But seeking the good of his wife and her children likely means a stepfather will lead through his wife, especially early in the marriage. This honors the bonds that exist and helps to ensure that the family experiences God's blessings. He will support her role, negotiate decisions behind closed doors, and set a spiritual focus in the home, all while building a relationship with his stepchildren.

So how should stepfathers handle "training" or "instruction" in righteousness? Is that their job too? Absolutely, yes! Stepfathers can be wonderful role models and spiritual teachers to their stepchildren and, I believe, are called by God to fulfill such a role. Regrettably, however, not all stepfathers are willing to accept this responsibility. I'll never forget a phone call from a mother whose second husband simply refused to be a spiritual influence on her two daughters. For many men, shirking this responsibility is done out of ignorance, but in her case it was not. Her husband was an elder in their church, taught marriage enrichment courses, and had been a wonderful, godly father to his own children (now grown with families of their own). After his wife died of cancer, he remarried but didn't feel the need to give time, energy, or influence to his stepdaughters. Since he had raised his family, he didn't think it was his responsibility to be an active spiritual leader. Instead, he played golf, kept to himself in the house, and attended to his personal interests. What a waste of positive spiritual influence!

Stepfathers need to understand that spiritual leadership is not a convenient volunteer endeavor—it is a calling from God. When you give your life in marriage to another woman, you are also committing yourself to the care, discipline, and spiritual training of her children. You cannot pick your roles. Accept the full assignment (or don't sign on at all).

The good news is, most stepfathers want to be a positive spiritual influence on their stepchildren—I hope you are one of them. Yet you must exercise wisdom as you grow into this role. In other words, the responsibility for the spiritual training of your stepchildren is yours, but the process of application will be different than the one used by biological fathers.

Initially, for example, stepfathers will want to focus on connecting with their stepchildren (as discussed in chapter 7). With older children it may take months before you've earned the right to verbally teach God's truths. Until then, train by modeling a Christlike lifestyle. Show yourself to be a man of God in your words, deeds, and especially in how you respond to your stepchild's biological father. All of this helps build a respectable bond with your stepchildren (and wife) and strengthens your spiritual influence.

Wise stepfathers also show Christ to their stepchildren by influencing their mother (his wife). By working with her behind the scenes to establish an expectation of godly behavior in the home, rules that support honoring God, and involvement with a local body of believers, a stepfather can have dramatic impact. Leading the family in prayer, orchestrating family spiritual times (having devotions, singing worship songs, sharing stories of God's activity in his life), and reading a Scripture passage at breakfast are just some ways a stepfather can gently lead his family while relationships are growing.

Finally, let me remind stepfathers that the reason Christians obey God is because we trust him to have our ultimate good at heart. For example, God doesn't declare sex outside of marriage a sin because he is trying to steal our fun. He does so because sex within a covenantal marriage relationship provides for our pleasure and protects us from harm. Likewise, your first task as a stepfather is to gain trust from your stepchildren so that they never question your intentions. They need to be confident at all times that you have their best interests at heart. Otherwise, your influence will be mediocre at best. But once trust is developed, you will have tremendous spiritual influence.

"Children, obey your parents in the Lord, for this is right. 'Honor your father and mother'—which is the first commandment with a promise—'that it may go well with you and that you may enjoy long life on the earth' " (Ephesians 6:1–3). This passage establishes that respect is due parents and that children should honor them with obedience. Viewing their stepparent as someone to be respected and obeyed is not a problem for many stepchildren. Yet others will have a hard time due to loyalty conflicts or the feeling that their biological parent is being removed from their rightful place of authority.

Putting the right frame on the expectation of honor toward a stepparent is helpful. A father might suggest to his children, "Honor your stepmother as you would a teacher or an older woman at church. She is not your mom, but she is due the same honor as your principal at school." In addition, you might teach your children that God expects children to show respect for all adults. "Rise in the presence of the aged, show respect for the elderly and revere your God. I am the Lord" (Leviticus 19:32). "Gray hair is a crown of splendor; it is attained by a righteous life" (Proverbs 16:31). God expects people to have a basic respect for older adults. I believe you can teach your children to honor their stepparents just as they would any older adult. This affirms the place of their other biological parent and helps to create an expectation of obedience in your home.

Scripture is full of wisdom for stepfamilies. Knowing how to best apply it in your home sometimes takes patience and guidance from others. Nevertheless, many passages on love, showing kindness, communication, and the roles of husbands and wives are just waiting to bless your life. Let God's Word guide you to be a stronger family. Be open to the depth of God's wisdom and provision for your life. Be in the Word. Share it as a couple. Share it as a family. Make it your road map for life.

SPIRITUAL FORMATION IN STEPFAMILY CHILDREN

It was a heartfelt question that I didn't know how to answer. "My kids have been through a lot," *Kara* began. "They have witnessed anger and manipulation, fights between their dad and me, six rough years living with a poor single mom, and now they have lived through a difficult stepfamily transition with three stepsiblings. How is all this going to impact their faith development?" I don't really know. I don't think anyone does.

Without question, the loss of an intact family due to a parent's death or divorce will have significant impact on a child's faith formation. Unfortunately, there has been very little research into what the positive or negative impact will be. We simply cannot say for sure. Some stepfamily children will likely demonstrate an increase in spiritual growth due to the trials they experience, as did many people in the Bible who experienced spontaneous spiritual growth due to hardship. In 2 Corinthians 1:8–11 the apostle Paul points out that a time of great stress led him to a deeper reliance on God. For some children and adults, loss and pain lead to a greater trust in the Lord. But parents need to face the fact that, while some positive outcome is possible, the impact on many children will be detrimental.

Family and Faith

God's plan for making himself known to children has always been centered on the family. Psalm 78:1–8 captures the essence of that plan:

> O my people, hear my teaching;
>> listen to the words of my mouth.
> I will open my mouth in parables,
> I will utter hidden things, things from of old—
>> what we have heard and known,
>> what our fathers have told us.
> We will not hide them from their children;
>> we will tell the next generation
>> the praiseworthy deeds of the Lord,
>> his power, and the wonders he has done.
> He decreed statutes for Jacob
>> and established the law in Israel,
>> which he commanded our forefathers
>> to teach their children,
> so the next generation would know them,
>> even the children yet to be born,
>> and they in turn would tell their children.
> Then they would put their trust in God

and would not forget his deeds
but would keep his commands.
They would not be like their forefathers—
a stubborn and rebellious generation,
whose hearts were not loyal to God,
whose spirits were not faithful to him.

Children come to know God when the stories around them point to God's mighty works and love. And it is parents who are handed the responsibility to tell their children the stories of God. Parents tell these stories in three ways.

Share the biblical story of God's work in the world and the sacrifice of Jesus Christ. Parents and stepparents must be diligent in impressing upon children the commandments of God. In Deuteronomy 6:7–9 Moses instructs the people to share the commands of God throughout the natural rhythms of everyday living. When you're driving to school, coaching a soccer team, or making decisions about money, share with your children how your relationship to God is influencing your thinking and behavior. The goal is to train your children to quite naturally think of God in the big and little moments of life.

Share your personal faith stories. Telling children the stories of God also occurs when parents and stepparents share their personal stories, including their peaks and valleys and times of plenty and drought. Most adults have never told their children how they came to know the Lord or about the key people throughout their life that have deepened their conviction and knowledge of God. This is one of the most significant stories parents can share, because it extends beyond the biblical stories of God's work in the world to modern times—even to the child's own heritage. Even sharing the valleys or dark days of your spiritual walk is helpful. Instead of showing your children or stepchildren that you were weak (as many people fear), it shows how God can be counted on to extend mercy. It also reveals the imperfections of our faith and conveys the value of "coming home to the Lord." Simply put, sharing your faith story adds an array of color to the black and white of the Bible.

Recently some friends of ours had a difficult time being open to God's direction when a military commitment was to take them far from extended family to an unfamiliar part of the country. They struggled with what they hoped to see happen, but when their prayers were answered "No," *Greg* and *Elisa* eventually found peace in submission and blind trust. Because their two daughters were too young to comprehend the significance of the trial, I suggested they write their girls a letter about the experience—a letter the girls would read in adolescence when the testimony of Mom and Dad's faith would mean something. Through this letter a current natural rhythm of life could still be a teachable moment later in life.

Live your faith. Telling the stories of God includes parents living out an unmistakable faith story in front of their children. Modeling a dedicated walk is far and above the most important story parents "tell" their children. Years ago someone shared with me part of a poem that captures the importance of example.

I'd rather see a sermon than hear one any day.
I'd rather one should walk with me than merely show the way.
The eye's a better pupil and more willing than the ear,
Fine counsel is confusing, but example's always clear.
　—Edgar A. Guest (1881–1959)

Life is a story. If your life story isn't oriented around a relationship with Christ, your children will view Sunday school and family devotions as interesting experiences, but nothing of true lasting significance. In order for truth to come alive, it must be lived out in front of our children. Otherwise, truth is just one concept in a world full of alternative philosophies.

Fathers, tell a specific story about God. It occurred to me years ago that as a father I had a tremendous task: to be the first positive impression my children would have of God. Children generally formulate their first picture and impression of their heavenly Father based on their experience with their earthly father. Just as God created man in his image, men (we dads) "create" God in our image.[6] If you are distant and unavailable, your children may have difficulty sensing God's presence or trusting his work in their life. If you explode in anger when your children make mistakes, guess from whom they will run after giving in to sin? If you are rigid and punitive, God easily becomes someone to fear, not draw near to. Consider Martin Luther's statement: "I have difficulty praying the Lord's Prayer because whenever I say 'Our Father,' I think of my own father, who was hard, unyielding, and relentless. I cannot help but think of God in that way." Your influence and behavior as a father is critical to your child's spiritual development. Some stepfathers will also have this kind of influence on their stepchildren, especially stepfathers of young children who become their second concrete image of God. Since your stepchildren have a biological father, who is also creating an image of God, you can never be sure to what extent your stepchildren are "listening" to your behavior. The task, then, is to live as if your example is all they will ever hear.

Will we ever be perfect fathers? I know I'm not. (Asking my children for forgiveness happens much more often than I'd like.) But the challenge is to give our children a taste of who God is—a taste that arouses their thirst for more. We are God's ambassadors; not just of his message but of his image. We have the opportunity to model for our children a heavenly Father who is thrilled with the presence of his children and who longs to be with them. That kind of introduction to God comes primarily through our life story. Dad and Stepdad, what kind of story is your child reading from your life?

Families also have a life story. It can be one of faithfulness or selfishness, sacrifice or self-preservation, warmth or coldness, safety or insecurity, unconditional love or conditional rejection. All of these aspects of family combine to create a culture that either encourages or discourages spiritual relationship with God. If a child's experience of family is one of chaos, where parents are not in charge and children having few boundaries learn self-indulgence, why would the difficult and narrow road of discipleship be attractive? If the family is abusive or neglectful, anger is easily shifted toward God, who—from the child's perspective—seems to have abandoned the child. On the other hand, wouldn't children who experience love, limits, and stability in their home be more likely to find a relationship with Christ? What if a child witnesses love between the marital partners? Wouldn't that improve the chances of a growing faith? One body of research discovered that adolescents whose parents were happily married were almost fifteen times more likely to take God seriously than teens whose parents were unhappily married.[7] So what about children whose parents divorce and remarry?

Divorce and Faith Formation

Early in this new millennium a friendly debate has developed between researchers over the long-term impact of divorce on children. Many of the conclusions are based on the well-being, short-term and long, of children. Unfortunately, well-being is generally limited to aspects like academic performance, juvenile delinquency, vocational aptitude, and the presence of mood disturbances or drug problems. But what of moral behavior?

One well-respected researcher, Mavis Hetherington, who concluded that only 20 percent of children from divorced homes have long-term emotional, psychological, and behavioral difficulties following parental divorce, also recognized what I call a significant impact in moral behavior.[8] When compared to their parents—who were mostly raised in the '60s, no less—children of divorce emerged more self-serving and materialistic. Hetherington cites a number of specific examples related to sex, cohabitation, and childbearing: While 10 percent of their parents were sexually active by age fifteen, half of the children of divorce were; less than 5 percent of their parents cohabited before marriage, but half of the children did; 20 percent of their parents said cohabitation was a good trial marriage compared to 80 percent of the children. Finally, she noted that almost 20 percent of children of divorce gave birth out of wedlock and 58 percent had had an abortion.[9]

Without question, the challenges of parental divorce and stepfamily adjustment impact child and young adult spiritual decision-making and behavior, which in turn brings complicating consequences to adult spirituality. In addition to an impact in moral behavior, there also seems to be an impact in understanding the biblical narrative and matters of faith.

Elizabeth Marquardt has conducted numerous interviews with children of divorce and discovered that many of them cannot relate to key characters in Bible stories.[10] For example, to a child with one parent who has remained distant, the father in the parable of the Prodigal Son is unrecognizable. Even worse, when a parent abandons the faith, children experience a role reversal in which their parent is the prodigal and they are the ones left waiting for the parent's return. Other children of divorce find it difficult to keep the fourth commandment—to honor their father and mother. It's almost as if kids say, "If they didn't honor each other in marriage, why should I have to honor them?" Clearly, children whose parents have divorced bring a host of complicating emotions to their understanding of God, his Word, and matters of faith.

Even as I write these words I am well aware of how depressing this must be to you who desperately want to raise faithful children. It is also likely resurrecting your anger and guilt over a past you cannot change (don't look now, it's pursuing you again). But all hope is not lost. I remind you again of chapter 1 and the discussion of Jehovah-Rophe—the God who heals. The Creator of the universe can turn the bitter waters of life sweet once again. Part of that healing is made easier when your current stepfamily is strengthened and you model the lifestyle you want your children to adopt. While the transitions through divorce and remarriage undoubtedly derail normative faith formation stages within children, a strong, stable stepfamily, I believe, can set children back on track much of the time. Furthermore, you must intentionally create a culture of faith within your home; make the story of God come alive for your children and stepchildren.

What If the Values Being Taught in the Other Home Conflict With the Christian Faith?

"I really want my two children to love the Lord and have a relationship with their father. But when they spend time with their dad and stepmom, they are exposed to a lifestyle that goes against what the Bible teaches. What can we do? I'm tempted to discourage them from going to see their dad." *Judy's* question is one I hear repeated around the country. Christian parents want their children to grow in faith. But what can you do when the other household is leading the sheep away from the Shepherd?

Before offering specific suggestions, let me address Judy's temptation to limit the contact between her children and their father. While her desire to protect the faith of her children is understandable, becoming a barrier between the other biological parent and his children is not recommended. When this happens, children often grow to resent the parent who blocks access to the other parent. In the end, you weaken your spiritual influence. In addition, the other parent may feel cheated and retaliate, exposing your children to more conflict.

Guarding your children from every negative influence is simply not within your power. You must find other ways of influencing your children. Here are some suggestions.

First, admit that you cannot control what is taught or demonstrated in the other home. Too many people are still trying to change their ex-spouse, even after they've been divorced for years. (If you couldn't change your spouse during your marriage, what makes you think you can change this person after your divorce?) Letting go of control forces you to let God be in control of what you can't change and make the most of your time with your children.

Influence your children toward the Lord while they are in your home. All parents need to *model* the Christian walk and *impress* on their children the decrees of God (Deuteronomy 6:4–9). But you will also have to *inoculate* them. Inoculations are controlled injections of a virus; they allow the body to develop antibodies that can combat a live virus, if ever encountered. Spiritual inoculations present viewpoints that oppose the Word of God and then teach biblical concepts that help children combat them. For example, you might view and discuss a TV program that glorifies greed, and then show children a spiritual view of money and stewardship.

Children who have one parent not living a Christian life will need inoculation to help them deal with an environment that is hostile to their growing faith. It is critical, however, that you remain neutral about the other parent; the inoculation cannot be a personal attack. A comment like "Your father shouldn't be lying to his boss—he's so self-centered" pulls on children's loyalties and burdens them with your hostility. Ironically, it also diminishes your influence as they react defensively against your negativity. A more appropriate response would be, "Some people believe lying is fine when it serves a purpose. But God is truth and wants us to be honest as well. Telling the truth like God does helps us build and keep our relationship with him. Let's talk about that. . . ."

You may have to endure years of prodigal living as your children try out the values of the other home. This is a truth that many parents fear. Children may experiment with the "easier" lifestyle of the other home, especially during the teen years when they are deciding whether the faith they've been handed (inherited faith) will become their own (owned faith).[11] Lovingly admonish them toward the Lord (not away from the other parent), and be close enough to reach when they turn around.

Pray daily for the strength to walk in the light, and introduce your children to Jesus at each and every opportunity. Your model is a powerful bridge to their personal commitment to Christ. Do all that you can to take your kids "by the hand and lead them in the way of the Master" (Ephesians 6:4, THE MESSAGE).

Questions for Discussion

FOR ALL COUPLES

1. What boundaries do you have in place to deter unhealthy sexual attractions? Which ones might you need to add?
2. What aspects of healthy sexuality have you discussed with your children?
3. How much time have you dedicated to reading the Bible and learning its wisdom for your home? Pray together now and ask God to make his love come alive in your lives.
4. What fears do you have regarding your children's faith formation?
5. What strategies for faith training did this chapter suggest that you are not doing well?
6. How well does your walk match your talk?
7. How are the spiritual values of your child's two homes different? What are you doing to inoculate them against non-Christian messages?

FOR PRE-REMARITAL COUPLES

1. Discuss the potential impact of sexuality on your family and boundaries you will adopt.
2. Prior to remarriage I believe it is very important for couples to seriously consider scriptural guidelines for remarriage. I strongly encourage you to arrange a meeting with your minister to discuss this matter.
3. Discuss God's design for husband-wife roles in marriage. What does it mean, practically speaking, for the husband to be the head or servant-leader of the home (Ephesians 5:21–33)? What does it mean for a woman to be a husband—and child—lover (Titus 2:4–5)?

4. Discuss your expectations for the stepparent regarding spiritual training.

5. Begin now to make prayer and informal, spontaneous discussions about God's role in your life a regular family practice. Develop your game plan for spiritual formation for yourselves and your children.

CHAPTER TEN

Smart Step Seven: STEP Over

Into the Promised Land: Stories of those who are making it

"After the death of Moses . . . the Lord said to Joshua . . . 'You and all these people, get ready to cross the Jordan River into the land I am about to give to them . . . as I promised Moses. . . . Be strong and courageous, because you will lead these people to inherit the land I swore to their forefathers to give them. Be strong and very courageous. Be careful to obey all the law my servant Moses gave you; do not turn from it to the right or to the left, that you may be successful wherever you go' " (Joshua 1:1–3, 6–7).

Is there hope for the weary? Yes, there is.

Because of their lack of faithfulness, God prohibited the Israelites from entering the Promised Land for forty years; the journey could have taken only a week. At the end of their long wilderness wandering, I'm certain they were weary. But as they finally stood on the brink of their destination, the reward for completing the journey lay just ahead. All they had to do was cross the Jordan and lay claim to the land God had promised.

But God could see that they needed some final encouragement. Moses, their steadfast leader, was dead, and Joshua had been granted leadership. And once they crossed the Jordan into the Promised Land, a fury of battles awaited them as they claimed the land. Joshua and the people needed a boost to their courage, and the Lord gave it to them: "Be strong and courageous . . . for the Lord your God will be with you wherever you go" (Joshua 1:9).

The trip to the Promised Land for most stepfamilies is sprinkled with uncertainty and frustrating dilemmas. Yet many have done more than survive the journey; they have learned to thrive with what their Crockpot produces. Rarely does a stepfamily turn out to be what each cook in the beginning dreamed it would be. However, for those who remain open to accepting the relationships that develop, imperfections and all, the new family can be an enjoyable and fulfilling one.

Perhaps you are standing on the brink of your Promised Land and don't even know it. Just one more river to cross and a few more battles to face, and the reward is yours. Yet you need some final encouragement.

This chapter shares the stories of a few who, to one degree or another, are tasting the fruits of the Promised Land. Some of the accounts are from a stepfamily member's point of view; others are shared by me. You'll notice that experiencing Promised Land Payoffs does not mean the end of hard work. Family life presents challenges from the cradle to the grave. Yet attaining some measure of stepfamily integration does create a spirit of togetherness and love that makes dealing with life's circumstances so much easier. I offer these stories to inspire and challenge you. These are not perfect people, just fellow travelers.

If, after reading their stories, you'd like to offer encouragement to others, you can submit your Promised Land journey online. Go to *www.SuccessfulStepfamilies.com*, click on Promised Land Stepfamilies, and write your story (anonymously, if you prefer). It will be shared with thousands of others who are themselves seeking hope and inspiration.

"Not Exactly What I Planned, But Life Has Been Good"

BARRY *My life didn't exactly go as planned. I never intended to be a public schoolteacher, and I never intended to be a stepparent. Both of those things have happened, and I wouldn't trade those experiences for the whole world. I prayed for years about one day having the right kind of wife, and God most graciously answered that prayer in a way that exceeded my hopes. I married Lisa seventeen years ago (at age thirty-four) for all the right reasons. We had become the best of friends and that relationship blossomed into the kind of love that makes for a strong marriage. Our commitment to each other was based completely on our commitment to God. Our plan, from the very beginning, was to put him first.*

Lisa had two children: Kevin, thirteen, and Haley, five. Lisa had been divorced for about three years, and, as expected, Kevin was not entirely thrilled with the "dude" Mom was going to marry. Haley was excited and told me a day before the wedding that she would be calling me Dad. I felt more than a little uncomfortable with that, since her real dad lived about twenty miles away.

We thought it was a brilliant idea to involve both kids in the wedding—Kevin as best man and Haley as flower girl. It worked out quite well, but I'm not entirely sure that it was good for Kevin. It was clear that he was fond of me, but his feeling of being disloyal to his dad was also obvious.

Maybe our situation is unique, but the kids' father seemed to relinquish "dadship" to me over the next few years. He did pay the required child support (with occasional prodding) but lost touch with the kids more and more as time passed. Kevin spent several weekends with him at first, but Haley really spent very little time with him at all. The frequency of those visits decreased; he eventually moved away. It has been quite difficult, at times, to keep my opinions to myself, but I think both Lisa and I have been pretty successful at avoiding criticizing the kids' father and thus increasing their feelings of disloyalty. While his actions made my role simpler, I have always felt sorry for him in that he missed getting to know two wonderful people.

It would have been helpful if I had had some kind of training in the art of stepparenting. Like most, I was shooting from the hip. It seemed reasonable that I could not immediately become a real parent. It was evident that we could easily have problems if I tried to be the primary disciplinarian of the family, especially with Kevin. Lisa filled that role very well until the kids and I had a good working relationship. I'm not really sure how long that took, although it was certainly longer with Kevin than with Haley. I think it may have been four or five years before he was very comfortable with me.

Life with a stepfamily has hardly been problem-free. Name almost

*any kind of bad decision a teenager can make and our kids have made
it. The heartaches caused by these decisions can truly test a parent's
faith and emotional stability. I suspect the pain is about the same for a
stepparent as for a biological one. It is easy to see how that pressure can
strain even a good marriage. Lisa and I leaned on each other and our
faith to get us through. There were times when some outside advice
would have been good. However, I didn't know about any stepparent
support groups, and our church didn't have one then. Most of our
friends couldn't relate to stepfamily problems and their innate complexity, because theirs were traditional nuclear families. We depended
upon the power of prayer to survive (sometimes it seems like survival).*

*Our family has survived so far; perhaps we can say prevailed rather
than survived. Both Kevin and Haley (now thirty and twenty-two) have
indeed grown up. Kevin is married with two fine sons; he is ready to
face parenthood. Haley is now an unwed mom with an infant daughter. We know that hers will be an uphill struggle as a single mother, but
we believe that she has matured greatly in the past year, and she has
turned in the right direction for help.*

*Getting kids past age twenty-one is not the end of parenthood.
Problems and heartaches are still present. I'm not really sure if either
Kevin or Haley has made any kind of resolution about their biological
father. He does keep in touch to a degree, but both harbor a great deal
of anger and resentment. Lisa and I wish we could help, but we have
no idea how to do it.*

*Even with all the problems, being a stepparent has been a faith-
building experience. Both Lisa and I realize that we could not have
survived without direct help from God. Knowing that the Lord helps
you in very practical, everyday ways does wonders for your faith.*

*It is most rewarding to know that you can have a good adult rela-
tionship with a stepchild. Kevin and I are friends. He lets his boys know
that I am "paw-paw." Earlier I mentioned that Haley started calling me
Dad before the wedding day—it overwhelms me that she has kept that
commitment even till now. Never one time has she ever said or hinted
that I am not her real father.*

Life hasn't been exactly as I planned, but life has been good.

"God Has Taught Us a Lot"

CINDY RAYMOND *Eleven years ago I entered the doors of this church to attend a divorce recovery seminar. After a year of bouncing back and forth between churches, God led me to make Second Baptist a home for my two boys and me. God used the next five years to teach me about his love and faithfulness, his provision and plan, and most important, his forgiveness and healing.*

My husband came to Second Baptist through similar circumstances. After years of living as a single dad, his daughters came to live with him full time. In his search to provide something more for his girls, he made Second Baptist their home as well.

As God designed it, we met at a wedding. We ran into each other again several weeks later at a Wednesday night service. As we spent more and more time together, we found we had a lot in common. We had both been married and divorced for about the same length of time. We both wanted something different for our children and ourselves. We both wanted our children raised in a Christ-centered home. We believed we should set a godly example while we dated. We were both very conscious of trying to do things God's way. We had been given a second chance, and all the pieces fit.

I have two boys. He has two girls. We weren't the Brady Bunch, but that must be because we don't have an Alice. Surrounded by family and friends, we had a wedding in December with our children standing with us. We weren't marrying only as a couple; we were marrying as a family. We were all active participants in the charges and vows. As we left for a brief honeymoon, we were full of hope and eager to start the journey together.

As we celebrated our first Christmas, a new life, and a new year, the fragile stability of our new family began to crumble. One morning we woke up like Dorothy and Toto to find we weren't in Kansas anymore. I assumed (a critical error, don't ever assume anything in a stepfamily) our relationship with each other and with each other's children would just get better after we said "I do." But three weeks into the marriage my husband's older daughter decided to leave our home and move back with her mother.

Nothing had prepared us for the storms that awaited us following that one decision. We knew we were in God's will, but we were ill equipped to deal with the challenges we would face. Some of our challenges were extreme, but some of them are faced by every stepfamily. We had to cope with weekend visitations, holiday traditions constantly changing, extended family households with different moral values, and broken promises by ex-spouses. We had to face emergency room visits involving old and new extended families, three trips to court to modify custody issues, calls from the school counselor, and family wanting to support us but not having a clue as to what to say or do. We had weeks of feeling discouraged and defeated. We knew about God's design for the family—but how did that design fit the stepfamily?

We faced unmet expectations. Our husband-wife relationship took a beating every time a new crisis arose. Trying to keep God number one and our relationship number two became a daily struggle. The stresses of defending our children took its toll. Trying to make everything equal and fair was exhausting. I had heard divorce was easier the second time around so I began to consider, "I know I'll live through another divorce and life will go on. . . ." But we had done marriage differently this time. We made a covenant with God, and divorce was not an option. (Some days that covenant and our foundation in Christ were all we had.)

God has taught us a lot over the last six years. He loves us and wants us to succeed, and he is rewarding our efforts. We haven't done it alone. We sought godly counsel. We have surrounded ourselves with strong Christian friends who have challenged us to remain faithful no matter how hopeless the situation looks. We have learned to expect the unexpected. We are learning about patience, grace, and forgiveness. Some days we still wonder if we will ever be "blended." In fact, we still have crises to deal with. Just this year one son had knee surgery, my husband was diagnosed with cancer, and our other son broke his leg. The difference is we are handling these situations as a family and not separate parts of a whole. God has given us both a strong determination to survive the odds. And we both know there is one thing that never changes—our commitment to Christ and knowing our hope is in him and that he has a plan for our lives.

"We're Having Problems Making This New Family Work"

PERRY, FAMILY THERAPIST *Kevin and Jamie had been married just seven months when they decided to see their congregation's family therapist. Their newly formed stepfamily, comprised of themselves and Kevin's three daughters, seemed to start off well but was taking a predictable turn into frustration. Kevin and Jamie's initial reason for seeking counseling was to improve the level of trust and communication in their marriage and to help their stepfamily integrate. Despite their amazingly proactive attitude, it didn't take long for some typical stepfamily problems to surface.*

Kevin is a talented, hardworking carpenter, and Jamie is a creative graphic artist. Jamie had been married twice before; Kevin once. His three were thirteen, twelve, and nine years old at the time they remarried. The three girls visited their mother twice each month and had a strong loyalty to her. The rules in Mom's house and Dad's house were quite different, and the girls frequently voiced their disdain for Jamie's need for cleanliness. The girls showed a preference for their mom and her ways whenever they could. Jamie took this very personally. It was especially difficult for her because she had always wanted children of her own, but a tubal pregnancy and struggles with infertility had kept her from having children. Coming into the marriage with Kevin, she fantasized about a mother-daughter relationship with his girls. After all, their mother had, in Kevin's opinion, been a terrible model for the girls. Jamie thought it was a perfect match—girls who needed a Christian mother and a woman who needed a mother's role. This expectation set up a conflict that would threaten the marriage.

Kevin admittedly was not adept at making decisions and handling conflict with his ex-spouse. Combined with his desire for Jamie and his girls to form a close bond, Kevin began to turn responsibilities regarding the girls over to her. He even let Jamie negotiate with his ex-wife, since arguments and anger were always the result whenever he spoke directly to her. This, however, only set Jamie up for further conflict with the girls, who resented her high structure, expectations, and authority.

Early in therapy Kevin and Jamie began to understand that the process of integration doesn't happen instantly, and they began grieving the unrealistic expectation that love would occur quickly. They learned to compartmentalize their marital relationship and give Kevin exclusive time with his girls (Jamie spent time with her craft hobby as a deterrent to feeling left out). Kevin stepped up to the plate and started dealing with his girls and ex-wife directly, taking Jamie out of the middle. Jamie learned that trying to force herself into the mother role only brought resistance from her stepdaughters. For example, instead of openly criticizing their mother, she learned to compliment her (and save her criticism for private conversations with Kevin). This freed Jamie from the burden of fighting with the girls and reduced the jealousy between Jamie and Kevin's ex-wife.

Despite these changes, a pervasive resentment that the family was not "working like a real family" continued for both Kevin and Jamie. Kevin resented Jamie for not "loving my girls the way she should." Jamie openly criticized the girls when she felt treated like an outsider. The girls responded predictably. "If she calls us slobs, then why not be one?" The stress of distant stepmother-stepdaughter relationships was taking a great toll on the family. With time, Jamie came to understand that her stepdaughters' loyalty to their mother just wouldn't make room for her (and her critical attitude wasn't helping). She needed to lower her expectations and give them her permission to honor their mother. For Jamie, that was a significant but challenging step.

Relationship struggles early in the marriage primarily centered around the relationship triangle of Kevin, Jamie, and her stepdaughters. Once some of those issues began to settle down, other marital struggles became salient. The couple complained of communication problems and had different opinions on how to experience intimacy and fun. Recurring conflicts, such as the division of household chores and how much say Jamie should have in Kevin's negotiations with his ex-wife, were not handled with much success. Jamie would aggressively pursue the issues, while Kevin would withdraw from what he felt was a no-win situation. The resulting distance only added to their frustration and negativity. But time and effort in therapy allowed the couple to learn how to communicate as a team. Negative cycles of interaction were broken, and the two began to speak to one another with respect. Anger and frustration were channeled and controlled. Kevin learned to listen to Jamie's frustrations without defending his daughters and gained strength in expressing his feelings. Jamie found ways to accept her outsider position and have compassion on her stepdaughters. For both, tongue-lashing diminished and a sense of partnership increased.

Kevin and Jamie were becoming a smart stepfamily. With much effort they had come to accept their differentness as a stepfamily and applied proven principles to their problems. In the meantime, the Crockpot continued slow cooking, and eventually the family began to experience some rewards. Kevin and Jamie's marriage grew stronger and more satisfying. Jamie's relationship with her stepdaughters developed slowly to the point of sharing mutual respect and affection.

But a trip to the Promised Land didn't mean the end of stress. Kevin still gets frustrated when dealing with his ex-wife; Jamie still feels left out at times (even though she understands why); and the girls' journey into adolescence has reignited some of the philosophical parenting differences Kevin and Jamie debated early on. Such is life. The journey continues.

"A Work in Progress"

Shawn has one daughter, twenty-one. His first wife, *Andrea*, died of cancer at a young age. At forty-six, Shawn married a divorced mother of two: *Elisa*, fifteen, and *Bobbie*, eleven. While the stepfamily seemed to have a smooth beginning, it didn't take long for sides to be taken, and Shawn and Elisa's relationship became quite conflicted. Elisa's rejection of Shawn wasn't entirely personal (very often the rejection of a stepparent has more to do with the past than the present). Nevertheless, Shawn found it difficult not to feel wounded every time she would show her opposition. After much prayer and consideration, Shawn felt it necessary to reach out to Elisa and communicate his wishes and desires for their relationship.

His letter to Elisa illustrates a balanced understanding of stepfamily life at work. Shawn shows great compassion and objectivity, effectively communicating his position in relationship to Elisa. The letter didn't magically transport Shawn and Elisa to the Promised Land. Rather, the letter represents an intentional effort to keep stepping in the right direction. Observe perseverance at work, listening and understanding being conveyed, and patience winning out over pressure.

Dear Elisa,

We've never had the chance to sit down and share how we feel about my becoming a part of your household and vice versa. Since I'm not as good with words as you, this letter will share some of my thoughts and feelings so you will have the chance to understand more of where I am coming from.

First of all, I want you to know that it would have been my desire for your dad and mom to be together and that you and Bobbie grow up in a normal family relationship. That is the way God intended it, and it is the way that human beings were meant to live. But that is not reality; and it is reality that each of us must live with and function in.

I wish my first wife, Andrea, were still here as well and that Janice [Shawn's daughter] still had her mother to lean on and enjoy. But that is not the case. She is buried at a cemetery in Ohio. What is true is that Janice's mom would want her to go on with her life and become all she can be. With God's help, good lives can come from bad situations. God has given Janice many friends and stand-in mothers to help her go forward.

And I am thankful that God has given me a new companion, that your mom has joined my life, and that we have each other to lean on, to enjoy, and to build a new life with. We are stronger together than trying to make it alone on our own. And we can help you grow up to be all you can be better together than if your mom continued to struggle alone. I think you really know that already.

Given the realities that we have, here are some things I want for you.

I want for you to continue to have a loving and caring relationship with your father, Gary. He is your dad, and you should enjoy all that you can with him. He loves you and has done a good job of showing you that love. I know you love him too.

I want for you to continue to have the special relationship I see with your mom. My presence in her life should be one that helps her to love, support, and develop you. I am not here to take her away from you.

I want for the four of us (you, Bobbie, your mom, and me) and Janice (when she is here) to share this nice house and the life we have been given in a way that makes us all we can be—sharing, caring, supporting, and just enjoying life. This is not a combat zone. It is a refuge. There are plenty of other obstacles and enemies out there in the world. I once told a junior high school student that she needed to figure out who her friends were. All of us in this household are friends, and we will stand together against those outside who would tear us down.

I want to be there for you and to help you in whatever ways I am able. At the same time, I cannot allow you to "machine gun" me, and I will not voluntarily stand in the aim of your gunsights. I really believe your goals are the same as those of your mom and me. If we can get on the same page, we can all get on with God's plan for our lives.

Most of all, I want for you to find a place to stand in the midst of the chaos, uncertainty, and instability that life has placed you in. I once had the opportunity to spend a weekend with a wise man who had written a book called A Place to Stand. *In it he explained that only when we place our lives in God's hands and follow the path of Jesus can we really stand up to the difficulties that come our way. So I want for you a close relationship with God. I want you to be able to "cast your cares on Him, because he cares for you." A guy named Peter once wrote that to some folk whose families were being torn apart and whose lives had disintegrated. He promised them that God cares for them and that he would sustain them and guide them through the chaos. I want you to know the same peace that was available to those he was writing to.*

Finally, Elisa, I want you to become all that you can be. You have been given health, a very intelligent brain, a wonderful mother, a caring dad, an ability to articulate your thoughts that is well beyond your years, a talent for playing music and participating in the arts, a natural aptitude for cooking, and a tender heart that cares for animals like Aggie and people like your parents and your friends. Your mom has begun the process of polishing some of the rough edges in your life. These include some of the social skills such as your behavior in school and keeping an orderly room. Please try to view these as areas that will help you in the long run, even if they seem harsh or unreasonable at the present.

Elisa, I do not believe that God has presented the challenges you have faced already in life to have you fail. He does not want evil in your life, but he has allowed some difficulties to strengthen you for doing his purpose in the future. I want for you to trust that he is capable, that he does care for you . . . and then I want for you to choose to behave in ways that result in positive growth rather than ways that are destructive to yourself and others.

If you do these things, you will be happier and you will be able to better care for those around you. God has given you the responsibility of extending love, affection, and care to others—beginning with your dad, mom, and brother. I hope you will choose to rise above the pain, to know joy, and to become who you were meant to be. Another wise man has written that our problems are seldom caused by us, but they are ours. And it is in the way we step up to these problems that determines who we are, who we become, and how others view us.

Few of us can handle all of life alone. I can help you, but you must first invite me in. I will be here if and when you choose to do that.

Your stepfather,
Shawn

"A Spiritual Journey Home"

"You know what the meaning of life is?" asks Jack Palance's character in the movie *City Slickers*. "Just one thing. You stick to that and everything else just doesn't matter." He's right, you know. In the movie, the "one thing" is relative—it's anything you decide it to be. But the objective truth is that only a relationship with God really matters. You can have a wonderful career, beautiful children, a loving stepfamily, and still have no hope once your last breath has passed. It is a spiritual journey with Christ that gives eternal hope.

But the Christian has more reason to pursue God than just the hope of heaven. First Timothy 4:8 tells us that godliness has "promise for both the present life and the life to come." It's what I call the double pleasure of Christianity. The hope of heaven and the best and most fulfilling life possible here on earth. The Creator of the universe established an incredible truth when he formed mankind as a relational being: A loving, obedient relationship with God increases our ability to love one another. Loving God first enhances our earthly relationships.

Yet the spiritual journey of many in stepfamilies is a rocky one. The heartache of divorce and the ensuing spiritual judgment that many receive from extended family and those in the church makes an active relationship with God difficult. In addition, the sense of being unworthy of God's grace often holds people back from claiming their life in Christ (see chapter 4).

This story, by one of my dearest and most respected friends, represents the journey of one prodigal back home. For James, building a successful stepfamily started with his willingness to step up. Perhaps yours will too.

James Caldwell:
A Message From a Fellow Sinner

Many of you reading this book had no active part in your divorce. I understand that many divorces have a "victim" and a "bad guy." This letter is to the "bad guys" who really, really want to walk out of the darkness and into the light and love of Jesus Christ.

Hi, my name is James. I am a serial sinner. I walked in a very dark world for thirty-seven years. My sins were many, and with each one my distance from God grew and my destructiveness increased. Why am I interested in stepfamilies and this book? Because I live in a stepfamily, and the author of this book demonstrated to me the acceptance of God when I decided to repent and be baptized into the family of God.

Faith in God, not man, is the key. Many times prior to my baptism two years ago, I attempted to get my life straight. I would attend church somewhere, justify the relationship I was in at the time, and because I needed acceptance, would look for people who believed in me. I would then set out to do better. That's where my spiritual effort would hit a snag. Eventually, I would drop out of the congregation and return to a sinful existence. The basic problem had to do with who was in control of my life—I was. God was not allowed to be Chief Architect.

Every time my halfhearted repentance failed, more of my friends and family began to give up on me, and I grew more deeply ashamed. Each cycle would result in fewer people who accepted me as a person and more reluctance on my part to go back and try to be "good" again.

Does this cycle sound familiar? If it does, read on. Until we, the adults in stepfamilies, overcome the sin that enslaves us, we will be powerless to effect positive change in our families. The fact that you are reading this book demonstrates one thing: you have a desire to change. Somewhere in your heart is the longing to come home. Relationship with God is what you are longing for. He is calling you to be a part of his kingdom. God wants you to come home. The question is *how?* It's easy to feel defeated. *What will the people of the church think if I come back? Will they let me?* If you share these doubts, understand they come from Satan's influence. He wants to keep you on ice, helpless under his control. But you must not let what other people think keep you from pursuing a relationship with Jesus Christ.

The first step is to realize that "all have sinned and fall short of the glory of God" (Romans 3:23). We are not the only sinners. Maybe our sins are more public, perhaps even more numerous. But the reality is we are all sinners, and salvation is offered to all of us.

The second step is the recognition that we are helpless. No matter how much we want to be better, we can't in our own strength. What can we do? We can claim God's redemptive power and rely on His Spirit to help us change our lives.

Step three is the tough one: repentance. The Samaritan woman at the well (John 4) and the woman caught in the act of adultery (John 8) were both made whole through faith in Christ. The departing words of Jesus to one woman still ring in my ears: "Go and sin no more." But that is so tough. Whether your habit is alcohol, drugs, sex, pornography, workaholism, or just plain laziness, God and only God can lift it. The miracle of salvation does not protect us from future temptation; that is a daily battle. To win, we must arm ourselves with God's words, surround ourselves with fellow believers, and pursue God with greater enthusiasm than we pursued evil. We must walk away from the activities, lifestyles, friends, and habits that led to sin. This distancing of ourselves from these things is a crucial element in beginning to build the family we really want.

Does this guarantee success? No. There are no foolproof recoveries. Am I holding myself up to say, "Look at me"? Hardly. I live in shame of my past and in hope of my future. Is the effort worth it? For me—yes. For instance, since my baptism, I have seen my two stepchildren baptized. The legacy God has started in my step-children is wonderful. But a life rededicated to Christ will not negate the consequences of our previous sin. I have a son who does not speak to me. He is angry and resentful. God has promised salvation from my sins, but not the absence of consequences in this life for my sin. I experience pain daily. God has not promised to protect me from my past, and I have to be willing to accept and deal with all the consequences of it. My only hope is in him.

I love Jesus. I truly believe he has come into my life and has changed me. God accepts us as we are—dirty, hopeless, scared, and alone. He has the power to change death to life. The path is simple: confessing your sins, ask the Lord of lords to make his home with you, repent of your sins, and die to yourself in the grave of baptism. Then work harder for you and your family than you ever have at anything before. Strive for the goal of Christlike-ness.

I have wasted eighteen years serving selfish impulses and being a member of Satan's army. I hope that reading this gives you the courage to walk toward Jesus, taking your spouse and your children with you. No one person alone has the power to effect lasting change. Our belief and hope must be in God. He alone has the power to bring hope out of hopelessness, life out of death, and light into the darkness. Ron's willingness to take the time to share the hope of Jesus with my family has opened our eyes to the fact that God has been reaching out to us with love and care for all these years. God has not placed limits on his ability to forgive; man has done that. God is waiting to forgive and to build something special inside every human being—even you! A fresh start is available to all of us. A fresh start that can impact the kind of home your great-grandchildren will experience. God is with you in the journey.

Questions for Discussion

FOR ALL COUPLES

1. Which story do you most identify with? Why?
2. In what ways is your life not exactly what you planned? In what ways

is your life blessed, in spite of your plan?

3. What has God taught you about surrendering to his will through your family experiences?

4. What are your attitudes and feelings about those who seek counseling? How would you know if seeking outside help was a good idea?

5. Shawn's letter to his stepdaughter struck a good balance between his feelings and his stepdaughter's. Discuss that balance and what you need to change to achieve balance in your home.

6. In what ways do you need to step up to God? What parts of your life are you striving to give over to him?

Consider sharing your story at *www.SuccessfulStepfamilies.com*. You might inspire another couple to keep their journey alive.

CHAPTER ELEVEN

Smart Questions, Smart Answers

"Fools think they need no advice, but the wise listen to others" (Proverbs 12:15 NLT).

For a number of years I have been collecting questions from step-families in an attempt to understand which issues seem to be the most common. This chapter addresses some pressing questions that have not been specifically addressed in the previous chapters.

I have solicited the expertise of a number of stepfamily researchers, practitioners, and clinicians in answering some of these key questions. They have graciously volunteered their wisdom and practical knowledge for your benefit.

Anger and Unresolved Emotions

My ex-wife is bad-mouthing my new wife and me. How can we get her to see this is making life more difficult for the kids?

Anger and unresolved emotions from the previous marital breakup often lead ex-spouses to criticize each other in an effort to gain loyalty from their children or seek revenge for perceived inequalities during the marriage. In addition, the biological mother in question is probably feeling threatened by the stepmother's presence. Biological parents need to be reminded that children will always be loyal to them (unless *they* cut off contact). Bad-mouthing a stepmother is unnecessary. Children can respect and obey a stepmother—even care for her deeply—and it won't ever change the strong bond they have with a biological parent.

To help alleviate this mother's misguided fear, the stepmother and husband should each communicate to his ex-wife their desire to cooperate and not hinder the children's relationship with their mother. The stepmother, in particular, should say in a phone call or e-mail, "I want you to know that your relationship with *Beth* and *Amy* is critical to them. Please understand that I will never try to replace you or hinder your relationship with them. In fact, I'm wondering what you would like me to do to help them feel more in touch with you. Do you have any ideas? From this day forward, my commitment to you and the children is to encourage their love and respect. If there is anything I can do differently, please let me know." This may or may not impact the mother's criticism. But the hope is that this message will help her to feel less threatened and, therefore, have less need to be negative about the stepmother.

Do what you can to be Christ to anyone in the other home—even if he or she is extremely negative. You may not be able to effect any practical change in an ex-spouse, but don't be guilty of not trying.

When Does the Integration Period Begin?

Does the seven-year integration period include dating before marriage, or does this period officially begin at the wedding?

Without a doubt, what takes place prior to the wedding, including how much time is allowed for grieving losses and how much time the couple spends in courtship, impacts the length of time required for integration. However, no matter how much time is spent together before the wedding, a significant number of emotional and psychological shifts take place within both children and adults after a wedding that also impact the length of integration time.[1] What was once a warm dating relationship is now a legal, psychological tie that brings people from different families into the same house, sharing the same food and toilet paper. It's just not the same as courtship. Things change.

For example, after the wedding stepparents often feel an increase in spiritual and parental responsibility for the children. "Before the wedding they were her kids," said *Tom*. "I kept my hands off and my opinions to myself. But after we married, I felt like I needed to be a part of what was going on. After all, they were living in my house and interacting with my children." Biological parents, on the other hand, may resist an increase in stepparent involvement, perceiving it a threat to their children. Or the opposite may occur. They may hand off too much responsibility to the new stepparent, since "we're a whole family now." In addition, stepchildren who didn't mind "Mom's boyfriend" being around may resent their step-father getting in the way. And when he was Mom's boyfriend, their biological father didn't say much. After the wedding, however, they may start receiving pressuring messages not to enjoy his presence. These post-wedding psychological shifts represent new territory for the couple. In fact, it may feel as if they've started over in some ways.

The stepparent-stepchild relationship often dictates the speed of the stepfamily integration process (see chapter 7). Many factors, including the age of the children and their previous family experiences, affect how quickly a bond develops with a stepparent. Do your homework before the wedding. Move slowly through courtship and give yourself and the children plenty of time to grieve losses. Then make the children aware of your decision to marry and give them some time to get used to the idea. Involve them in the wedding when possible.[2] Daily renew your commitment to them and express unconditional love. But keep in mind that real step-family life begins with marriage. Many adjustments will have to be made, even in the best of circumstances. Take them one day at a time and keep walking with God.

Relationships With Adult Stepchildren

How do I develop a relationship with my two stepchildren who were adults when we married?

Answered by Susan J. Gamache, Ph.D., R. Psych[3]

Stepparents coming into a family with grown children can help develop positive relationships with adult children by keeping a few points in mind.

First, there is a wide variety of stepparent-stepchild relationships ranging from "almost identical to Mom or Dad" to "not at all like Mom or Dad" and everything in between. New stepparents to adult stepchildren need to remember that these young people are far beyond the age when they are available for more parents. However, they can still enjoy a warm, supportive relationship with Mom or Dad's new partner.

Begin by simply noticing what the young person finds meaningful or interesting in life. You do not need to like it yourself to appreciate that it is important to them. You can do a lot for a smooth beginning by accepting them as they are. A word of caution here: The family already has a long history that you cannot change. If you are noticing things that seem strange or uncomfortable for you, speak to your partner about them. Try to understand how it got to be this way. The better you and your partner can communicate about these aspects of family life, the easier it will be for you to compassionately accept the family idiosyncrasies. If things are very strained between your partner and his or her children, you will not be able to fix it. Sometimes just being a "fair witness" to what is going on can be a valuable contribution and can make you a safe person for family members to get close to. However, getting hooked into trying to get the family to change is a good way to alienate everyone.

Second, families go on forever. You have all the time you need to establish warm relationships. If the stepchildren are college age and not terribly interested in family, this is natural. Be patient. Once grandbabies are on the scene, a whole new family life cycle will begin.

Third, you may find yourself developing stronger ties with young stepgrandchildren than with their parents. In other words, the grandchildren may consider you Granny or Gramps, while their parents don't consider you a parent. This may feel a bit awkward, but it makes perfect sense. Young children are wide open to attachment with adults. Providing your relationship with them is warm and responsive, the young children will include you in their grandparent category. This provides another way to connect with adult stepchildren. Your support of them as young parents will bring you all closer together.

Memories of a Deceased Parent

How do you include memories of a stepson's deceased mother comfortably so he doesn't think everyone has forgotten her, but so that it doesn't inhibit his involvement and acceptance of his new family?

This stepmother's question reveals a common misunderstanding: letting people remember the past or relish its memories will create barriers to future attachments. It does not. Indeed, just the opposite is true. By

displaying pictures of the boy's deceased mother and listening to his stories of her life, this stepmother is paving a way for her stepson to accept
and respect her. It is not a threat to the new family for them to acknowledge the past. In fact, denying people their memories and sadness goes a
long way to sabotaging the new family.

To step forward, this stepfamily will entertain occasional and spontaneous conversations about the mother's death (a typical grieving pattern
for children) and be interested in the boy's feelings about her. If he goes
through a period of time in which he wants to discuss her frequently, the
biological parent should take an active role in the conversations. In effect,
the two (including other biological children if present) are grieving
together. This is a healthy form of family mourning. A stepparent who
encourages and allows such conversation, sometimes in her presence, is
giving her new family a wonderful gift over time.

Discipline of Nonresidential Children

**What kind of discipline should we have when our daughter visits in
the summer? Should we treat her as a visitor and try to keep the peace
or establish consequences to be enforced regarding acting out behaviors
and responsibility?**

It is tempting to be permissive with nonresidential children. Biological
parents want so badly for their children to feel good about their visit that
they frequently exempt them from house rules. This, in effect, forces everyone else in the home to accommodate the visiting child (giving far too
much power to a child). This is sure to build resentment between a stepparent and the biological parent or between residential children and the
biological parent who is displaying the double standard. The assumption
that "taking it easy on them" is the best way to give them a good experience is faulty.

Visiting children should be expected to follow house rules and participate in chores like everyone else. They will need extra reminders of the
rules and a little "grace space" as they make adjustments, but in the end,
structure is good for everyone.

A Biological Parent's Rejection

My daughter's father won't call her or pick her up for his weekend visit. When she asks why she can't see her dad, what is the best thing to say?

Watching your child suffer rejection from an uninvolved and uninterested parent is heartbreaking. I've observed that a parent who promises time together and then repeatedly breaks the promise can be even harder on children. Their hopes are raised, only to be dashed on the rocks of disappointment again and again.

Jennifer's father, *Roger*, lived across the state from her and her stepfamily. He had remarried and had a new son. Roger's new marriage and stepfamily, together with a growing career, took a lot of his time. However, his guilt in not making time to be with his daughter led him to (with good intentions) promise her special weekend visits that never happened.

As Jennifer entered adolescence, she gave constant attention to the horizon, that is, to wondering if her daddy would finally keep his promises. She became increasingly oppositional toward her stepfather and mother and was unmotivated in school. Though previously a good student, her grades were failing fast and so was her mother's tolerance of her behavior. A complicating issue was Roger's subtle invitation for Jennifer to come live with him in a couple years. He conveniently blamed his ex-wife for Jennifer's trouble in school and implied everything would be better when they could finally be together. This kept father and daughter sharing a shallow intimacy brought about by the fantasy of empty promises.

Eventually Jennifer began to ask why her father didn't care to be with her. Her increasing age and cognitive abilities gave her a new ability to see through the empty promises her father had repeated numerous times. When she finally admitted her father's deception, she sank into depression and self-blame. Her mother asked what she should say to help Jennifer.

I reminded her mother that no explanation would take away the pain. Parents cannot take away a child's grief; they can only help them cope with reality. I suggested that it was okay for this mother to share her anger toward Roger, but that she should then turn any conversations toward Jennifer and her feelings. In response to Jennifer's statement, "It's like Dad thinks paying child support is enough," her mother might say, "This is extremely hard for you, huh? It feels like your father doesn't really care. My heart is so sad for you. Tell me more about how you're feeling." Such a response communicates an understanding of her pain and validates her experience. Jennifer's mother should not openly criticize Roger ("He is a selfish man") or make excuses for him ("He's just so busy at work"). Focusing on Jennifer's feelings and helping her to develop a plan for how she will relate to her father is the best approach.

Finally, for those with younger children, a neutral explanation of why a parent is uninvolved works best. "Sometimes moms and dads do things because they don't feel good or because they are confused about what is important. [Now turn the focus back to the child's feelings.] You seem to be feeling hurt over this. Tell me about it."

Severing Bonds With an Ex-Spouse

My husband's ex-wife seems to rely on him for the most basic needs. My husband talks with his ex-wife often (sometimes daily) to discuss their children. How do I deal with feeling that she is intruding on our new marriage?

The bonds with ex-spouses are often perpetuated by unhealthy patterns. We've already discussed how anger and pain tie two people together. It is my experience that when ex-spouses are still able to call on each other for personal favors, guilt and obligation are the two dynamics at work. In chapter 6 we discussed the need to sever marital bonds and retain parental ones when spouses divorce. Personal favors, like fixing the lawn mower, comforting an ex who is hurting, or giving financial advice fall within the realm of marital exchanges. When you or your ex-spouse calls on the other for such favors, you are perpetuating an unhealthy bond. One of you has remarried, so there is no longer an obligation to conduct such favors.

New spouses are generally the first to point out what to them is an unhealthy attachment. It makes sense, of course, for them to do so because it feels to be a threat to the new marriage. Frequently their spouse will defend their actions or not recognize what is happening. Defensiveness of ongoing personal interaction usually indicates a sense of obligation or guilt that is keeping the patterns alive.

Jim's ex-wife would call him to fix the screen door and he would rush over to do it. His third wife, Ann, couldn't understand why he felt the need and wondered if it represented a flicker of romantic interest in her. But to understand his sense of obligation, look at how the divorce and remarriage occurred. Jim had an affair with Ann that eventually ended his marriage. The affair and remarriage took place during a time of spiritual rebellion. Later, when Jim realized his sin, he confessed, repented, and returned to the Lord. It was at this time that his eyes were opened to the consequences his sin had on both his children and his ex-wife. He couldn't help but feel he had to make it up to them. At the same time, his ex-wife still longed for Jim to come home. Her emotional attachments to Jim were very strong, and she enjoyed any opportunity to talk with him. Veiled as issues related to the children, she would call Jim and ask personal favors like fixing the door. Jim would respond, thinking, *I've left her without someone to help her. I need to do this for her.* What Jim didn't realize was that responding to his ex-wife's requests fed her interest in him, resulting in more and more requests.

While the spiritual and practical consequences of Jim's affair and divorce are tremendous (particularly on his children), the truth of the matter is this: He is now married to Ann and should honor that commitment completely. Yes, his relationship with his children is important, and he should strive to be the best father and co-parent possible. His obligations to cooperate with his ex-wife regarding the children are still in place. However, a line should be drawn between parental and marital issues.

The next time a request is made, Jim should take time to evaluate (he doesn't have to give his ex an immediate answer on the phone) whether it is a parental or personal (marital) issue. If it is personal, he needs to respond kindly and respectfully with a *no*. For example, "I know in the past I would help you with house maintenance, but I don't think fixing the screen door is my obligation. I'm going to have to say no this time. How did Mark do on his math test?"

Finally, conversations about the children can be excessive and, therefore, personal as well. The amount of time that you and your ex-spouse speak about the children can create a false personal intimacy. Let your co-parental conversations be respectful, businesslike, and only as long as necessary. Then invest your extra time in your children and new marriage.

Reducing Friction and Tension

What is my role as the biological parent in reducing friction and tension in our home?

Answered by Craig A. Everett, Ph.D.[4]

Stepfamilies do not often work well as democracies, even when the children are adolescents. Some form of hierarchy for the parents is necessary, particularly in the early stages of forming a stepfamily (perhaps over the initial two years together). In most [step] families it is hard for the stepparent to assume much power or authority over the other parent's children. Even if this were possible, it would not be recommended because the needs of the children dictate that they have time to become familiar with and accept the new stepparent into their lives. The process of accomplishing this will vary greatly among families and often depends on the following six issues:

1. The ages and relative maturity of the children;
2. The children's preparation for and adjustment to their parents' divorce;
3. The manner in which the stepparent was introduced to the children following the divorce (or before in some cases);
4. The stepparent's relative comfort, patience, and personal resources in dealing with these stepchildren;
5. The ability of the biological parent to balance her/his new role as spouse with one's continuing role as a biological parent;
6. The relative support (as compared to sabotaging) for the biological parent and for the stepfamily that is displayed and communicated to the children by their other biological parent.

Even when remarried parents have completed family therapy and/or educational programs to enhance their understanding of stepfamily dynamics and to improve their communications and decision-making, the biological parent must remain in control of the parenting team and have the recognized power to structure and discipline when necessary. The biological parent's power can be defined and negotiated in private consultation with the stepparent. But when the stepfamily is interacting, the biological parent's power must be clearly understood and respected by the children and the stepparent.

In stepfamilies with high levels of friction and tension, particularly after the early transitions, this hierarchy is often unclear and weak. The children may perceive that their parent is in continual conflict over parenting with the stepparent. They may perceive that their parent has given authority to the stepparent, whom they neither know nor trust. They may also react toward what they perceive to be an intrusion by the stepparent into their lives and home. The biological parent may feel unsupported by his or her partner in parenting issues, and the stepparent may feel uninvolved and useless in the family.

All of these dynamics in a stepfamily can lead to internal friction and tension. The biological parent, in consultation with the new partner, needs to assert a sense of leadership and maintain a clear parenting hierarchy so that the children can feel safe and their lives can feel predictable.

Dr. Everett has offered good advice. And because this issue is a common one for biological parents, I'd like to tackle it from another angle. *Triangulation* is a term used by family therapists to describe a relational process between three people. The triangle typically involves two people whose relationship is unstable and a third person whose presence adds stability by diffusing the two-person discomfort. (Sounds technical, doesn't it?) Here's how triangulation frequently works in a stepfamily.

A stepparent and a stepchild begin to get on each other's nerves, perhaps by criticizing one another or being uncooperative. In order to bring stability to the tension, the biological parent intervenes and coaches the two parties on how to better get along. After all, who better to intervene than the one person who has a vested interest in everyone liking one another, right? Wrong. The triangulation process brings temporary stability to the two-person conflict, but sometimes it creates long-term difficulties.

While triangles can be helpful during a time of transition, a habitual pattern of triangulation can actually prevent problem solving. Biological parents should seek the delicate balance of supporting and listening to the two parties without becoming their rescuer. When a biological parent is forced into bridging every gap between a stepparent and stepchild, the two cannot ever bridge the gap themselves—they are dependent upon the biological parent for help. The irony of this stuck pattern is that the conflict is actually extended long-term due to the biological parent's involvement.

Reducing tension occurs when listening to a child's frustration is balanced with validating his concerns (without necessarily agreeing with the child's position, because agreement forms a dangerous parent-child alliance against the stepparent). It means saying, "It's time for you and Bob to work this out. Let me know how it goes." Likewise, Bob may express his frustrations about his stepchild, but still needs to himself find a way to build a bridge to the child and resolve the conflict.

This same principle applies to stepsibling (and sibling) conflict. An adult who always intervenes in child conflict robs the children of the opportunity to negotiate, learn to make trades, or find other solutions to their problems. Someone complains, "Mom, Jared took my computer game without asking." Instead of offering a solution, de-triangulate yourself and encourage the two to resolve the problem. Say, "I can see you're upset. What did Jared say when you spoke to him about that?" When the child says, "Nothing. I haven't said anything to him," you say, "Then maybe you should. I'm sure you can work this out." Then monitor the conversation from a distance. Eventually they will establish their own bridge and their own relationship.

Wanting your decision to remarry to bring joy to your children and spouse—and not pain—means wanting everyone to get along. *Not every person in your stepfamily will be happy all the time. Learn to live with other people's anxiety and unhappiness.* Even though it makes you uncomfortable, their anxiety with one another actually helps motivate them to change. If you try to help them feel better all the time, you rob them of a much-needed motivator for change.

Fair Treatment of Biological and Stepgrandchildren

How do you get grandparents to be fair toward their stepgrandchildren?

Grandparents frequently find themselves in awkward situations. Loyalty conflicts lead them to make inadvertent and purposeful decisions that reflect their close ties. For example, out of loyalty to their son, grandparents may not spend much time with grandchildren who have primary residence with their former daughter-in-law. Or the awkwardness of supporting their biological grandchildren through a difficult time of transition may lead them to be less than fair in Christmas gift-giving. To give equally expensive gifts to grandchildren and stepgrandchildren may feel like a betrayal toward their grandchildren, who are already feeling loss in the stepfamily.

No matter the motivation for previous grandparent behavior, biological parents have the responsibility to communicate their expectation that grandparents treat each child the same. This may put grandparents in an even more awkward situation (in their minds), but the standard of fairness or equity remains. Note that it is the biological parent's obligation to articulate this expectation; in most situations the stepparent doesn't carry enough clout to make the request.

To set the boundaries, say something like, "I know our situation may not be exactly as you would have it, and you can really help out the kids by doing a few things. Please treat all the children equally in things such as gift-giving and attending performances and celebrations. You can spend time with Josh and Julie [biological grandchildren] without Maddie and Camron [stepgrandchildren]. Over time, let's let Maddie and Camron show us how much time they would like with you. If they are open to it, you can really support our family by spending some time with them. I know sometimes you get in a tight spot between me and the other household, so if you ever have questions, please don't hesitate to call."

In some situations, the boundaries have been clearly articulated, but the grandparents are not interested in honoring them. You may have to set even firmer ones. "We have spoken a number of times about fair gift-giving at birthdays, but you continue to spend lots of money on Josh and Julie and barely any on Maddie and Camron. Until you can acknowledge all the children in our family fairly, we will not allow you to give gifts to any of the kids. This is important to our family and to the kids. We hope you can comply." Sometimes standing up for your family means drawing lines in the sand and sticking to them.

Differences Between Children

How do you blend children with personalities that are so different? It seems as if I am favoring my child and overly punishing my stepchild.

Answered by Francesca Adler-Baeder, Ph.D.[5]

This question is often asked by a parent in a first family about siblings and by a stepparent about stepsiblings. Children are unique individuals from the day they are born, interacting with their environments (and the people in those environments). Although we tend to think of parenting as something we "do" to children (a unidirectional model of influence), in fact, parenting is a bi-directional model of influence, meaning there is action and reaction going both ways. It makes sense, then, that each parent-child relationship has its own characteristics. Viewing parenting in this way explains why it is very difficult to interact with all children in one family exactly the same way. Differences are to be expected. The difficulty is that children become very astute at comparing and picking up on differences. They communicate these differences as "preferences" or "better or worse" treatment, or "you love her more," rather than as simply different relationships. They also are generally not capable of acknowledging or even understanding the part they play in the relationship and in your behaviors.

With sibling relationships, comparisons should be addressed by the parent with reassurances that one child is not loved more than the other, but that each one is loved "differently." In stepfamilies, responses are more complicated. In most cases a parent does have stronger emotional attachment and love for his or her biological child than the stepchild. It is okay to admit this to yourself. Step relationships take time to develop, and love relationships don't always develop between a stepparent and a stepchild; don't allow yourself to be pushed into comparing a child with a stepchild. For example, a response to a stepchild's accusation (or question) might be, "I have a different relationship with every member of this family. I don't compare them. Every member of this family is cared for, respected, and valued. We have family rules and values that apply to every person in this family."

So yes, you may be more attached to your biological child than your stepchild, and yes, different children's behaviors may elicit different responses from you. That said, there is still much that an adult can do to promote fairness and to give children (both biological and stepchildren) feelings of being cared for and valued.

Check that your "labels" for the children don't drive your responses and exaggerate qualities. In many families, there appears to be a "good kid" (who works to please parents) and a "bad kid" who is more spirited and tends to push the limits. Over time, labels (created either consciously or subconsciously by parents) set up a cycle of expected behaviors. We find validation for those expectations and express the label to the child in some form, which, in turn, sets up the child to live up to the label. "You're so lazy," "You forget everything—you have no sense of responsibility," and "You *stay* in trouble" become self-fulfilling prophecies. Also, when these attributions develop, it is highly likely that parents don't see or don't focus on behaviors to the contrary. One technique for counteracting this phenomenon when a negative cycle is established is to consciously verbalize the response "That's not like you" and then label the child what you want her to be: "You're a thoughtful person; it's not like you to walk into your sister's room and take a sweater without asking." It is much more likely that the child will begin to live up to the positive labels.

Notice positive behavior. Sometimes children establish patterns of negative behavior because this behavior gets attention—and negative attention is better than no attention. "Catch them being good" is a guideline in parenting the early years and should be a parenting tool throughout development. Research tells us that increasing the amount of positive interactions decreases the amount of negative interactions in a relationship (this is true in marriages as well). Make a point of spending more one-on-one time with your stepchild in positive activities. You may begin to see more balance in the children's behaviors and your responses to them.

Establish family rules and be consistent in enforcing them. It is much better to have a plan for behavior management than to think of consequences on the spot when misbehavior occurs. This is an especially useful approach for new stepfamilies, since stepparents should ease into a disciplinarian role with stepchildren. Enforcing "rules of the house" the way that a baby-sitter or other caregiver would is recommended for stepparents. Rules and consequences can be established with children's input. Following through, then, can be matter-of-fact. Consistency is the key to fairness among children in the household: similar responses to similar behaviors. If one has more consequences than the other, it will be understood that this is a result of their choices, not differences in your feelings for them.

Bullying Within the Stepfamily

What do you do when your child is bullying his stepbrother? It is hard not to defend my son or blame my stepson.

Answered by Sandra Volgy Everett, Ph.D.[6]

Aggressive behavior—bullying—toward other family members cannot be tolerated, regardless of whether the children are biological or step-children. Often in stepfamilies these conflicts among the children are symptomatic of difficulties the family as a whole is having in becoming attached and bonded. Such conflicts may also indicate that the adults are having difficulty creating a united co-parenting partnership. The feelings of loyalty that parents and children have toward each other often lead to differences in how discipline is understood and carried out. When your role as stepparent differs from your role with your own children, resentment and bitterness between family members can result. Of course, this can affect other areas of family functioning as well.

It is important to manage your discipline issues consistently with all the children in your family; have equal expectations based on ages and ability levels. If a child is bullying another child, take a firm stance against such aggression and create appropriate, consistent consequences for the aggressing child, whether the child is a biological child or a stepchild. It is also important to teach your children to work out their differences and feelings within a family discussion (or family meeting) rather than in an aggressive manner.

Stepfamilies often find it difficult to create appropriate discipline methods because of the history each family brings to the new stepfamily. Each is accustomed to the way discipline was handled in their prior family, and neither wishes to give up the familiarity of those methods for new ones that may not feel as comfortable or predictable. Initially, children will often resent new discipline methods, especially if those methods are more structured, consistent, or rigid than the methods they knew previously. It will help them to accept the new methods if their biological parent promotes and encourages acceptance, and if the two of you present a united front regarding the new manner in which issues will be handled.

One of the things that drew *Tim* to *Maria* was her ability to plan and structure her life. Tim had always struggled to be organized in his life and work—and in his parenting. Maria's ability to structure the family schedule and create a higher expectation for behavior had definite advantages, yet it also created many conflicts. Tim's children were not used to her high standards, nor did they take kindly to her expectation that they, too, become organized with their possessions and schoolwork. In the end, Maria kept trying to hold the children to a level of accountability that Tim would not support. Conflict between their children was common, and both parents felt defeated by the other.

Help your children accept new discipline and parenting methods by defining them in a family meeting. This way, children can have input and express their opinions. Open discussion allows for the expression of their frustration and for learning communication methods that may keep them from resorting to aggressive means of resolving disputes.

Respect for a Stepparent

My stepson doesn't follow rules or treat me with respect. My spouse feels this is allowing him the freedom to express his emotions. What should I do? How do I explain the double standard to my children?

The first issue here is the stepparent's authority. If this situation is happening within the first few years, a number of things must be in place to empower this stepparent (see chapter 7). However, let's assume the couple is working together to establish household rules and that the biological parent has communicated them clearly. Let's also assume the biological parent has communicated an expectation that the stepparent is the adult in charge when the biological parent is not present and that they should be treated with respect. What else, then, is happening?

Communicating an expectation of respect for the stepparent but then allowing misbehavior and excusing it as "freedom of expression" is a double standard that will sabotage the stepfamily's integration. Either a difference in parenting style or strong emotion is driving this biological parent. He may not really agree to the household rules or may be concerned about his son's anger over his remarriage. However, preserving his relationship with his son by sabotaging his wife's position (by not requiring respect and obedience) brings more long-term harm than good. It not only undercuts the stepmother's power, it forces a double standard on his stepchildren. Furthermore, it slowly erodes the marriage as she comes to learn he can't be trusted to support her in the family. This is not good.

Approach your husband and inquire about his fears for his son. The temptation is to approach your husband and explain why he is treating you poorly and sabotaging your position in the family. However, that is sure to instigate defensiveness on his part (you've probably already tried that, and it didn't work; why would it work now?). Try a different approach.

Focus on what he is feeling and what is driving his behavior. Help him wrestle with his fears or concerns. Then, when he feels you are on his side, explain how his behavior is harming his son (not you) long-term by destabilizing your stepfamily. Gain his cooperation and work together to find a solution. If necessary, seek outside help. Someone else may have a voice with your husband that you simply don't have.

A Hostile Noncustodial Parent

How do you deal with a hostile noncustodial biological mother (my ex-wife) who paints a wicked picture of us ("they are bad and selfish")? My wife (stepmother) doesn't stand a chance. Not only are conversations with my ex very one-sided (her way or no way), but the children are obviously influenced by her.

Answered by Jean McBride, M.S. LMFT[7]

Remarried couples face many challenges as they bring their new stepfamily together and begin to take steps to actually feel like a family. Perhaps one of the most complicated and emotionally charged of these challenges is dealing with the children's other parent. Until recently there have been almost no models of how parents and stepparents can work together for the good of the children. Instead, people have operated from more of a fear-based, adversarial position, where biological parents and stepparents competed for the coveted title of "real parent" in the eyes of the children. To effectively address this question, there are a number of points to consider.

Research tells us that stepmothers have a more difficult time establishing relationships with their stepchildren than do stepfathers. There are several reasons for this. The role of mother brings with it an automatic respect and reverence. In addition, a cultural mythology says "Mothers always know how to care for their children" and "A mother's touch will make everything better." This is a tough act for a new stepmother to follow. Biological mothers often fear that stepmothers are replacing them, which creates enormous anxiety and jealousy. In turn, stepmothers feel unimportant, devalued, and often invisible. Children feel the tug-of-war between their mother and stepmother and do their best to get out of the middle. To a child's way of thinking, liking a stepmother often translates into being disloyal to a biological mother.

Divorce is a complicated and multifaceted event in the life of a family. Each member of the family may experience intense feelings of loss, sadness, grief, anger, loneliness, despair, fear, and abandonment, to name just a few. There also may be feelings of relief, hope, and freedom. Intense feelings are often demonstrated through actions. In the question above, there is a good chance that the biological mom is communicating her feelings through her hostility and attempts to get the children on her side.

How does a new stepfamily stand a chance of succeeding in the face of this kind of pressure? Here are a few suggestions:

Develop an attitude of compassion for everyone in the family. There are no easy roles here. Children, biological parents, and stepparents all struggle to do the best they can under the circumstances.

Focus on the things over which you have control. For example, a stepmother can choose to react to what the children's mother says and does, or she can spend her energy more productively getting to know her stepchildren and letting them get to know her. Allow this "getting to know you" period to be slow and gentle with few expectations. Some events will go well and others will not. Accept both as part of the normal development of a stepfamily.

Remember the adage "Slow and steady wins the race"? Children respond best to structure and predictability. For a new stepfamily, sometimes the best course of action is to simply keep at it.

Plan for time together as a couple. Build into your weekly schedule time to connect with each other, even if it is only a shared cup of tea or a quick walk around the block. When the couple is strong, the partners can handle just about anything.

Plan for time alone. Take good care of yourself. Carve out a bit of alone time where you can recharge your emotional and physical batteries. Be ruthless about your self-care.

Set good boundaries. Make every effort to communicate well and cooperate with the children's other parent. And at the same time, be clear about your own boundaries. Know where you are able to compromise and where you aren't. Keep the tone of the interactions businesslike and focused on solving problems.

Keep the children out of disagreements. Handle the business of co-parenting without involving the children. Avoid calling the other parent names or setting her up to look bad in the eyes of the children. Don't get snagged by the temptation to act as badly as the other parent does.

Expand your sense of humor. Focus on the joy in your life instead of the misery. Set a goal to laugh with your family every day.

Questions for Discussion

FOR ALL COUPLES

1. Take turns sharing (as a couple and in your group) which questions are most relevant to your situation. Discuss the answers that were helpful and why.
2. What additional questions do you have? Propose them to your spouse and/or group, then brainstorm possible solutions. You decide which solutions you might employ.

PART THREE

A Message
to the Church

Stepfamily ministry represents the next challenge for American churches. Stepfamilies are a field ripe for harvest. But the workers are few. Most of the current ministry to stepfamilies is a grassroots effort; in other words, the ministry being done in most churches today is being done by the stepfamilies themselves. Very few ministers and church leaders have put stepfamily ministry on their list of priorities—at least not yet.

To the stepfamilies reading this book: You are part of the church. And as members of God's family, you have an opportunity to serve in his kingdom. As members of his church, you have a responsibility to be involved in ministry. My prayer is that this chapter will encourage you to initiate a local stepfamily educational group. Begin, perhaps, by sharing this chapter (or entire book) with your minister. Then discuss the ideas in this chapter and how you might begin a local stepfamily ministry. Believing that some ministry leaders will read this chapter first, I have repeated some information from other sections of the book, hoping that they, too, will catch a vision for stepfamily ministry.

To the ministers reading this book: Stepfamilies, if they do not already, will soon comprise a significant population of your ministry audience. The need is real, and you can help. Please read on to find out how.

CHAPTER TWELVE

Ministering to Stepfamilies

Please respond if you can help. I'm not sure what to do. I have been married two times and have one son by each marriage. My current wife has been growing increasingly hostile toward my first son. Just yesterday she complained that I am spending too much time with him and not enough with our son. She's bitter, jealous, and possessive (she even wants him written out of my will), and I'm caught in the middle. No matter what I do, somebody loses. I know it doesn't help that my first son's mother shows up my current wife (they're always competing)—and once again, I'm stuck in the middle. Any suggestions you might have would be greatly appreciated.

—E-mail from a father

Ministering to stepfamilies will be one of the greatest challenges of the new millennium. Clearly, the relational and spiritual issues of stepfamily members are opportunities for the church to touch people's lives with the power of the gospel. However, the church is far behind in its understanding of stepfamily life and has been slow to offer assistance. As a result, Satan and his forces are having their way with generations of people. Adults and children are discouraged, disillusioned, and therefore, distracted from active service in God's kingdom.

Satan's best line of attack is (and always has been) against the home. If he can prevent a stepfamily from integrating successfully, for example, he can take captive multiple generations. Depression, anxiety, drug use, and other unhealthy attachments (to food, work, etc.) become temporary coping mechanisms for adults and adolescents who suffer from unhealthy family circumstances. Unhealthy behaviors then sabotage and take the place of healthy, intimate family relationships. In addition, children experience conditional love as they witness their parents engaging in serial velcro marriage (stick and peel at will). What results for children is a cynical view of marriage and a tendency toward distrust when they do become married. Not all stepfamilies are unhealthy, but most could benefit greatly from practical education and a solid support system. The church is perfectly positioned to provide both.

I should, of course, remind us that Satan's efforts to hamstring families and stepfamilies are not new. I do receive countless e-mails from stepfamilies throughout the world, but the "e-mail" at the beginning of this chapter is not an e-mail at all. It is, in fact, a fictional retelling of the story of Abraham, Sarah, and Hagar found in Genesis 16 and 21. In contrast to the modern day stepfamily, their "expanded family" included a man with two wives instead of a wife and ex-wife, but the dynamics are the same as those in stepfamilies today. Truly, the church must find a way to respond or the next generation will unnecessarily repeat the same mistakes we've seen for centuries.[1]

FAMILY LIFE MINISTRY

Churches have long supported the family as the primary vehicle for spiritual formation in children (see Psalm 78; Deuteronomy 6) and spiritual maturity in adults. The family in America has been undergoing drastic changes in the last fifty years, and churches, on the whole, are lagging in their attempts to minister effectively to changing family compositions. More specifically, stepfamilies, while encompassing a large number of children and adults in America, continue to be overlooked by most church family ministries.

I believe the church must always hold up as the marital standard God's ideal for one man and one woman for life. Nothing should replace this standard. But for those who find themselves in a stepfamily, the church must provide healing from brokenness or loss and equipping for the future. *We must be just as serious about preventing divorce in second and third marriages as we are in preventing a first marriage divorce. But I regret to report that the church currently is not serious about stepfamily enrichment or divorce prevention.* Consider these compelling statistics about American stepfamilies:

- Forty-six percent of marriages today are remarriages for one or both partners.[2] The rate of divorce for remarriages with stepchildren is 50 percent higher than in those without.[3]
- Approximately one-third of all children under the age of eighteen are living in a marital or nonmarital cohabiting stepfamily home.[4]
- One out of three Americans is now a stepparent, stepchild, stepsibling, or some other member of a stepfamily, and more than half of Americans living today will live in at least one step-situation during their lifetime.[5]
- By the year 2010 it is predicted there will be more stepfamilies in the U.S. than any other type of family.[6]
- The remarriage divorce rate continues at 60 percent.[7] Put another way, 50 percent of U.S. children will see their parents divorce and 50 percent of those children will see at least one parent divorce a second time.

Despite the prevalence of stepfamilies and the remarriage divorce rate, stepfamilies remain one of the most neglected groups in churches today. I'm thankful, however, that churches and faith-based organizational "sleeping giants" are beginning to awaken to the incredible opportunities for stepfamily ministry and community outreach. Stepfamilies lack a clear, coherent image of the 3-D puzzle they seek to build; churches can integrate scriptural principles with valuable research and give them the tools they need through practical training programs. Thus, the opportunities for familial and spiritual growth, for the churched and unchurched alike, are remarkable. But many barriers still exist.

BARRIERS TO STEPFAMILY MINISTRY

The first barrier is that most church leaders don't perceive the need. We can't begin to address stepfamily concerns until we realize and acknowledge they exist. Despite the vast number of stepfamilies in the general population, they remain invisible to many church leaders for a number of reasons.

First, churches have fewer stepfamilies. It is not uncommon for the number of stepfamily households in a given congregation to number only 6 percent compared to 25–30 percent of the general U.S. population.[8] The problem, then, is that church leaders sometimes do not interact with the congregational or community stepfamilies enough to notice their increasing numbers or experience their struggles. And even when they do, finding practical, biblically centered resources to aid in pastoral care has been difficult (until this book). Further, stepfamily couples who feel outnumbered by first marriage households may not assertively ask their leaders for help. In other words, we may have more stepfamilies in churches than the numbers suggest due to an underreporting by the stepfamily couples themselves.

"Closet stepfamilies," as I have come to call them, sit in our pews every Sunday, refusing to be identified as a stepfamily. They fear judgment for the past and reminders of their differentness. Recently, the leader of our stepfamily support group and I attended a conference on stepfamilies. I asked him how many stepfamilies he knew of in our church. In addition to those well known to me, he listed six couples that I had no idea were remarried couples. I was stunned. Even in a church that openly welcomes and ministers to stepfamilies and that has supported my stepfamily seminar ministry, we have stepfamily couples who fear "coming out of the closet." Truly, shame and a sense of unworthiness are among our greatest barriers to effective stepfamily ministry. Churches must begin to program stepfamily educational opportunities, but more important, we must convey a message of acceptance, or few will take advantage of the programs offered.

A second reason there are fewer stepfamilies in local congregations is that frequently they are *spiritually marginalized.* This comes about for a variety of reasons. The first is *personal spiritual shame and guilt* from divorce or past sin. The same shame or fear that drives some into the closet drives others away from God and the church. One person said, "I am not sure if I am accepted by God in regard to remarriage. I am almost afraid to read the Bible because I'm not sure what I might find." This doubt and shame moves people away from God for fear of judgment and away from Christians they perceive as "better people" than they are.

In addition, many divorced and remarried persons are marginalized due to being *socially shunned* or *spiritually judged* by the church. A perfect example is the couple I mentioned in chapter 3 who were told straight out by a minister, "I'm sorry. Your background and past might infect everyone else, so we can't have you at our church." Stepfamilies are made to feel like unclean outsiders, second-class Christians who don't fit socially or ideologically. This marginalizes remarried couples and gives them a strong sense of unworthiness.

After attending my *Building a Successful Stepfamily* seminar, a remarried father told one of his elders, "I'm so glad I came this weekend. I never thought I could step foot in a church again." He obviously felt unworthy and unacceptable. By hosting the seminar, that church made a statement: God's grace is available here. If you feel you're unworthy of God's forgiveness—come join our club.

Occasionally stepfamilies looking for a church home will visit a congregation and find subtle messages in church language and programming that separate them from other couples. For example, the advice given in parent education courses often doesn't come close to addressing the daily struggles of stepparents, and questions regarding ex-spouses go unanswered because no one knows how to advise. The inadvertent but unfortunate message becomes "You don't belong here," and stepfamilies hear it loud and clear. As one woman said, "I got so discouraged going to my church, because no one listened to my pleas for assistance. It was as if my needs were unimportant."

A third barrier to developing a stepfamily ministry is that *churches don't want to perceive the need.* I know as a full-time family life minister that local church ministry is a tough, stressful profession. Ministers are coping with ever-changing technology; differing baby-boomer, buster, and millennial generation leadership styles; preaching to a postmodern audience; shifting musical preferences; and polarized churches (with some members holding out for the status quo, while others are pushing for radical changes in ministry methodology). The list of challenges before ministers is endless. And now, in order to understand stepfamilies, church leaders are being asked to rethink their most commonly held notions of marriage and family life. This would require, at a minimum, stepping back from standard family advice, retooling, and looking afresh at the ministry audience.

On top of everything else ministers are trying to handle, that is a difficult challenge.

That's why most local stepfamily ministries are grassroots efforts. Tired of struggling in isolation, stepfamily couples are getting together with other couples to form support/educational groups. A few materials exist to help provide biblically based guidance, but most important, couples are finding support from others with similar struggles. Organizations like mine—*www.SuccessfulStepfamilies.com*—are trying to help.

I know you are busy. But when you can, extend encouragement and a small budget to the stepfamilies in your church. Encourage stepfamily couples to continue working from the ground up. Educate yourself and others when you can, but be sure to bless their local ministry efforts. Use this book to educate yourself and encourage leaders to purchase copies for other couples. Use the discussion questions for group support. I'll say more about support groups later.

The fourth key barrier to stepfamily ministry pertains to *theological struggles with marriage and divorce*. It is beyond the scope of this book to address marriage, divorce, and remarriage from a scriptural standpoint. Suffice it to say that each minister and church needs to study carefully the biblical text in order to arrive at a doctrinal position. I have not answered all of my own questions. Just when I think I've got it all figured out, another question arises that is not easily answered by Scripture. But I have determined that divorce is not the "unforgivable sin," and once remarried, no matter what their background, every couple should work to honor their vows.

Ministering to stepfamilies does not mean we are pro-divorce or pro-adultery any more than believing in hospitals makes one pro-illness.[9] Stepfamily ministry is not about condoning someone's past or lowering God's standard for marriage. God's standard is that people honor their marriage covenants. Sometimes we are confused in thinking that all God desires is that we live with one person our entire life (you can live with someone and not love him or her as you promised), when what God wants is people who remain faithful to their commitments and live them out to the best of their ability. God hates divorce (Malachi 2:16) because it involves covenant breaking; he never breaks a covenant, and he doesn't want us to either. But first-marriage couples can stay married and still not honor their covenant to love, honor, and cherish. The point I'm making is that remarriage, too, is a covenant that should be honored. Persons may need to repent for previous decisions that led to a remarriage, but once the promise is made, we should help couples keep their commitment.

Oddly enough, some would have me encourage divorce among the remarried. My TV and radio appearances have made me the easy target of many whose theology is closed to the idea of remarriage. One woman wrote me a letter accusing me of encouraging people to "marry in adultery" and suggested that I "should be telling them to get out of the new marriage so they can get their hearts right with God." How can intentionally breaking a new covenant (the sin of divorce) be part of getting right with God? This can only make sense to those who refuse to recognize the new marriage as a legitimate union. While again repeating that a thorough exploration of Scripture is beyond the scope of this book, for this issue I would simply point to Jesus' conversation with the woman at the well (John 4:1–26). In verse 18 Jesus points out that she has had five husbands and is now living with a man to whom she is not married. (Note that Jesus delineated carefully between previous marriages and a current cohabiting relationship.) If it were impossible for this serial marital partner to be married beyond her first marriage, then Jesus would have said that she was married once and had lived with five other men. But he didn't. Apparently, whether a marriage starts off right or not, once a couple makes a covenant promise to marry, they are indeed married and ought to honor that promise. While not excusing the circumstances surrounding the decision to wed, I believe our obligation after the wedding is to equip the couple to make their marriage smart and successful.

Stepfamily ministry, then, is about divorce prevention. It is also about reducing the pressures of stepfamily life that hold people back from serving in God's kingdom and prevent parents from raising children to know the Lord. Furthermore, when the body of Christ extends itself as a supportive community, stepfamilies will find direction and courage to continue through their wilderness wanderings toward the Promised Land.[10] The church has a message that can crush Satan's attack on the stepfamily home: First, *God forgives the imperfect people in stepfamilies just as he does the imperfect people in traditional, biological families*; and second, *God's strength and healing are available to any who come to him in faithfulness.* It is time for the church to articulate that message of redemption and hope and to become a spiritual extended family for stepfamilies.

PRACTICAL MINISTRY SUGGESTIONS

I am very excited about the seminar. I am really looking forward to the insight the seminar will provide. We have programs to deal with first time marriages but nothing to address the needs of second marriages. So many couples are so ill prepared to handle the unique issues of step-families. We went into our marriage knowing we were doing things right in God's eyes but were and still can be totally overwhelmed by the issues that arise. I have seen so many friends not make it the second time around because we, the church, have not had the tools to help them.
—Cindy Raymond, Second Baptist Church, Houston

The following are some practical ways your church can begin to minister to stepfamilies.

Communicate messages of hope and determination to the step-families in your congregation. The "wilderness wanderings" can be long and frightening (see chapter 1), but there is a Promised Land of marital fulfillment, interpersonal connectedness, child well-being, and spiritual redemption. Admonish them not to give up (divorce or accept mediocrity) but to trust God and endure the journey in order to reach the Promised Land.

Maintain an outreach (evangelistic) mentality. You may have only a few stepfamilies in your congregation, but you have a lot in the surrounding community. Educate your leadership and staff to consider stepfamily ministry as an outreach effort. Design your classes (titles, meeting times, etc.) with the unchurched in mind.

Start an educational group or Bible class for stepfamilies. This book was written with discussion questions so groups could learn and grow together. Recruit a well-adjusted stepfamily couple and perhaps a non-stepfamily ministry couple to co-lead the discussion group. The leadership team should then spend time in prayer as they read and study this book. Announce your plans to begin a group and purchase a copy of this book for everyone who attends. Ask the group to read a given chapter and then come together to discuss how it applies in their homes. It is likely that you'll need to spend more than one meeting on each chapter.

Keep the group open, allowing remarried couples or pre-remarriage individuals to enter and exit the group whenever they desire. My experience is that couples will gravitate to the group when they are in need.

Once stabilized, couples may stop attending. Don't be discouraged by a fluctuating attendance, just be faithful to help at a time of need. Pre-remarriage couples can benefit from listening to the realities of stepfamily life and learn from the solutions discovered by other groups' members.

At Southwest (my home church) we discovered that once a group of people bond, it may be difficult for new persons to enter the group. Much like a stepfamily, outsiders (those new to the group) feel disconnected when they first attend. After a couple of years the established core of the group (insiders) have a common history together that is difficult to penetrate. Don't be afraid of starting a new group every two years or so. You can encourage the established group to turn their study toward matters of discipleship and spiritual maturity. The new group will address elementary principles of stepfamily living and offer one another encouragement.

Finally, let the group decide how often they meet (every Sunday morning, bi-weekly, or once per month) and consider calling it an "educational group" rather than "support group." I have found it easier for men to attend an educational meeting. "Support group" raises their fears about having to share deep, personal feelings and implies they can't handle life on their own.

Once you have launched your group, contact the Stepfamily Association of America about establishing a local chapter and explore additional Christian resources for further group study. (Visit us at our Web site: *www.SuccessfulStepfamilies.com.*)

When a stepfamily visits your congregation, educate your welcome team not to ask too many questions about why last names are different. Asking a stepfather to explain why his last name is Jones, hers is Mackey, and her children's is Epstein may feel like an inquisition and lead to more guilt and shame. Greet them as you would any other family. If you have an educational group, let them know about it but don't require them to attend. Many will find it a comfort to connect with other stepfamilies, others will not want to be pigeonholed. Initially, let them hide their past if they need to.

Sensitize your children's Bible class teachers to stepfamily complexities. For example, during preparation for Mother's Day and Father's Day activities, you might give children the option of making two cards, one for a biological parent and one for their stepparent (but only if the child wants to). In addition, use language from the pulpit that acknowledges stepmothers and stepfathers; encourage their role and sympathize with their struggles.

Also, find out who is authorized to pick up children after Bible class and who is not. For example, some parents will end their visitation weekend by dropping off their children at the Sunday night children's choir. In order to avoid confusion, custodial parents should put in writing who is authorized to pick up children. Perhaps begin each quarter with a parent-teacher conference to meet the adults in both households and get the pick-up arrangements documented.

Get your youth ministry in touch.

- Biological parents need to sign medical release forms. Stepparents generally do not have the legal right to provide consent for medical treatment unless the right to make such decisions has been documented. Appendix A contains a form that gives stepparents permission to make emergency medical decisions. Have the form notarized and keep it on file. Also, if the youth group is traveling, make sure the other parent knows about your travel plans, especially if the stepparent is traveling as a chaperone. A consent-to-travel form, that when signed by the other biological parent ensures permission for stepchildren to travel with stepparents, can be obtained from the Stepfamily Association of America (*www.saafamilies.org*).

- I recommend that Bible class curriculum include case studies that deal with common adolescent stepfamily struggles. For example, how to honor stepparents in view of Ephesians 6:1–3 while struggling with feelings of disloyalty toward biological parents, conflicts with stepsiblings, and uninvolved biological parents. Teens need a place to talk about such matters with youth leaders who understand their experiences.

Discuss stepparenting and remarriage pressures when doing general marriage and family enrichment classes or sermons. Speak to their needs whenever possible. In classes on parenting, for example, discuss how stepparents might handle a situation differently, and on occasion study case examples from stepfamily situations. Also, examine common biblical texts addressing family life to see how they apply (or apply differently) to stepfamily situations (see chapter 9).

Pre-remarital counseling needs to educate couples about stepfamily dynamics. Most pre-remarriage couples have little practical knowledge of stepfamily life or the struggles they are likely to experience. You must consider it your job to help couples to critically analyze both their relationship strengths and their potential stepfamily dynamics.[11] In order to conduct solid pre-remarital counseling, help couples with all of the issues that first-married couples face. Then make the issues of stepfamily life a major counseling priority. If you do not, you may be giving couples a false sense of security about their future.

I highly recommend that you require couples with children from previous relationships to read this book as part of their pre-remarriage counseling. Discuss the chapters privately or in a pre-remarital class. Then put couples in touch with those who are living the journey. For example, open your stepfamily educational group to single parents and couples considering remarriage. Ask them simply to attend the meetings and listen to the reality stories. Establish a mentoring program so that pre-remarriage couples and newly remarried couples can talk with older couples who have crossed the "sea of opposition" (see chapter 1). Consider it a priority to give couples an accurate picture of the puzzle they are trying to create.

I also recommend that ministers make use of the Prepare-MC profile.[12] This inventory serves as a tool to help identify couples' strengths and growth areas, as well as helping you to make priorities with your sessions. You only have so many opportunities to meet; making the most of those sessions is important.

Session topics will include all those generally related to Christian marriage, such as expectations of your partner, the Ephesians 5 marriage (roles of submission and servant-leadership), spiritual intimacy, communication and conflict resolution skills, goals for your marriage, and sexuality. However, sessions must also focus on stepfamily life. Who attends the sessions is left to your discretion, but it is a good idea to have a combination of adults and children as they discuss expectations for one another, roles, stepparent authority, and how children will refer to their stepparent. Ex-spouses may be invited to a session with the couple (only if conflict and hostility can be contained) to negotiate co-parenting responsibilities. Children-only sessions can help children discuss their losses and fears relative to the new family. If you do not feel competent to handle such ses-

sions, call on a therapist you trust to help with these pre-remarital sessions.[13]

Finally, schedule post-wedding six-month and twelve-month follow-up
sessions to gauge the couple's and stepfamily's adjustment process. Coach
them through difficulties if necessary and provide support along the way.

**Host a stepfamily seminar, sponsor a stepfamily retreat, or offer a
short course for stepfamily adults—but do something!** One of the pio-
neers in Christian stepfamily education, Dick Dunn, believes that while 60
percent of remarried couples will divorce, 80 percent of them could have
survived the wilderness wanderings with just a little information and support.[14] I believe he is right. And the church is perfectly positioned to offer
both. So what are you doing to minister to the soon-to-be largest family
group in America?

A CALL TO MINISTRY

What would you say to someone who suggested that you could not
minister to or evangelize half of your community's population? Let's just
say someone told you to be insensitive to the needs of all the women in
your community (approximately half the population). Would you embrace
that restriction? Perhaps you would feel better if you were told to ignore
the men. My guess is, either way, you would not feel good about neglecting
half the population of your community.

The current projections in this country suggest that one of every two
Americans will live in a stepfamily situation at some point in their lifetime.
It may be as a stepparent, stepchild, stepsibling, stepgrandparent, or step-
uncle, but 50 percent of us will live in at least one step situation. Can you
imagine neglecting all those people or being irrelevant to their family
needs? Probably not. Stepfamily ministry is a tremendous opportunity for
churches across America. But it must begin with a willingness to re-tool
yourself and expand your ministry to expanded families. The great-grandchildren of the stepfamilies in your church and community need you to
be faithful in the task of strengthening their ancestors. Indeed, stepfamily
couple education and stepfamily enrichment are necessary and vital
aspects of ministry in this new millenium. The only question is, when will
you begin?

APPENDIX A

MEDICAL PERMISSION TO TREAT MINOR CHILD[1]

Date _____

To Whom It May Concern:

Regarding _____
GIVE FULL NAME OF CHILD, ADDRESS, DATE OF BIRTH, SOCIAL SECURITY NUMBER

_____

As the parents of the above-named child, _____
NAME OF STEPPARENT

has our permission to authorize emergency medical treatment for this child.

Known allergies are: _____
LIST ANY KNOWN ALLERGIES TO FOOD, MEDICATION, ETC., OR WRITE "NONE"

_____

This child's regular doctor is: _____

_____
GIVE NAME, COMPLETE ADDRESS, AND TELEPHONE NUMBER

This child is insured under medical policy _____

_____
GIVE COMPANY, POLICY NUMBER, LISTED INSURED'S NAME AND ID

SIGNATURE	SIGNATURE
PARENT NAME	PARENT NAME
PARENT ADDRESS	PARENT ADDRESS
WORK PHONE	WORK PHONE
HOME PHONE	HOME PHONE
NOTARY PUBLIC	NOTARY PUBLIC
DATE	DATE
MY COMMISSION EXPIRES	MY COMMISSION EXPIRES

NOTE: This letter must be notarized.

Resources

RESOURCES FOR STEPFAMILIES AND CHURCHES

Marriage Education Programs, Organizations, and Web Sites
Deal, Ron L. "Successful Stepfamilies: Christian Resources for Church and Home." *www.SuccessfulStepfamilies.com*

FamilyLife. *www.familylife.com*

Family Medallion. *www.familymedallion.com*. Planning to get remarried? This site provides medallions that parents can give their children during the wedding ceremony. A wonderful way to reassure children and start your family.

Focus on the Family. *www.family.org*

Marriage Alive International. *www.marriagealive.com*. 888–690–6667.

Marriage Savers. *www.marriagesavers.org*. 9500 Michaels Court, Bethesda, MD 20817–2214. 301–469–5870.

PAIRS International. *www.pairs.com*. Pairs Foundation, Ltd. 1056 Creekford Drive, Weston, FL 33326.

PREP and Christian PREP: Prevention and Relationship Enhancement Program. *www.prepinc.com*. P.O. Box 102530, Denver, CO 80250–2530. 303–759–9931.

The Second Wives Club. *www.secondwivesclub.com*

Stepfamily Association of America (SAA). *www.SAAfamilies.org*. 650 J Street, Suite 205, Lincoln, NE 68508. 800–735–0329.

Stepfamily Living. *www.steplife.com*

Books and Study Resources
Barnes, Bob. *Winning the Heart of Your Stepchild*. Grand Rapids: Zondervan, 1992.

Deal, Ron. L. *Building A Successful Stepfamily*. Audio seminar. Little Rock: FamilyLife, 2001. Over nine hours of presentation material on six audiocassettes with an accompanying study manual. An excellent resource for individuals and groups. Order from *www.SuccessfulStepfamilies.com*.

———. *7 STEPS to Stepfamily Success*. Video seminar. This 75-minute presentation captures the key elements outlined in this book. Can be used by educational groups. Order from *www.SuccessfulStepfamilies.com*. (2000).

Douglas, Edward, and Sharon Douglas. *The Blended Family: Achieving Peace and*

Harmony in the Christian Home. Franklin, Tenn.: Providence House Publishers, 2000.

Dunn, Dick. *New Faces in the Frame: A Guide to Marriage and Parenting in the Blended Family*. Nashville: LifeWay Press, 1997. A twelve-week Bible study curriculum for adult groups.

Lauer, Robert, and Jeannette Lauer. *Becoming Family: How to Build a Stepfamily That Really Works*. Minneapolis: Augsburg Fortress, 1999.

Leman, Kevin. *Bringing Peace and Harmony to the Blended Family*. Dallas: Sampson Ministry Resources, 2000.

Nelsen, Jane, Cheryl Erwin, and Stephen Glenn. *Positive Discipline for Your Stepfamily: Nurturing Harmony, Respect, and Joy in Your New Home*. Roseville, Calif.: Prima Publishing, 2000.

Pratt, Lonni Collins. *Making Two Halves a Whole: Studies for Parents in Blended Families*. Colorado Springs: David C. Cook, 1995. A thirteen-week Bible study curriculum for adult groups.

Smith-Broersma, Margaret. *Devotions for the Blended Family*. Grand Rapids: Kregel, 1994.

———. *Devotions for Couples in Blended Families*. Grand Rapids: Kregel, 1996.

Sposto, Steve, and Dena Sposto. *Fruits of the Spirit: The Stepfamily Spiritual Journey*. A small-group resource self-published by Stepfamily Living. *www.steplife.com*, 2002.

Townsend, L.L. *Pastoral Care With Stepfamilies: Mapping the Wilderness*. St. Louis: Chalice Press, 2000.

Visher, E., and J. Visher. *Stepping Together: Creating Strong Stepfamilies*. (New York: Brunner/Mazel), 1997. A curriculum for stepfamily groups available from the Stepfamily Association of America. A Christian supplement, by Vannesa Henneke, is also available.

BUILD YOUR STEPFAMILY

If you are looking for a live semiar, or more in-depth resources for stepfamilies, please visit *www.SuccessfulStepfamilies.com*.

A home study audio seminar—"Building a Successful Stepfamily"—is also available from Ron L. Deal. Through this seminar you will learn realistic expectations, how to "cook" a stepfamily, how to help children adjust to stepparents and living in two households, how to improve your ex-spouse relationship, and the best parent and stepparent roles for raising healthy kids.

Also available is *Smart Steps*, a dynamic interaction-filled twelve-hour curriculum for adults and children living in stepfamilies, by Francesca Adler-Baeder, Ph.D., in cooperation with Cornell Cooperative Extension and the Stepfamily Association of America, with a Christian supplement by Ron L. Deal.

Endnotes

Introduction

1. Elizabeth Einstein, Workshop: "Strengthening Our Stepfamilies: A Developmental Approach," November 7, 1997, Harding University, Searcy, Arkansas.

Chapter One

1. Elizabeth Einstein, Workshop: "Strengthening Our Stepfamilies: A Developmental Approach."
2. E. M. Hetherington and J. Kelly, *For Better or For Worse: Divorce Reconsidered* (New York: W. W. Norton & Company, 2002).
3. James Bray, *Stepfamilies: Love, Marriage, and Parenting in the First Decade* (New York: Broadway Books, 1998), 12.

Chapter Two

1. H. T. Blackaby and C. V. King, *Experiencing God: Knowing and Doing the Will of God* (Nashville: LifeWay Press, 1990), 108–25.
2. I am well aware that some marriages are extremely dangerous due to physical or sexual abuse toward a spouse or children. The matter of perseverance in the face of evil and dangerous circumstances changes dramatically. I would not encourage anyone in physical jeopardy to stay in a situation where the marriage covenant has been broken and there is little hope of reconciliation of the marriage. If you find yourself in such a circumstance, please seek professional help immediately.
3. James Bray, *Stepfamilies: Love, Marriage, and Parenting in the First Decade.*
4. Patricia Papernow, *Becoming a Stepfamily: Patterns of Development in Remarried Families* (New York: Gardner Press, 1993), 387.
5. Ibid., 387.
6. Ibid., 330–31.

Chapter Four

1. Adapted from E. Einstein and Albert L. Einstein, *Strengthening Your Stepfamily* (Circle Pines, Minn.: American Guidance Service, Inc., 1986).
2. Patricia Papernow, *Becoming a Stepfamily*, 387.

Chapter Five

1. Based on 1985 U.S. Census Bureau data.
2. U.S. Bureau of Statistics, 1995.
3. A. J. Norton and L. F. Miller, "Marriage, Divorce, and Remarriage in the 1990s." Current Population Reports (Series P23-180) (Washington D.C.: Government Printing Office, 1992).
4. E. M. Hetherington and J. Kelly, For Better of For Worse: Divorce Reconsidered.
5. Carroll D. Osburn, The Peaceable Kingdom: Essays Favoring Non-Sectarian Christianity (Abilene, Tex.: Restoration Perspectives, 1993), 127–28.
6. Excerpted from Max Lucado, When the Angels Were Silent. Used by permission of Multnomah Publishers, Inc.
7. Source unknown; story used by Max Lucado.
8. John Gottman, Why Marriages Succeed or Fail (New York: Simon & Schuster, 1994).
9. Patricia Papernow, Becoming a Stepfamily, 54.

Chapter Six

1. Carol R. Lowery, "Psychotherapy With Children of Divorced Families." In M. Textor, ed., The Divorce and Divorce Therapy Handbook (Northvale, N.J.: Jason Aronson, Inc., 1989), 225–41.
2. W. F. Horn, "A Misconception About Divorce," Fatherly Advice column in Washington Times (August 29, 2000). See also, P. F. Fagan and R. Rector, "The Effects of Divorce on America," The Heritage Foundation Backgrounder Executive Summary (June 5, 2000), The Heritage Foundation, Washington, D.C.
3. J. Wallerstein, The Unexpected Legacy of Divorce: A Twenty-Five-Year Landmark Study (New York: Hyperion Books, 2000).
4. E. M. Hetherington and J. Kelly, For Better of For Worse: Divorce Reconsidered, 228.
5. J. H. Bray, "Children in Stepfamilies: Assessment and Treatment Issues." In D. K. Huntely, ed., Understanding Stepfamilies: Implications for Assessment and Treatment (Alexandria, Va.: American Counseling Association, 1995), 59–72.
6. ———. "Children's Development During Early Remarriage." In E. M. Hetherington and J. Arasteh, eds., Impact of Divorce, Single Parenting, and Stepparenting on Children (Hillsdale, N.J.: Erlbaum, 1988), 279–98.
7. R. J. Haurin, "Patterns of Childhood Residence and the Relationship to Young Adult Outcomes," Journal of Marriage and the Family, 54 (1992), 846–60.
8. G. D. Sandefur, S. S. McLanahan, and R. A. Wojtkiewicz, "The Effects of Parental Marital Status During Adolescence on High School Graduation," Social Forces, 7 (1992), 103–21.
9. W. S. Aquilino, "Family Structure and Home-Leaving: A Further Specification of the Relationship," Journal of Marriage and the Family, 53 (1991), 999–1010.
10. A. Thornton, "Influence of the Marital History of Parents on the Marital and Cohabitational Experiences of Children," American Journal of Sociology, 96 (1991), 868–94.
11. E. M. Hetherington, "Families, Lies, and Videotapes," Journal of Research on Adolescence, 1 (1991), 323–48.
12. Patricia Papernow, Becoming a Stepfamily.
13. James Bray, Stepfamilies: Love, Marriage, and Parenting in the First Decade, 83.
14. Tom Worthen, ed., Broken Hearts' Healing: Young Poets Speak Out on Divorce, abridged version (Logan, Utah: Poet Tree Press, 2001), 27. Used with permission.

15. Patricia Papernow, *Becoming a Stepfamily.*

16. Tom Worthen, ed., *Broken Hearts' Healing: Young Poets Speak Out on Divorce,* 19. Used with permission.

17. Emily Visher and John Visher, *How to Win As a Stepfamily* (New York: Brunner/Mazel, 1996), 110–12.

18. Adapted from Everett & Volgy, *Healthy Divorce* (San Francisco: Jossey-Bass, Inc., 1994), and Visher & Visher, *How to Win As a Stepfamily.*

19. List for item #12 developed from M. Engel, "President's Message," *Stepfamilies,* Vol. 18, No. 2, 1998.

20. Constance Ahrons, *The Good Divorce: Keeping Your Family Together When Your Marriage Comes Apart* (New York: Harper Collins, 1994), 55–56. Used with permission of HarperCollins Publishers Inc.

21. Ibid., 57.

22. Ibid., 52–57.

23. Emily Visher and John Visher, *How to Win As a Stepfamily,* 93.

24. V. Rackley, "Forgiveness in Relationships," personal communication airing on *Life-Talk* with Ron L. Deal, KBTM 1230 AM radio, Jonesboro, Ark., 1997.

25. Patricia Papernow, "Dealing Across Households: Scripts to Get by On," cassette recording (Williamsburg, Va.: Stepfamily Association of America, 1995). Used with permission.

26. I am very grateful to Dr. Papernow for her input into these scripts. They are a marvelous tool—I hope they will bless you.

Chapter Seven

1. R. M. Hoffman, "Why Is Stepmothering More Difficult Than Stepfathering?" *Step-families, www.saafamilies.org* (Summer 1995).

2. Jean McBride, *Encouraging Words for New Stepmothers* (Fort Collins, Col.: CDR Press, 2001), xv.

3. R. H. Lauer and J. C. Lauer, *Becoming Family: How to Build a Stepfamily That Really Works* (Minneapolis: Augsburg Fortress, 1999), 147.

4. M. Fine, "The Role of the Stepparent: How Similar are the Views of Stepparents, Parents, and Stepchildren?" *Stepfamilies, www.saafamilies.org* (Fall 1997).

5. James Bray, *Stepfamilies: Love, Marriage, and Parenting in the First Decade.*

6. Ibid.

7. K. Pasley, D. Dollahite, and M. Ihinger-Tallman, "What We Know About the Role of the Stepparent," *Stepfamilies, www.saafamilies.org,* (2000).

8. James Bray, *Stepfamilies: Love, Marriage, and Parenting in the First Decade.*

9. K. Pasley, "What is Effective Stepparenting?" *Stepfamilies, www.saafamilies.org* (Summer 1994).

10. K. Pasley, D. Dollahite, and M. Ihinger-Tallman, "What We Know About the Role of the Stepparent."

11. Dr. Susan Gamache, *Building Your Stepfamily: A Blueprint for Success* (Vancouver, B.C.: BC Council for Families).

12. E. B. Visher and J. S. Visher, *Old Loyalties, New Ties: Therapeutic Strategies with Step-families* (New York: Brunner/Mazel, 1998).

13. While a stepparent is building emotional bonds with stepchildren, he or she still has practical matters to attend to. For example, a lack of legal bonds with stepchildren

makes handling medical emergencies difficult. Obtaining permission to make medical decisions is important; see Appendix A.

14. James Bray, *Stepfamilies: Love, Marriage, and Parenting in the First Decade.*
15. E. Einstein and Albert L. Einstein, *Strengthening Your Stepfamily.*
16. Ibid.
17. Ibid.
18. Based on the work of Dr. Susan Gamache in *Building Your Stepfamily: A Blueprint for Success.*
19. Dr. Susan Gamache, "Parental status: A new construct describing adolescent perceptions of stepfathers." (Ph.D. diss., University of British Columbia, 2000).
20. M. A. Fine, "The Stepfather and Stepchild Relationship" (presented at the Stepfamily Association of America Training Institute, Kansas City, Mo., April 1990).
21. E. M. Hetherington and J. Kelly, *For Better or For Worse*, 201–202.

Chapter Eight

1. R. Emery, *Renegotiating Family Relationships: Divorce, Child Custody, and Mediation* (New York: Guilford Press, 1994) 26–28.
2. E. B. Visher and J. S. Visher, *How to Win As a Stepfamily*, 97–100.
3. K. Pasley, "Relations Across the Generations: The Complications of Divorce and Remarriage," *Stepfamilies, www.saafamilies.org*, (Spring 1995).
4. E. B. Visher and J. S. Visher, *Old Loyalties, New Ties: Therapeutic Strategies With Stepfamilies.*
5. Adapted from Visher and Visher, *Old Loyalties, New Ties: Therapeutic Strategies with Stepfamilies.*
6. Patricia Papernow, *Dealing Across Households: Scripts to Get by On*, cassette recording.
7. K. Leman, *Living in a Stepfamily Without Getting Stepped On: Helping Your Children Survive the Birth Order Blender* (Nashville: Thomas Nelson, 1994).
8. It seems that both sides may be right. Informal studies show that couples who favor pooling their money into an "ours pot" are no more or less satisfied with their money management than those who keep money separate. In either case, the legal realities of marriage are binding enough that pooling is not necessary to make the couple financially linked and interdependent.
9. Margorie Engel, *Managing Stepfamily Money: Yours, Mine, and Ours* (Lincoln, Neb.: Stepfamily Association of America Press, 2000). Used with permission.
10. Ibid.

Chapter Nine

1. J. Giles-Sims, "Current Knowledge About Child Abuse in Stepfamilies." In *Stepfamilies: History, Research, and Policy*, ed. M. Sussman and I. Levin (New York: The Haworth Press, 1997).
2. Dr. Francesca Adler-Baeder, personal communication (June 2001).
3. E. M. Hetherington and J. Kelly, *For Better or For Worse: Divorce Reconsidered*, 198.
4. This is not to imply in any way that victims make their offenders abuse them. Offenders are solely to blame for their actions.
5. Bryan Chapell, *Each for the Other: Marriage As It's Meant to Be* (Grand Rapids: Baker Books, 1998), 35.
6. Ron L. Deal, "Fathers: Our First Impression of God," *Today's Father* 5, no.1 (1997): A1 (Shawnee Mission, Kans.: National Center for Fathering).

7. D. K. Lewis, C. H. Dodd, and D. L. Tippens, *The Gospel According to Generation X. The Culture of Adolescent Belief* (Abilene, TX: ACU Press, 1995).
8. E. M. Hetherington and J. Kelly, *For Better or For Worse: Divorce Reconsidered.*
9. Ibid., 271–72.
10. E. Marquardt, "Children of Divorce: Stories of Exile," *The Christian Century* (February 2001).
11. J. H. Westerhoff III, *Will Our Children Have Faith?* (San Francisco: Harper and Row, 1976).

Chapter Eleven

1. S. Browning, "Why Didn't Our Two Years of Dating Make the Remarriage Easier?" *Stepfamilies, www.saafamilies.org* (Summer 2000), 6.
2. Dr. Roger Coleman has created a medallion that can be given to children during the wedding ceremony. The act reassures children of their place in the new family and symbolically represents the commitment that stepparents make to care for their stepchildren. A wonderful resource for engaged couples: *www.familymedallion.com.*
3. Susan J. Gamache is an individual, marital, and family therapist in private practice in Vancouver, British Columbia. She is the author of *Building Your Stepfamily: A Blueprint for Success* and a board member of the Stepfamily Association of America.
4. Craig A. Everett is a marital and family therapist in private practice and co-director of the Arizona Institute for Family Therapy, Tucson, Arizona. He is co-author of *Healthy Divorce: Fourteen Stages of Separation, Divorce, and Remarriage* (Jossey-Bass, 1994/1998).
5. Francesca Adler-Baeder, Ph.D., CFLE, Assistant Professor and Extension Specialist for Children, Youth, & Families, Department of Human Development and Family Studies, Auburn University, Auburn, Alabama.
6. Sandra Volgy Everett is a clinical and child psychologist and family therapist in private practice and co-director of the Arizona Institute for Family Therapy in Tucson, Arizona. She is co-author of *Healthy Divorce: Fourteen Stages of Separation, Divorce, and Remarriage* (Jossey-Bass, 1994/1998).
7. Jean McBride is president and CEO of The Center for Divorce & Remarriage, Inc. and CDR Press. She is in private practice in Fort Collins, Colorado, where she specializes in working with divorce and remarriage. Jean is the author of *Encouraging Words for New Stepmothers, Hopeful Steps: A Gentle Guide for the Stepfamily Journey* (audiotapes), and *Quick and Easy Brochures About Divorce.* Jean serves on the board of directors of the Stepfamily Association of America.

A Message to the Church

1. To be clear, I am not suggesting that stepfamilies are mistakes. They are not. The mistakes come in how people manage stepfamily dynamics.
2. R. F. Stahmann and W. Hiebert, *Premarital and Remarital Counseling* (San Francisco: Jossey-Bass, 1997).
3. E. M. Hetherington and J. Kelly, *For Better or For Worse: Divorce Reconsidered.*
4. L. L. Bumpass, R. K. Raley, and J. A. Sweet, "The Changing Character of Stepfamilies: Implications of cohabitation and nonmarital childbearing," *Demography* 32 (1995): 425–36. Best estimates suggest that 25 percent of stepfamilies are actually cohabiting couples.
5. J. Larson, "Understanding Stepfamilies," *American Demographics* 14 (1992): 360.

6. E. B. Visher and J. S. Visher, "Stepparents, the Forgotten Family Member," Second World Congress on Family Law and the Rights of Children and Youth (June 1997).

7. A. J. Norton and L. F. Miller, "Marriage, Divorce, and Remarriage in the 1990s," Current Population Reports (Series P23–180) (Washington, D.C.: Government Printing Office, 1992).

8. P. A. Yankeelov and D. R. Garland, "The families in our congregations: Initial research findings," *Family Ministry: Empowering Through Faith* 12 (1988): 3, 23–56.

9. I am grateful to Dr. Susan Gamache for sharing this analogy with me.

10. L. L. Townsend, *Pastoral Care With Stepfamilies: Mapping the Wilderness* (St. Louis: Chalice Press, 2000).

11. R. F. Stahmann and W. Hiebert, *Premarital and Remarital Counseling* (San Francisco: Jossey-Bass 1997).

12. D. Olson, PREPARE/ENRICH, (Minneapolis: Life Innovations). Available at 1–800–331–1661 or *www.lifeinnovations.com*

13. Not all therapists are created equal. A surprising number are not trained in stepfamily dynamics and can be more harmful than helpful. To find a therapist you trust, ask these questions: (1) What specific training have you had in stepfamily therapy? (2) How would you treat a stepfamily situation differently than a biological family? (3) What books would you recommend on the subject? (4) Are you a Christian and how does that make a difference in your counseling? If the counselor cannot sufficiently answer these questions or has little specific training, do not make referrals to him or her.

14. Dick Dunn, personal communication, 2001.

Appendix A: Medical Permission to Treat Minor Child

1. This information first appeared in *The Divorce Decisions Workbook* (McGraw-Hill) by Dr. Margorie Engel. Permission to use granted by the author. (New York: N.Y., 1992).

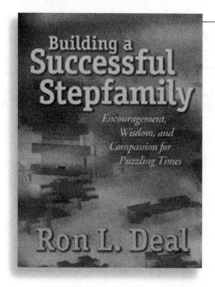